Oscar Fingal O'Flahertie Wills Wilde (16 October 1854 – 30 November 1900) was an Irish poet and playwright. After writing in different forms throughout the 1880s, he became one of London's most popular playwrights in the early 1890s. He is best remembered for his epigrams and plays, his novel The Picture of Dorian Gray, and the circumstances of his criminal conviction for homosexuality, imprisonment, and early death at age 46. Wilde's parents were successful Anglo-Irish intellectuals in Dublin. Their son became fluent in French and German early in life. At university, Wilde read Greats; he proved himself to be an outstanding classicist, first at Trinity College Dublin, then at Oxford. He became known for his involvement in the rising philosophy of aestheticism, led by two of his tutors, Walter Pater and John Ruskin. After university, Wilde moved to London into fashionable cultural and social circles. (Source: Wikipedia)

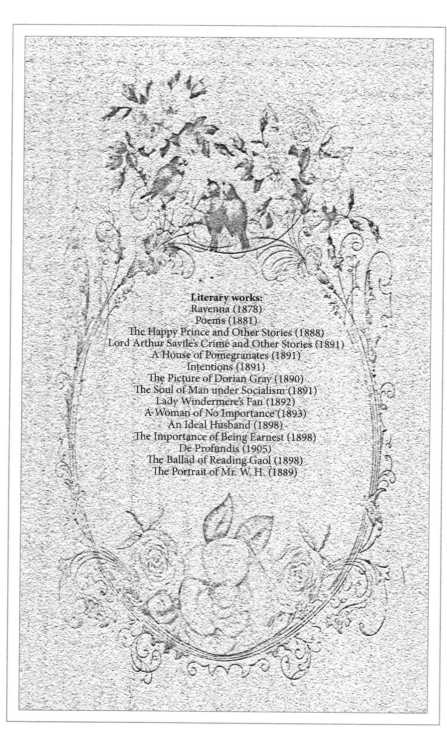

Literary works:
Ravenna (1878)
Poems (1881)
The Happy Prince and Other Stories (1888)
Lord Arthur Savile's Crime and Other Stories (1891)
A House of Pomegranates (1891)
Intentions (1891)
The Picture of Dorian Gray (1890)
The Soul of Man under Socialism (1891)
Lady Windermere's Fan (1892)
A Woman of No Importance (1893)
An Ideal Husband (1898)
The Importance of Being Earnest (1898)
De Profundis (1905)
The Ballad of Reading Gaol (1898)
The Portrait of Mr. W. H. (1889)

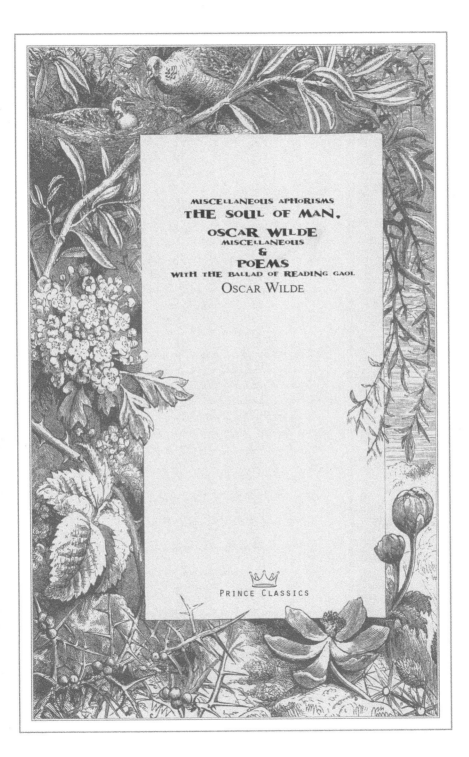

MISCELLANEOUS APHORISMS

THE SOUL OF MAN,

OSCAR WILDE
MISCELLANEOUS
&
POEMS
WITH THE BALLAD OF READING GAOL

OSCAR WILDE

PRINCE CLASSICS

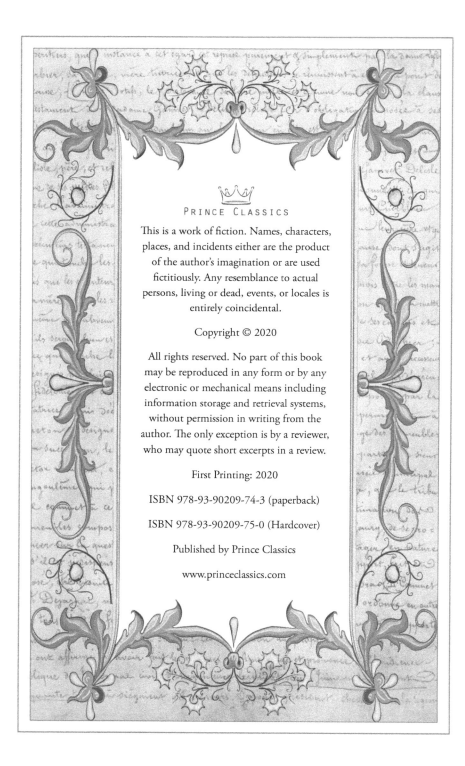

PRINCE CLASSICS

This is a work of fiction. Names, characters, places, and incidents either are the product of the author's imagination or are used fictitiously. Any resemblance to actual persons, living or dead, events, or locales is entirely coincidental.

Copyright © 2020

First Printing: 2020

ISBN 978-93-90209-74-3 (paperback)

ISBN 978-93-90209-75-0 (Hardcover)

Published by Prince Classics

www.princeclassics.com

Contents

MISCELLANEOUS APHORISMS

THE SOUL OF MAN,

OSCAR WILDE
MISCELLANEOUS
&
POEMS
WITH THE BALLAD OF READING GAOL

MISCELLANEOUS APHORISMS: THE SOUL OF MAN

SEBASTIAN MELMOTH

(OSCAR WILDE)

The mystery of love is greater than the mystery of death.

Women are made to be loved, not to be understood.

It is absurd to have a hard and fast rule about what one should read and what one shouldn't. Moren than half of modern culture depends on what one shouldn't read.

Women, as someone says, love with their ears, just as men love with their eyes, if they ever love at all.

It is better to be beautiful than to be good, but it is better to be good than to be ugly.

Nothing looks so like innocence as an indiscretion.

Misfortunes one can endure, they come from outside, they are accidents. But to suffer for one's faults—ah! there is the sting of life.

Beauty is the only thing that time cannot harm. Philosophies fall away like sand, creeds follow one another, but what is beautiful is a joy for all seasons, a possession for all eternity.

Questions are never indiscreet; answers sometimes are.

Twenty years of romance make a woman look like a ruin; but twenty years of marriage make her something like a public building.

The only thing that one really knows about human nature is that it changes.

Anyone can sympathise with the sufferings of a friend, but it requires a very fine nature to sympathise with a friend's success.

Selfishness is not living as one wishes to live, it is asking others to live as one wishes to live: and unselfishness is letting other people's lives alone, not interfering with them.

A man who does not think for himself does not think at all.

Nowadays people seem to look on life as a speculation. It is not a speculation. It is a sacrament. Its ideal is love. Its purification is sacrifice.

In old days nobody pretended to be a bit better than his neighbour. In fact, to be a bit better than one's neighbour was considered excessively vulgar and middle class. Nowadays, with our modern mania for morality, everyone has to pose as a paragon of purity, incorruptibility, and all the other seven deadly virtues. And what is the result? You all go over like ninepins—one after the other.

All sympathy is fine, but sympathy with suffering is the least fine mode.

If you pretend to be good the world takes you very seriously. If you pretend to be bad it doesn't. Such is the astounding stupidity of optimism.

It is most dangerous nowadays for a husband to pay any attention to his wife in public. It always makes people think that he beats her when they're alone. The world has grown so suspicious of anything that looks like a happy married life.

Actors are so fortunate. They can choose whether they will appear in tragedy or in comedy, whether they will suffer or make merry, laugh or shed tears. But in real life it is different. Most men and women are forced to perform parts for which they have no qualifications. The world is a stage, but the play is badly cast.

Men know life too early; women know life too late-that is the difference between men and women.

He who stands most remote from his age is he who mirrors it best.

There is only one thing in the world worse than being talked about, and that is not being talked about.

Life is not governed by will or intention. Life is a question of nerves and fibres and slowly built-up cells, in which thought hides itself and passion has its dreams.

Man is a being with myriad lives and myriad sensations, a complex, multiform creature that bears within itself strange legacies of thought and passion, and whose very flesh is tainted with the monstrous maladies of the dead.

As long as a woman can look ten years younger than her own daughter she is perfectly satisfied.

There is always something infinitely mean about other people's tragedies.

Public and private life are different things. They have different laws and move on different lines.

When one is placed in the position of guardian one has to adopt a very high moral tone on all subjects. It's one's duty to do so.

I have always been of opinion that a man who desires to get married should know either everything or nothing.

An engagement should come on a young girl as a surprise, pleasant or unpleasant, as the case may be. It is hardly a matter that she could be allowed to arrange for herself.

If the lower classes don't set us a good example what on earth is the use of them? They seem, as a class, to have absolutely no sense of moral responsibility.

If a woman cannot make her mistakes charming she is only a female.

The world was made for men and not for women.

It is always with the best intentions that the worst work is done.

If you wish to understand others you must intensify your own individualism.

Why do you talk so trivially about life? Because I think that life is far too important a thing ever to talk seriously about it.

What a pity that in life we only get our lessons when they are of no use to us.

It is better to have a permanent income than to be fascinating.

Relations are simply a tedious pack of people who haven't got the remotest knowledge of how to live nor the smallest instinct about when to die.

Charity creates a multitude of sins.

My experience is that as soon as people are old enough to know better they don't know anything at all.

Truth is a very complex thing and politics is a very complex business. There are wheels within wheels. One may be under certain obligations to people that one must pay. Sooner or later in political life one has to compromise. Everyone does.

Men can love what is beneath them—things unworthy, stained, dishonoured. We women worship when we love; and when we lose our worship we lose everything.

The proper basis for marriage is a mutual misunderstanding.

The one advantage of playing with fire is that one never gets even singed. It is the people who don't know how to play with it who get burned up.

There are moments when one has to choose between living one's own life fully, entirely, completely, or dragging out some false, shallow, degrading existence that the world in its hypocrisy demands.

When one is in town one amuses oneself. When one is in the country one amuses other people. It is excessively boring.

Romance is the privilege of the rich, not the profession of the unemployed. The poor should be practical and prosaic.

An acquaintance that begins with a compliment is sure to develop into a real friendship. It starts in the right manner.

The truths of metaphysics are the truths of masks.

Science can never grapple with the irrational. That is why it has no future before it in this world.

The happy people of the world have their value, but only the negative value of foils. They throw up and emphasise the beauty and the fascination of the unhappy.

In this world there are only two tragedies. One is not getting what one wants, and the other is getting it. The last is much the worst—the last is a real tragedy.

Disobedience in the eyes of anyone who has read history is man's original virtue. It is through disobedience that progress has been made—through disobedience and rebellion.

It is not wise to find symbols in everything that one sees. It makes life too full of terrors.

Comfort is the only thing our civilisation can give us.

Politics are my only pleasure. You see nowadays it is not fashionable to flirt till one is forty or to be romantic till one is forty-five, so we poor women who are under thirty, or say we are, have nothing open to us but politics or philanthropy. And philanthropy seems to me to have become simply the refuge of people who wish to annoy their fellow-creatures. I prefer politics. I think they are more ... becoming.

One's past is what one is. It is the only way by which people should be judged.

In a very ugly and sensible age the arts borrow, not from life, but from each other.

It is always a silly thing to give advice, but to give good advice is fatal.

Secrets from other people's wives are a necessary luxury in modern life.

So, at least, I am told at the club by people who are bald enough to know better. But no man should have a secret from his own wife. She invariably finds it out. Women have a wonderful instinct about things. They discover everything except the obvious.

Life holds the mirror up to art, and either reproduces some strange type imagined by painter or sculptor or realises in fact what has been dreamed in fiction.

I feel sure that if I lived in the country for six months I should become so unsophisticated that no one would take the slightest notice of me.

To recommend thrift to the poor is both grotesque and insulting. It is like advising a man who is starving to eat less.

A thing is not necessarily true because a man dies for it.

I am always saying what I shouldn't say; in fact, I usually say what I really think—a great mistake nowadays. It makes one so liable to be misunderstood.

Experience is the name everyone gives to their mistakes.

The true perfection of man lies, not in what man has, but in what man is.

The basis of every scandal is an absolute immoral certainty.

People talk so much about the beauty of confidence. They seem to entirely ignore the much more subtle beauty of doubt. To believe is very dull. To doubt is intensely engrossing. To be on the alert is to live, to be lulled into security is to die.

Every effect that one produces gives one an enemy. To be popular one must be a mediocrity.

It is a sad truth, but we have lost the faculty of giving lovely names to things. Names are everything. I never quarrel with actions, my one quarrel is with words. That is the reason I hate vulgar realism in literature. The man who could call a spade a spade should be compelled to use one. It is the only thing he is fit for.

A high moral tone can hardly be said to conduce very much to either one's health or one's happiness.

There are terrible temptations that it requires strength—strength and courage—to yield to. To stake all one's life on one throw—whether the stake be power or pleasure I care not—there is no weakness in that. There is a horrible, a terrible, courage.

Nowadays it is only the unreadable that occurs.

All charming people are spoiled. It is the secret of their attraction.

There is more to be said for stupidity than people imagine. Personally, I have a great admiration for stupidity. It is a sort of fellow-feeling, I suppose.

All men are monsters. The only thing to do is to feed the wretches well. A good cook does wonders.

There is no such thing as an omen.

Destiny does not send us heralds. She is too wise or too cruel for that.

Crying is the refuge of plain women but the ruin of pretty ones.

Love art for its own sake and then all things that you need will be added to you. This devotion to beauty and to the creation of beautiful things is the test of all great civilisations; it is what makes the life of each citizen a sacrament and not a speculation.

It is always worth while asking a question, though it is not always answering one.

It takes a thoroughly good woman to do a thoroughly stupid thing.

With a proper background women can do anything.

Chiromancy is a most dangerous science, and one that ought not to be encouraged, except in a 'tête-à-tête.'

One should never take sides in anything. Taking sides is the beginning of sincerity, and earnestness follows shortly afterwards, and the human being becomes a bore.

The work of art is beautiful by being what art never has been; and to measure it by the standard of the past is to measure it by a standard on the reflection of which its real perfection depends.

There are three kinds of despots. There is the despot who tyrannises over the body. There is the despot who tyrannises over the soul. There is the despot who tyrannises over soul and body alike. The first is called the prince. The second is called the pope. The third is called the people.

Costume is a growth, an evolution, and a most important, perhaps the most important, sign of the manners, customs, and mode of life of each century.

I really don't see anything romantic in proposing. It is very romantic to be in love, but there is nothing romantic about a definite proposal. Why, one may be accepted. One usually is, I believe. Then the excitement is all over. The very essence of romance is uncertainty.

What consoles one nowadays is not repentance but pleasure. Repentance is quite out of date.

Ideals are dangerous things. Realities are better. They wound, but they are better.

Unless one is wealthy there is no use in being a charming fellow.

Shallow sorrows and shallow loves live on. The loves and sorrows that are great are destroyed by their own plenitude.

An eternal smile is much more wearisome than a perpetual frown. The one sweeps away all possibilities, the other suggests a thousand.

To disagree with three-fourths of England on all points is one of the first elements of vanity, which is a deep source of consolation in all moments of spiritual doubt.

Women live by their emotions and for them, they have no philosophy of life.

As long as war is regarded as wicked it will always have a fascination. When it is looked upon as vulgar it will cease to be popular.

There is only one thing worse than injustice, and that is justice without her sword in her hand. When right is not might it is evil.

We spend our days, each one of us, in looking for the secret of life. Well, the secret of life is in art.

The truth isn't quite the sort of thing that one tells to a nice, sweet, refined girl.

If one plays good music people don't listen, and if one plays bad music people don't talk.

How fond women are of doing dangerous things. It is one of the qualities in them that I admire most. A woman will flirt with anybody in the world as long as other people are looking on.

Englishwomen conceal their feelings till after they are married. They show them then.

Moderation is a fatal thing. Nothing succeeds like excess.

Actions are the first tragedy in life, words are the second. Words are perhaps the worst. Words are merciless.

Life is terrible. It rules us, we do not rule it.

In art there is no such thing as a universal truth. A truth in art is that whose contradictory is also true.

One's days are too brief to take the burden of another's sorrows on one's shoulders. Each man lives his own life, and pays his own price for living it. The only pity is that one has to pay so often for a single fault. One has to pay over and over again, indeed. In her dealings with man Destiny never closes her accounts.

Pleasure is Nature's test, her sign of approval. When we are happy we are always good, but when we are good we are not always happy.

The people who love only once in their lives are really the shallow people. What they call their loyalty and their fidelity I call either the lethargy of custom or their lack of imagination.

Better to take pleasure in a rose than to put its root under a microscope.

Of Shakespeare it may be said that he was the first to see the dramatic value of doublets and that a climax may depend on a crinoline.

Plain women are always jealous of their husbands; beautiful women never are! They never have time. They are always so occupied in being jealous of other people's husbands.

What between the duties expected of one during one's lifetime and the duties exacted from one after one's death land has ceased to be either a profit or a pleasure. It gives one position and prevents one from keeping it up.

A man who moralises is usually a hypocrite, and a woman who moralises is invariably plain. There is nothing in the whole world so unbecoming to a woman as a nonconformist conscience. And most women know it, I am glad to say.

It was a fatal day when the public discovered that the pen is mightier than the paving-stone and can be made as offensive as a brickbat.

A map of the world that does not include Utopia is not worth even glancing at, for it leaves out the one country at which Humanity is always landing. And when Humanity lands there it looks out, and, seeing a better country, sets sail. Progress is the realisation of Utopias.

What is the difference between scandal and gossip? Oh! gossip is charming! History is merely gossip, but scandal is gossip made tedious by morality.

All beautiful things belong to the same age.

It is personalities, not principles, that move the age.

Modern pictures are, no doubt, delightful to look at. At least, some of them are. But they are quite impossible to live with; they are too clever, too assertive, too intellectual. Their meaning is too obvious and their method too clearly defined. One exhausts what they have to say in a very short time, and then they become as tedious as one's relations.

To know nothing about our great men is one of the necessary elements of English education.

The truth is rarely pure and never simple. Modern life would be very tedious if it were either and modern literature a complete impossibility.

You may laugh, but it is a great thing to come across a woman who thoroughly understands one.

The majority of people spoil their lives by an unhealthy and exaggerated altruism.

The number of women in London who flirt with their own husbands is perfectly scandalous. It looks so bad. It is simply washing one's clean linen in public.

The chief thing that makes life a failure from the artistic point of view is the thing that lends to life its sordid security—the fact that one can never repeat exactly the same emotion.

We teach people how to remember, we never teach them how to grow.

Vulgar habit that is people have nowadays of asking one, after one has given them an idea, whether one is serious or not. Nothing is serious except passion. The intellect is not a serious thing and never has been. It is an instrument on which one plays, that is all. The only serious form of intellect I know is the British intellect, and on the British intellect the illiterate always plays the drum.

It is absurd to divide people into good and bad. People are either charming or tedious.

It is only the modern that ever become old-fashioned.

It is only the Philistine who seeks to estimate a personality by the vulgar test of production.

Musical people are so absurdly unreasonable. They always want one to be perfectly dumb at the very moment when one is longing to be absolutely deaf.

Nothing is so dangerous as being too modern. One is apt to grow old-fashioned quite suddenly.

The fact of a man being a poisoner is nothing against his prose. The domestic virtues are not the true basis of art.

To the philosopher women represent the triumph of matter over mind, just as men represent the triumph of mind over morals.

The only way a woman can ever reform a man is by boring him so completely that he loses all possible interest in life.

The only horrible thing in the world is 'ennui.' That is the one sin for which there is no forgiveness.

French songs I cannot possibly allow. People always seem to think that they are improper, and either look shocked, which is vulgar, or laugh, which is worse.

It has often been made a subject of reproach against artists and men of letters that they are lacking in wholeness and completeness of nature. As a rule this must necessarily be so. That very concentration of vision and inversity of purpose which is the characteristic of the artistic temperament is in itself a mode of limitation. To those who are preoccupied with the beauty of form nothing else seems of so much importance.

The work of art is to dominate the spectator. The spectator is not to dominate the work of art.

One should sympathise with the joy, the beauty, the colour of life. The less said about life's sores the better.

You can't make people good by act of Parliament—that is something.

Art creates an incomparable and unique effect, and having done so passes on to other things. Nature, on the other hand, forgetting that imitation can be made the sincerest form of insult, keeps on repeating the effect until we all become absolutely wearied of it.

It is perfectly monstrous the way people go about nowadays saying things against one behind one's back that are absolutely and entirely true.

A true artist takes no notice whatever of the public. The public are to him non-existent.

One should never trust a woman who tells one her real age. A woman who would tell one that would tell one anything.

Nothing is so aggravating as calmness. There is something positively brutal about the good temper of most modern men. I wonder we women stand it as well as we do.

The truth is a thing I get rid of as soon as possible. Bad habit, by the way, makes one very unpopular at the club ... with the older members. They call it being conceited. Perhaps it is.

My own business always bores me to death. I prefer other people's.

Don't be led astray into the paths of virtue—that is the worst of women. They always want one to be good. And if we are good, when they meet us they don't love us at all. They like to find us quite irretrievably bad and to leave us quite unattractively good.

Men are such cowards. They outrage every law in the world and are afraid of the world's tongue.

Wicked women bother one. Good women bore one. That is the only difference between them.

To know the principles of the highest art is to know the principles of all the arts.

I don't believe in the existence of Puritan women. I don't think there is a woman in the world who would not be a little flattered if one made love to her. It is that which makes women so irresistibly adorable.

When I am in trouble eating is the only thing that consoles me. Indeed, when I am in really great trouble, as anyone who knows me intimately will tell you, I refuse everything except food and drink.

When one is going to lead an entirely new life one requires regular and wholesome meals.

The soul is born old, but grows young. That is the comedy of life. The body is born young, and grows old. That is life's tragedy.

One can survive everything nowadays except death, and live down anything except a good reputation.

The past is of no importance. The present is of no importance. It is with the future that we have to deal. For the past is what men should not have been. The present is what men ought not to be. The future is what artists are.

Men become old, but they never become good.

By persistently remaining single a man converts himself into a permanent public temptation. Men should be more careful; this very celibacy leads weaker vessels astray.

I think that in practical life there is something about success, actual success, that is a little unscrupulous, something about ambition that is scrupulous always.

Every man of ambition has to fight his century with its own weapons. What this century worships is wealth. The god of this century is wealth. To succeed one must have wealth. At all costs one must have wealth.

I love scandals about other people, but scandals about myself don't interest me. They have not got the charm of novelty.

Moderation is a fatal thing. Enough is as bad as a meal. More than enough is as good as a feast.

The English can't stand a man who is always saying he is in the right, but they are very fond of a man who admits he has been in the wrong. It is one of the best things in them.

Life is simply a 'mauvais quart d'heure' made up of exquisite moments.

There is the same world for all of us, and good and evil, sin and innocence, go through it hand in hand. To shut one's eyes to half of life that one may live securely is as though one blinded oneself that one might walk with more safety in a land of pit and precipice.

Married men are horribly tedious when they are good husbands and abominably conceited when they are not.

Between men and women there is no friendship possible. There is passion, enmity, worship, love, but no friendship.

Everybody is clever nowadays. You can't go anywhere without meeting clever people. This has become an absolute public nuisance.

I don't think man has much capacity for development. He has got as far as he can, and that is not far, is it?

I am not quite sure that I quite know what pessimism really means. All I do know is that life cannot be understood without much charity, cannot be lived without much charity. It is love, and not German philosophy, that is the explanation of this world, whatever may be the explanation of the next.

I do not approve of anything that that tampers with natural arrogance. Ignorance is like a delicate exotic fruit: touch it, and the blossom is gone.

The whole theory of modern education is radically unsound. Fortunately, in England, at any rate, education produces no effect whatsoever. If it did it would prove a serious danger to the upper classes, and probably lead to acts of violence in Grosvenor Square.

No woman should ever be quite accurate about her age. It looks so calculating.

Emotion for the sake of emotion is the aim of art, and emotion for the sake of emotion is the aim of life and of that practical organisation of life that we call society.

Men of the noblest possible moral character are extremely susceptible to the influence of the physical charms of others. Modern, no less than ancient,

29

history supplies us with many most painful examples of what I refer to. If it were not so, indeed, history would be quite unreadable.

I am not in favour of long engagements. They give people the opportunity of finding out each other's character before marriage, which I think is never advisable.

It is a terrible thing for a man to find out suddenly that all his life he has been speaking nothing but the truth.

The two weak points in our age are its want of principle and its want of profile.

Thirty-five is a very attractive age. London society is full of women who have of their own free choice remained thirty-five for years.

Never speak disrespectfully of society. Only people who can't get into it do that.

It is always painful to part with people whom one has known for a very brief space of time. The absence of old friends one can endure with equanimity. But even a momentary separation from anyone to whom one has just been introduced is almost unbearable.

To be natural is to be obvious, and to be obvious is to be inartistic.

One is tempted to define man as a rational animal who always loses his temper when he is called upon to act in accordance with the dictates of reason.

The essence of thought, as the essence of life, is growth.

What people call insincerity is simply a method by which we can multiply our personalities.

In a temple everyone should be serious except the thing that is worshipped.

We are never more true to ourselves than when we are inconsistent.

There is always something ridiculous about the emotions of people whom one has ceased to love.

Intellectual generalities are always interesting, but generalities in morals mean absolutely nothing.

To be in society is merely a bore, but to be out of it simply a tragedy.

We live in an age when unnecessary things are our only necessities.

One should never make one's début with a scandal. One should reserve that to give an interest to one's old age.

What man has sought for is, indeed, neither pain nor pleasure, but simply life. Man has sought to live intensely, fully, perfectly. When he can do so without exercising restraint on others, or suffering it ever, and his activities are all pleasurable to him, he will be saner, healthier, more civilised, more himself. Pleasure is nature's test, her sign of approval. When man is happy he is in harmony with himself and his environment.

Society often forgives the criminal, it never forgives the dreamer.

It is so easy for people to have sympathy with suffering. It is so difficult for them to have sympathy with thought.

Conversation should touch on everything, but should concentrate itself on nothing.

There is a luxury in self-reproach. When we blame ourselves we feel that no one else has a right to blame us. It is the confession, not the priest, that gives us absolution.

There are only two kinds of people who are really fascinating—people who know absolutely everything and people who know absolutely nothing.

The public is wonderfully tolerant; it forgives everything except genius.

Life makes us pay too high a price for its wares, and we purchase the meanest of its secrets at a cost that is monstrous and infinite.

This horrid House of Commons quite ruins our husbands for us. I think the Lower House by far the greatest blow to a happy married life that there has been since that terrible thing they called the Higher Education of Women was invented.

Once a man begins to neglect his domestic duties he becomes painfully effeminate, does he not? And I don't like that. It makes men so very attractive.

Experience is a question of instinct about life.

What is true about art is true about life.

One can always be kind to people about whom one cares nothing.

I like men who have a future and women who have a past.

Women, as some witty Frenchman put it, inspire us with the desire to do masterpieces and always prevent us from carrying them out.

In matters of grave importance style, not sincerity, is the vital thing.

The only way to behave to a woman, is to make love to her if she is pretty and to someone else if she is plain.

Women give to men the very gold of their lives. Possibly; but they invariably want it back in such very small change.

Define women as a sex? Sphinxes without secrets.

What do you call a bad man? The sort of man who admires innocence.

What do you call a bad woman? Oh! the sort of woman a man never gets tired of.

One can resist everything except temptation.

Don't let us go to life for our fulfilment or our experience. It is a thing narrowed by circumstances, incoherent in its utterance, and without that fine correspondence or form and spirit which is the only thing that can satisfy the artistic and critical temperament.

It is a dangerous thing to reform anyone.

One can always know at once whether a man has home claims upon his life or not. I have noticed a very, very sad expression in the eyes of so many married men.

A mother who doesn't part with a daughter every season has no real affection.

To be good is to be in harmony with oneself. Discord is to be forced to be in harmony with others.

A really grand passion is comparatively rare nowadays. It is the privilege of people who have nothing to do. That is the one use of the idle classes in a country.

There is no secret of life. Life's aim, if it has one, is simply to be always looking for temptations. There are not nearly enough of them; I sometimes pass a whole day without coming across a single one. It is quite dreadful. It makes one so nervous about the future.

All thought is immoral. Its very essence is destruction. If you think of anything you kill it; nothing survives being thought of.

What is truth? In matters of religion it is simply the opinion that has survived. In matters of science it is the ultimate sensation. In matters of art it is one's last mood.

It is so easy to convert others. It is so difficult to convert oneself.

A little sincerity is a dangerous thing, and a great deal of it is absolutely fatal.

Life cheats us with shadows, like a puppet-master. We ask it for pleasure. It gives it to us, with bitterness and disappointment in its train. We come across some noble grief that we think will lend the purple dignity of tragedy to our days, but it passes away from us, and things less noble take its place, and on some grey, windy dawn, or odorous eve of silence and of silver, we find ourselves looking with callous wonder, or dull heart of stone, at the tress of gold-flecked hair that we had once so wildly worshipped and so madly kissed.

There are two ways of disliking art One is to dislike it and the other to like it rationally.

There is nothing sane about the worship of beauty. It is too splendid to be sane. Those of whose lives it forms the dominant note will always seem to the world to be mere visionaries.

I am afraid that good people do a great deal of harm in this world. Certainly the greatest harm they do is that they make badness of such extraordinary importance.

A sentimentalist is a man who sees an absurd value in everything and doesn't know the marked price of any single thing.

Punctuality is the thief of time.

Self-culture is the true ideal for man.

There's nothing in the world like the devotion of a married woman. It's a thing no married man knows anything about.

No woman should have a memory. Memory in a woman is the beginning of dowdiness. One can always tell from a woman's bonnet whether she has got a memory or not.

There are things that are right to say but that may be said at the wrong time and to the wrong people.

The meaning of any beautiful created thing is, at least, as much in the soul of him who looks at it as it was in his soul who wrought it. Nay, it is rather the beholder who lends to the beautiful thing its myriad meanings, and makes it marvellous for us, and sets it in some new relation to the age, so that it becomes a vital portion of our lives and a symbol of what we pray for, or perhaps of what, having prayed for, we fear that we may receive.

The Renaissance was great because it sought to solve no social problem, and busied itself not about such things, but suffered the individual to develop freely, beautifully, and naturally, and so had great and individual artists and great and individual men.

In England people actually try to be brilliant at breakfast. That is so dreadful of them! Only dull people are brilliant at breakfast.

When one is in love one begins by deceiving oneself, and one ends by deceiving others. That is what the world calls a romance.

The secret of life is never to have an emotion that is unbecoming.

No artist is ever morbid. The artist can express everything.

The development of the race depends on the development of the individual, and where self-culture has ceased to be the ideal the intellectual standard is instantly lowered and often ultimately lost.

An idea that is not dangerous is unworthy of being called an idea at all.

To elope is cowardly; it is running away from danger, and danger has become so rare in modern life.

When a man is old enough to do wrong he should be old enough to do right also.

The Book of Life begins with a man and a woman in a garden. It ends with Revelations.

In married life three is company and two is none.

Out of ourselves we can never pass, nor can there be in creation what in the creator was not.

Don't tell me that you have exhausted life. When a man says that one knows that life has exhausted him.

When a woman marries again it is because she detested her first husband. When a man marries again it is because he adored his first wife. Women try their luck; men risk theirs.

The highest criticism really is the record of one's own soul. It is more fascinating than history, as it is concerned simply with oneself. It is more delightful than philosophy, as its subject is concrete and not abstract, real and not vague. It is the only civilised form of autobiography, as it deals, not with the events, but with the thoughts of one's life, not with life's physical accidents of deed or circumstance, but with the spiritual moods and imaginative passions of the mind.

To know anything about oneself one must know all about others.

Duty is what one expects from others, it is not what one does oneself.

After a good dinner one can forgive anybody, even one's own relations.

Talk to every woman as if you loved her and to every man as if he bored you, and at the end of your first season you will have the reputation of possessing the most perfect social tact.

Man—poor, awkward, reliable, necessary man—belongs to a sex that has been rational for millions and millions of years. He can't help himself; it is in his race. The history of women is very different. They have always been picturesque protests against the mere existence of common-sense; they saw its dangers from the first.

More marriages are ruined nowadays by the common-sense of the husband than by anything else. How can a woman be expected to be happy with a man who insists on treating her as if she were a perfectly rational being.

It is very vulgar to talk about one's business. Only people like stock-brokers do that, and then merely at dinner-parties.

It is awfully hard work doing nothing. However, I don't mind hard work when there is no definite object of any kind.

To do nothing at all is the most difficult thing in the world, the most difficult and the most intellectual. To Plato, with his passion for wisdom, this was the noblest form of energy.

To Aristotle, with his passion for knowledge, this was the noblest form of energy also. It was to this that the passion for holiness led the saint and the mystic of mediæval days.

Youth! There is nothing like it. It is absurd to talk of the ignorance of youth. The only people to whose opinions I listen now with any respect are persons much younger than myself. They seem in front of me. Life has revealed to them her latest wonder.

Romance lives by repetition, and repetition converts an appetite into an art.

I adore simple pleasures. They are the last refuge of the complex.

There is nothing like youth. The middle-aged are mortgaged to life. The old are in life's lumber-room. But youth is the lord of life. Youth has a kingdom waiting for it. Everyone is born a king, and most people die in exile—like most kings.

All crime is vulgar, just as all vulgarity is crime.

Society, civilised society at least, is never very ready to believe anything to the detriment of those who are both rich and fascinating. It instinctively feels that manners are of more importance than morals, and in its opinion the highest respectability is of much less value than the possession of a good chef. And, after all, it is a very poor consolation to be told that the man who has given one a bad dinner or poor wine is irreproachable in his private life. Even the cardinal virtues cannot atone for half-cold entrees.

While, in the opinion of society, contemplation is the gravest thing of which any citizen can be guilty, in the opinion of the highest culture it is the proper occupation of man.

Life is terribly deficient in form. Its catastrophes happen in the wrong way and to the wrong people. There is a grotesque horror about its comedies, and its tragedies seem to culminate in farce. One is always wounded when one approaches it. Things last either too long or not long enough.

If a woman wants to hold a man she has merely to appeal to what is worst in him.

We are all in the gutter, but some of us are looking at the stars.

Beauty has as many meanings as man has moods. It is the symbol of symbols. It reveals everything, because it expresses nothing. When it shows us itself it shows us the whole fiery-coloured world.

Men always want to be a woman's first love. That is their clumsy vanity. Women have a more subtle instinct about things. What they like is to be a man's last romance.

Anything approaching to the free play of the mind is practically unknown amongst us. People cry out against the sinner, yet it is not the sinful but the stupid who are our shame. There is no sin except stupidity.

One regrets the loss even of one's worst habits. Perhaps one regrets them the most. They are such an essential part of one's personality.

It is through art, and through art only, that we can realise our perfection; through art and through art only, that we can shield ourselves from the sordid perils of actual existence.

A man who can dominate a London dinner-table can dominate the world. The future belongs to the dandy. It is the exquisites who are going to rule.

It often happens that the real tragedies of life occur in such an inartistic manner that they hurt us by their crude violence, their absolute incoherence, their absurd want of meaning, their entire lack of style. They affect us just as vulgarity affects us. They give us an impression of sheer brute force, and we revolt against that. Sometimes, however, a tragedy that possesses artistic elements of beauty crosses our lives. If these elements of beauty are real the whole thing simply appeals to our sense of dramatic effect. Suddenly we find that we are no longer the actors but the spectators of the play. Or rather we are both. We watch ourselves, and the mere wonder of the spectacle enthrals us.

When a woman finds out that her husband is absolutely indifferent to her, she either becomes dreadfully dowdy or wears very smart bonnets that some other woman's husband has to pay for.

It is immoral to use private property in order to alleviate the horrible evils that result from the institution of private property.

It is a mistake to think that the passion one feels in creation is ever really shown in the work one creates. Art is always more abstract than we fancy. Form and colour tell us of form and colour-that is all.

It is sometimes said that the tragedy of an artist's life is that he cannot realise his ideal. But the true tragedy that dogs the steps of most artists is that they realise their ideal too absolutely. For when the ideal is realised it is robbed of its wonder and its mystery, and becomes simply a new starting-point for an ideal that is other than itself.

People who go in for being consistent have just as many moods as others have. The only difference is that their moods are rather meaningless.

It is only shallow people who require years to get rid of an emotion. A man who is master of himself can end a sorrow as easily as he can invent a pleasure.

Good women have such a limited view of life, their horizon is so small, their interests so petty. The fact is they are not modern, and to be modern is the only thing worth being nowadays.

Discontent is the first step in the progress of a man or a nation.

Men marry because they are tired, women because they are curious. Both are disappointed.

All men are married women's property. That is the only true definition of what married women's property really is.

I am not in favour of this modern mania for turning bad people into good people at a moment's notice. As a man sows so let him reap.

Nothing refines but the intellect.

It is very painful for me to be forced to speak the truth. It is the first time in my life that I have ever been reduced to such a painful position, and I am really quite inexperienced in doing anything of the kind.

The man who regards his past is a man who deserves to have no future to look forward to.

Just as it is only by contact with the art of foreign nations that the art of a country gains that individual and separate life that we call nationality, so, by curious inversion, it is only by intensifying his own personality that the critic can interpret the personality of others; and the more strongly this personality enters into the interpretation the more real the interpretation becomes, the more satisfying, the more convincing, and the more true.

Man is least himself when he talks in his own person. Give him a mask, and he will tell you the truth.

All women become like their mothers: that is their tragedy. No man does: that is his.

Women are a fascinatingly wilful sex. Every woman is a rebel, and usually in wild revolt against herself.

One should always be in love. That is the reason one should never marry.

No man came across two ideal things. Few come across one.

To become the spectator of one's own life is to escape the suffering of life.

The state is to make what is useful. The individual is to make what is beautiful.

A community is infinitely more brutalised by the habitual employment of punishment than it is by the occasional occurrence of crime.

The systems that fail are those that rely on the permanency of human nature and not on its growth and development.

Jealousy, which is an extraordinary source of crime in modern life, is an emotion closely bound up with our conceptions of property, and under socialism and individualism will die out. It is remarkable that in communistic tribes jealousy is entirely unknown.

All art is immoral.

He to whom the present is the only thing that is present knows nothing of the age in which he lives. To realise the nineteenth century one must realise every century that has preceded it and that has contributed to its making.

Few parents nowadays pay any regard to what their children say to them. The old-fashioned respect for the young is fast dying out.

The history of woman is the history of the worst form of tyranny the world has ever known; the tyranny of the weak over the strong. It is the only tyranny that lasts.

The happiness of a married man depends on the people he has not married.

There is no one type for man. There are as many perfections as there are imperfect men. And while to the claims of charity a man may yield and yet be free, to the claims of conformity no man may yield and remain free at all.

A practical scheme is either a scheme that is already in existence or a scheme that could be carried out under existing conditions.

All imitation in morals and in life is wrong.

The world has been made by fools that wise men may live in it.

Women love us for our defects. If we have enough of them they will forgive us everything, even our gigantic intellects.

Society is a necessary thing. No man has any real success in this world unless he has got women to back him—and women rule society. If you have not got women on your side you are quite over. You might just as well be a barrister or a stockbroker or a journalist at once.

The worship of the senses has often, and with much justice, been decried; men feeling a natural instinct of terror about passions and sensations that seem stronger than themselves, and that they are conscious of sharing with the less highly organised forms of existence. But it is probable the true nature of the senses has never been understood, and that they have remained savage and animal merely because the world has sought to starve them into submission or to kill them by pain instead of aiming at making them elements of a new spirituality, of which a fine instinct for beauty will be the dominant characteristic.

Women appreciate cruelty more than anything else. They have wonderfully primitive instincts. We have emancipated them, but they remain slaves, looking for their master all the same. They love being dominated.

Those who try to lead the people can only do so by following the mob. It is through the voice of one crying in the wilderness that the way of the gods must be prepared.

Circumstances are the lashes laid on to us by life. Some of us have to receive them with bared ivory backs, and others are permitted to keep on a coat—that is the only difference.

Criticism is itself an art.... It is no more to be judged by any low standard of imitation or resemblance than is the work of poet or sculptor. The critic occupies the same relation to the work of art that he criticises as the artist does to the visible world of form and colour or the unseen world of passion and thought. He does not even require for the perfection of his art the finest materials. Anything will serve his purpose.

It is very much more difficult to talk about a thing than to do it. In the sphere of actual life that is, of course, obvious. Anybody can make history, only a great man can write it.

If we lived long enough to see the results of our actions it may be that those who call themselves good would be filled with a wild remorse and those whom the world calls evil stirred with a noble joy. Each little thing that we do passes into the great machine of life, which may grind our virtues to powder and make them worthless or transform our sins into elements of a new civilisation more marvellous and more splendid than any that has gone before.

Children begin by loving their parents; as they grow older they judge them, sometimes they forgive them.

We live in an age that reads too much to be wise and that thinks too much to be beautiful.

One should absorb the colour of life, but one should never remember its details. Details are always vulgar.

It will be a marvellous thing—the true personality of man—when we see it. It will grow naturally and simply flowerlike, or as a tree grows. It will not be at discord. It will never argue or dispute. It will not prove things. It will know everything, and yet it will not busy itself about knowledge. It will have wisdom. Its value will not be measured by material things. It will have nothing, and yet it will have everything, and whatever one takes from it it will still have, so rich it will be. It will not be always meddling with others or asking them to be like itself. It will love them because they will be different. And yet, while it will not meddle with others, it will help all, as a beautiful thing helps us, by being what it is. The personality of man will be very wonderful. It will be as wonderful as the personality of a child.

Cynicism is merely the art of seeing things as they are instead of as they ought to be.

Three addresses always inspire confidence, even in tradesmen.

If one doesn't talk about a thing it has never happened. It is simply expression that gives reality to things.

No man is able who is unable to get on, just as no woman is clever who can't succeed in obtaining that worst and most necessary of evils, a husband.

The one charm of the past is that it is the past. But women never know when the curtain has fallen. They always want a sixth act, and as soon as the interest of the play is entirely over they propose to continue it. If they were allowed their way every comedy would have a tragic ending and every tragedy would culminate in a farce. They are charmingly artificial, but they have no sense of art.

Each time that one loves is the only time that one has ever loved. Difference of object does not alter singleness of passion. It merely intensifies it.

The real tragedy of the poor is that they can afford nothing but self-denial. Beautiful sins, like beautiful things, are the privilege of the rich.

Human life is the one thing worth investigating. Compared to it there is nothing else of any value. It is true that as one watches life in its curious crucible of pain and pleasure one cannot wear over one's face a mask of glass nor keep the sulphurous fumes from troubling the brain and making the imagination turbid with monstrous fancies and misshapen dreams. There are poisons so subtle that to know their properties one has to sicken of them. There are maladies so strange that one has to pass through them if one seeks to understand their nature. And yet what a great reward one receives! How wonderful the whole world becomes to one! To note the curious, hard logic of passion and the emotional, coloured life of the intellect—to observe where they meet, and where they separate, at what point they are in unison and at what point they are in discord—there is a delight in that! What matter what the cost is? One can never pay too high a price for any sensation.

There is only one class in the community that thinks more about money than the rich, and that is the poor. The poor can think of nothing else. That is the misery of being poor.

To live is the rarest thing in the world. Most people exist—that is all.

Personality is a very mysterious thing. A man cannot always be estimated by what he does. He may keep the law, and yet be worthless. He may break the law, and yet be fine. He may be bad without ever doing anything bad. He may commit a sin against society, and yet realise through that sin his true perfection.

Mediæval art is charming, but mediæval emotions are out of date. One can use them in fiction, of course; but then the only things that one can use in fiction are the only things that one has ceased to use in fact.

Man is complete in himself.

What is a cynic? A man who knows the price of everything and the value of nothing.

It's the old, old story. Love—well, not at first sight—but love at the end of the season, which is so much more satisfactory.

No nice girl should ever waltz with such particularly younger sons! It looks so fast!

Good resolutions are useless attempts to interfere with scientific laws. Their origin is pure vanity. Their result is absolutely nil. They give us now and then some of those luxurious, sterile emotions that have a certain charm for the weak. That is all that can be said for them. They are simply cheques that men draw on a bank where they have no account.

What is the difference between literature and journalism? Journalism is unreadable and literature is unread.

I hope you have not been leading a double life, pretending to be wicked and being really good all the time. That would be hypocrisy.

My husband is a sort of promissory note; I am tired of meeting him.

Conscience makes egotists of us all.

Never trust a woman who wears mauve, whatever her age may be, or a woman over thirty-five who is fond of pink ribbons. It always means that they have a history.

There is a fatality about good resolutions-they are always made too late.

We can have in life but one great experience at best, and the secret of life is to reproduce that experience as often as possible.

Anybody can be good in the country. There are no temptations there. That is the reason why people who live out of town are so absolutely uncivilised. Civilisation is not by any means an easy thing to attain to. There are only two ways by which man can reach it. One is by being cultured, the other by being corrupt. Country people have no opportunity of being either, so they stagnate.

What nonsense people talk about happy marriages! A man can be happy with any woman so long as he does not love her.

The things one feels absolutely certain about are never true. That is the fatality of faith and the lesson of romance.

In the common world of fact the wicked are not punished nor the good rewarded. Success is given to the strong, failure thrust upon the weak.

Nothing should be able to harm a man except himself. Nothing should be able to rob a man at all. What a man really has is what is in him. What is outside of him should be a matter of no importance.

Modern morality consists in accepting the standard of one's age. I consider that for any man of culture to accept the standard of his age is a form of the grossest immorality.

Perplexity and mistrust fan affection into passion, and so bring about those beautiful tragedies that alone make life worth living. Women once felt this, while men did not, and so women once ruled the world.

Sin is a thing that writes itself across a man's, face. It cannot be concealed. People talk sometimes of secret vices. There are no such things.

If a wretched man has a vice it shows itself in the lines of his mouth, the drop of his eyelids, the moulding of his hands even.

There are sins whose fascination is more in the memory than in the doing of them, strange triumphs that gratify the pride more than the passions and give to the intellect a quickened sense of joy, greater than they bring or can ever bring to the senses.

No civilised man ever regrets a pleasure, and no uncivilised man ever knows what a pleasure is.

As for a spoiled life, no life is spoiled but one whose growth is arrested. If you want to mar a nature you have merely to reform it.

Socialism itself will be of value simply because it will lead to individualism.

Some years ago people went about the country saying that property has duties. It is perfectly true. Property not merely has duties, but has so many duties that its possession to any large extent is a bore. If property had simply pleasures we could stand it, but its duties make it unbearable.

It is through joy that the individualism of the future will develop itself. Christ made no attempt to reconstruct society, and consequently the individualism that He preached to man could be realised only through pain or in solitude.

Most people become bankrupt through having invested too heavily in the prose of life. To have ruined oneself over poetry is an honour.

The only artists I have ever known who are personally delightful are bad artists. Good artists exist simply on what they make, and consequently are perfectly uninteresting in what they are.

What are the virtues? Nature, Renan tells us, cares little about chastity, and it may be that it is to the shame of the Magdalen, and not to their own purity, that the Lucretias of modern life owe their freedom from stain. Charity, as even those of whose religion it makes a formal part have been compelled to acknowledge, creates a multitude of evils. The mere existence of conscience, that faculty of which people prate so much nowadays, and are so ignorantly proud, is a sign of our imperfect development. It must be merged in instinct before we become fine. Self-denial is simply a method by which man arrests his progress, and self-sacrifice a survival of the mutilation of the savage, part of that old worship of pain which is so terrible a factor in the history of the world, and which even now makes its victims day by day and has its altars in the land. Virtues! Who knows what the virtues are? Not you. Not I. Not anyone. It is well for our vanity that we slay the criminal, for if we suffered him to live he might show us what we had gained by his crime. It is well for his peace that the saint goes to his martyrdom. He is spared the sight of the horror of his harvest.

Nowadays all the married men live like bachelors and all the bachelors like married men.

The higher education of men is what I should like to see. Men need it so sadly.

The world is perfectly packed with good women. To know them is a middle-class education.

Hesitation of any kind is a sign of mental decay in the young, of physical weakness in the old.

Our husbands never appreciate anything in us. We have to go to others for that.

Most women in London nowadays seem to furnish their rooms with nothing but orchids, foreigners and French novels.

The canons of good society are, or should be, the same as the canons of art. Form is absolutely essential to it. It should have the dignity of a ceremony as well as its unreality, and should combine the insincere character of a romantic play with the wit and beauty that make such plays delightful to us. Is sincerity such a terrible thing? I think not. It is merely a method by which we can multiply our personalities.

The tragedy of old age is not that one is old but that one is young.

A great poet, a really great poet, is the most unpoetical of all creatures. But inferior poets are absolutely fascinating. The worse their rhymes are the more picturesque they look. The mere fact of having published a book of second-rate sonnets makes a man quite irresistible. He lives the poetry that he cannot write. The others write the poetry that they dare not realise.

Being adored is a nuisance. Women treat us just as humanity treats its gods. They worship us, and are always bothering us to do something for them.

If a man treats life artistically his brain is his heart.

The 'Peerage' is the one book a young man about town should know thoroughly, and it is the best thing in fiction the English have ever done.

The world has always laughed at its own tragedies, that being the only way in which it has been able to bear them. Consequently whatever the world has treated seriously belongs to the comedy side of things.

The only difference between the saint and the sinner is that every saint has a past and every sinner has a future.

What is termed sin is an essential element of progress. Without it the world would stagnate or grow old or becomes colourless. By its curiosity it increases the experience of the race. Through its intensified assertion of individualism it saves us from the commonplace. In its rejection of the current notions about morality it is one with the higher ethics.

Formerly we used to canonise our heroes. The modern method is to vulgarise them. Cheap editions of great books may be delightful, but cheap editions of great men are absolutely detestable.

Individualism does not come to man with any claims upon him at all. It comes naturally and inevitably out of man. It is the point to which all development tends. It is the differentiation to which all organisms grow. It is the perfection that is inherent in every mode of life and toward which every mode of life quickens. Individualism exercises no compulsion over man. On the contrary, it says to man that he should suffer no compulsion to be exercised over him. It does not try to force people to be good. It knows that people are good when they are let alone. Man will develop individualism out of himself. Man is now so developing individualism. To ask whether individualism is practical is like asking whether evolution is practical. Evolution is the law of life, and there is no evolution except towards individualism.

The longer I live the more keenly I feel that whatever was good enough for our fathers is not good enough for us. In art, as in politics, 'les grand pères ont toujours tort.'

No woman is a genius. Women are a decorative sex. They never have anything to say but they say it charmingly.

Humanity takes itself too seriously. It is the world's original sin. If the cave men had known how to laugh history would have been different.

I wonder who it was defined man as a rational animal. It was the most premature definition ever given. Man is many things, but he is not rational.

Thought and language are to the artist instruments of an art.

To get into the best society nowadays one has either to feed people, amuse people, or shock people—that is all.

You should never try to understand women. Women are pictures, men are problems. If you want to know what a woman really means—which, by the way, is always a dangerous thing to do—look at her, don't listen to her.

Ordinary women never appeal to one's imagination. They are limited to their century. No glamour ever transfigures them. One knows their minds as easily as one knows their bonnets. One can always find them. There is no mystery in any of them. They ride in the park in the morning and chatter at tea parties in the afternoon. They have their stereotyped smile and their fashionable mauve.

Don't run down dyed hair and painted faces. There is an extraordinary charm in them—sometimes.

To have been well brought up is a great drawback nowadays. It shuts one out from so much.

The people who have adored me—there have not been very many, but there have been some—have always insisted on living on long after I had ceased to care for them or they to care for me. They have become stout and tedious, and when I meet them they go in at once for reminiscences. That awful memory of women! What a fearful thing it is! And what an utter intellectual stagnation it reveals!

Examinations are pure humbug from beginning to end. If a man is a gentleman he knows quite enough, and if he is not a gentleman whatever he knows is bad for him.

Credit is the capital of a younger son, and he can live charmingly on it.

The object of art is not simply truth but complex beauty. Art itself is really a form of exaggeration, and selection, which is the very spirit of art, is nothing more than an intensified mode of over-emphasis.

The popular cry of our time is: 'Let us return to Life and Nature, they will recreate Art for us and send the red blood coursing through her veins; they will shoe her feet with swiftness and make her hand strong.' But, alas! we are mistaken in our amiable and well-meant efforts. Nature is always behind the age. And as for life, she is the solvent that breaks up Art, the enemy that lays waste her house.

There are only two kinds of women—the plain and the coloured. The plain women are very useful. If you want to gain a reputation for respectability you have merely to take them down to supper. The other women are very charming. They commit one mistake, however—they paint in order to try and look young.

The way of paradoxes is the way of truth. To test reality we must see it on the tight-rope. When the verities become acrobats we can judge them.

Life imitates art far more than art imitates life.... The Greeks with their quick, artistic instinct understood this, and set in the bride's chamber the statue of Hermes or of Apollo, that she might bear children as lovely as the works of art that she looked at in her rapture or her pain. They knew that life gains from art not merely spirituality, depth of thought and feeling, soul-turmoil or soul-peace, but that she can form herself on the very lines and colours of art, and can reproduce the dignity of Pheidias as well as the grace of Praxiteles. Hence came this objection to realism. They disliked it on purely social grounds. They felt that it inevitably makes people ugly, and they were perfectly right.

Faithfulness is to the emotional life what consistency is to the life of the intellect—simply a confession of failure.

There are many things that we would throw away if we were not afraid that others might pick them up.

What a fuss people make about fidelity! Why, even in love it is purely a question for physiology. It has nothing to do with our own will. Young men want to be faithful and are not; old men want to be faithless and cannot—that is all one can say.

Modernity of form and modernity of subject-matter are entirely and absolutely wrong. We have mistaken the common livery of the age for the vesture of the muses, and spent our days in the sordid streets and hideous suburbs of our vile cities when we should be out on the hillside with Apollo.

Certainly we are a degraded race, and have sold our birthright for a mess of facts.

Nothing can cure the soul but the senses, just as nothing can cure the senses but the soul.

I can stand brute force, but brute reason is quite unbearable. There is something unfair about its use. It is hitting below the intellect.

Those who live in marble or on painted panel know of life but a single exquisite instant, eternal, indeed, in its beauty but limited to one note of passion or one mood of calm. Those whom the poet makes live have their myriad emotions of joy and terror, of courage and despair, of pleasure and of suffering. The seasons come and go in glad or saddening pageant, and with winged or leaden feet the years pass by before them. They have their youth and their manhood, they are children, and they grow old. It is always dawn for St Helena as Veronese saw her at the window. Through the still morning air the angels bring her the symbol of God's pain. The cool breezes of the morning lift the gilt threads from her brow. On that little hill by the city of Florence, where the lovers of Giorgione are lying, it is always the solstice of noon—of noon made so languorous by summer suns that hardly can the slim, naked girl dip into the marble tank the round bubble of clear glass, and the long fingers of the lute player rest idly upon the chords. It is twilight always for the dancing nymphs whom Corot set free among the silver poplars of France. In eternal twilight they move, those frail, diaphanous figures, whose tremulous, white feet seem not to touch the dew-drenched grass they tread on. But those who walk in epos, drama, or romance see through the labouring months the young moons wax and wane, and watch the night from evening into morning star, and from sunrise into sun-setting can note the shifting day with all its gold and shadow. For them, as for us, the flowers bloom and wither, and the earth, that green-tressed goddess, as Coleridge calls her, alters her raiment for their pleasure. The statue is concentrated to one moment of perfection. The image stained upon the canvas possesses no spiritual element of growth or change. If they know nothing of death it is because they know little of life, for the secrets of life and death belong to those, and to those only, whom the sequence of time affects, and who possess not merely the present but the future, and can rise or fall from a past of glory or of shame. Movement, that problem of the visible arts, can be truly realised by literature alone. It is literature that shows us the body in its swiftness and the soul in its unrest.

Behind every exquisite thing that exists there is something tragic. Worlds have to be in travail that the merest flower may blow.

Beauty is a form of genius—is higher, indeed, than genius, as it needs no explanation. It is one of the great facts of the world, like sunlight, or spring-time, or the reflection in dark water of that silver shell we call the moon. It cannot be questioned, it has its divine right of sovereignty.

The only way to get rid of a temptation is to yield to it. Resist it and your soul grows sick with longing for the things it has forbidden to itself.

Women spoil every romance by trying to make it last for ever.

He's sure to be a wonderful success. He thinks like a Tory and talks like a Radical, and that's so important nowadays.

Nowadays to be intelligible is to be found out.

We make gods of men and they leave us. Others make brutes of them and they fawn and are faithful.

The husbands of very beautiful women belong to the criminal classes.

To me beauty is the Wonder of wonders. It is only shallow people who do not judge by appearances.

The true mystery of the world is the visible, not the invisible.

The thoroughly well-informed man is the modern ideal. And the mind of the thoroughly well-informed man is a dreadful thing. It is like a bric-a-brac shop, all monsters and dust, with everything priced above its proper value.

Women have no appreciation of good looks in men—at least good women have none.

To influence a person is to give him one's own soul. He does not think

53

his natural thoughts or burn with his natural passions. His virtues are not real to him. His sins, if there are such things as sins, are borrowed. He becomes an echo of someone else's music, an actor of a part that has not been written for him.

Those who are faithful know only the trivial side of love; it is the faithless who know love's tragedies.

An artist should create beautiful things, but should put nothing of his own life into them. We live in an age when men treat art as if it were meant to be a form of autobiography. We have lost the abstract sense of beauty.

A man cannot be too careful in the choice of his enemies. I have not got one who is a fool. They are all men of some intellectual power, and consequently they all appreciate me.

The value of an idea has nothing whatever to do with the sincerity of the man who expresses it.

I like persons better than principles, and I like persons with no principles better than anything else in the world.

He who would lead a Christ-like life is he who is perfectly and absolutely himself. He may be a great poet, or a great man of science; or a young student at the university, or one who watches sheep upon a moor; or a maker of dramas, like Shakespeare, or a thinker about God, like Spinoza; or a child who plays in a garden, or a fisherman who throws his nets into the sea. It does not matter what he is as long as he realises the perfection of the soul that is within him.

The aim of life is self-development. To realise one's nature perfectly— that is what each of us is here for.

There is no such thing as a good influence. All influence is immoral— immoral from the scientific point of view.

Words have not merely music as sweet as that of viol and lute, colour as rich and vivid as any that makes lovely for us the canvas of the Venetian or the Spaniard, and plastic form no less sure and certain than that which reveals itself in marble or in bronze, but thought and passion and spirituality are theirs also—are theirs, indeed, alone.

There is nothing so absolutely pathetic as a really fine paradox. The pun is the clown among jokes, the well-turned paradox is the polished comedian, and the highest comedy verges upon tragedy, just as the keenest edge of tragedy is often tempered by a subtle humour. Our minds are shot with moods as a fabric is shot with colours, and our moods often seem inappropriate. Everything that is true is inappropriate.

The longer one studies life and literature the more strongly one feels that behind everything that is wonderful stands the individual, and that it is not the moment that makes the man but the man who creates the age.

To know the vintage and quality of a wine one need not drink the whole cask.

It is a sad thing to think of, but there is no doubt that genius lasts longer than beauty. That accounts for the fact that we all take such pains to over-educate ourselves.

The ugly and the stupid have the best of it in this world. They can sit at their ease and gape at the play. If they know nothing of victory they are at least spared the knowledge of defeat.

To have a capacity for a passion, and not to realise it is to make oneself incomplete and limited.

Even in actual life egotism is not without its attractions. When people talk to us about others they are usually dull. When they talk to us about themselves they are nearly always interesting, and if one could shut them up when they become wearisome as easily as one can shut up a book of which one has grown wearied they would be perfect absolutely.

Every great man nowadays has his disciples and it is invariably Judas who writes the biography.

Art finds her own perfection within, and not outside of, herself. She is not to be judged by any external standard of resemblance. She is a veil rather than a mirror. She has flowers that no forest knows of, birds that no woodland possesses. She makes and unmakes many worlds, and can draw the moon from heaven with a scarlet thread. Hers are the 'forms more real than living man,' and hers the great archetypes, of which things that have existence are but unfinished copies. Nature has, in her eyes, no laws, no uniformity. She can work miracles at her will, and when she calls monsters from the deep they come. She can bid the almond-tree blossom in winter and send the snow upon the ripe cornfield. At her word the frost lays its silver finger on the burning mouth of June, and the winged lions creep out from the hollows of the Lydian hills. The dryads peer from the thicket as she passes by, and the brown fauns smile strangely at her when she comes near them. She has hawk-faced gods that worship her, and the centaurs gallop at her side.

In literature mere egotism is delightful.

If we live for aims we blunt our emotions. If we live for aims we live for one minute, for one day, for one year, instead of for every minute, every day, every year. The moods of one's life are life's beauties. To yield to all one's moods is to really live.

Many a young man starts in life with a natural gift for exaggeration which, if nurtured in congenial and sympathetic surroundings, or by the imitations of the best models, might grow into something really great and wonderful. But, as a rule, he comes to nothing. He either falls into careless habits of accuracy or takes to frequenting the society of the aged and the well-informed. Both things are equally fatal to his imagination.

The spirit of an age may be best expressed in the abstract ideal arts, for the spirit itself is abstract and ideal.

As for believing things, I can believe anything provided that it is quite incredible.

'Know thyself' was written over the portal of the antique world. Over the portal of the new world 'Be thyself' shall be written. And the message of Christ to man was simply: 'Be thyself.' That is the secret of Christ.

London is full of women who trust their husbands. One can always recognise them, they look so thoroughly unhappy.

For those who are not artists, and to whom there is no mode of life but the actual life of fact, pain is the only door to perfection.

The English public always feels perfectly at its ease when a mediocrity is talking to it.

Men always fall into the absurdity of endeavouring to develop the mind, to push it violently forward in this direction or in that. The mind should be receptive, a harp waiting to catch the winds, a pool ready to be ruffled, not a bustling busybody for ever trotting about on the pavement looking for a new bun shop.

There is nothing more beautiful than to forget, except, perhaps, to be forgotten.

All bad art comes from returning to life and nature, and elevating them into ideals. Life and nature may sometimes be used as part of art's rough material, but before they are of any real service to art they must be translated into artistic conventions. The moment art surrenders its imaginative medium it surrenders everything. As a method realism is a complete failure, and the two things that every artist should avoid are modernity of form and modernity of subject-matter.

Men may have women's minds just as women may have the minds of men.

London is too full of fogs and serious people. Whether the fogs produce the serious people or whether the serious people produce the fogs I don't know.

How marriage ruins a man! It's as demoralising as cigarettes, and far more expensive.

He must be quite respectable. One has never heard his name before in the whole course of one's life, which speaks volumes for a man nowadays.

Literature always anticipates life. It does not copy it, but moulds it to its purpose.

As long as a thing is useful or necessary to us or affects us in any way, either for pain or pleasure, or appeals strongly to our sympathies or is a vital part of the environment in which we live, it is outside the proper sphere of art.

I couldn't have a scene in this bonnet: it is far too fragile. A harsh word would ruin it.

Music creates for one a past of which one has been ignorant and fills one with a sense of sorrows that have been hidden from one's tears.

Nothing is so fatal to personality as deliberation.

I adore London dinner parties. The clever people never listen and the stupid people never talk.

Learned conversation is either the affection of the ignorant or the profession of the mentally unemployed.

The Academy is too large and too vulgar. Whenever I have gone there, there have been either so many people that I have not been able to see the pictures—which was dreadful, or so many pictures that I have not been able to see the people—which was worse.

All art is quite useless.

Beauty, real beauty, ends where an intellectual expression begins. Intellect is in itself a mode of exaggeration and destroys the harmony of any face. The moment one sits down to think one becomes all nose or all forehead or something horrid.

The one charm of marriage is that it makes a life of deception absolutely necessary for both parties.

Secrecy seems to be the one thing that can make modern life mysterious or marvellous to us. The commonest thing is delightful if one only hides it.

Conceit is one of the greatest of the virtues, yet how few people recognise it as a thing to aim at and to strive after. In conceit many a man and woman has found salvation, yet the average person goes on all-fours grovelling after modesty.

It is difficult not to be unjust to what one loves.

Humanity will always love Rousseau for having confessed his sins not to a friend but to the world.

Just as those who do not love Plato more than truth cannot pass beyond the threshold of the Academe, so those who do not love beauty more than truth never know the inmost shrine of art.

There is a fatality about all physical and intellectual distinction: the sort of fatality that seems to dog, through history, the faltering steps of kings. It is better not to be different from one's fellows.

To be born, or at any rate bred, in a handbag, whether it had handles or not, seems to me to display a contempt for the ordinary decencies of family life that reminds one of the worst excesses of the French Revolution.

Vice and virtue are to the artist materials for an art.

There must be a new Hedonism that shall recreate life and save it from that harsh, uncomely Puritanism that is having, in our own day, its curious revival. It must have its service of the intellect, certainly, yet it must never accept any theory or system that will involve the sacrifice of any mode of passionate experience. Its aim, indeed, is to be experience itself and not the fruits of experience, bitter or sweet as they may be. Of the æstheticism that deadens the senses, as of the vulgar profligacy that dulls them, it is to know nothing. But it is to teach man to concentrate himself upon the moments of a life that is itself but a moment.

Art never expresses anything but itself. It has an independent life, just as thought has, and develops purely on its own lines. It is not necessarily realistic in an age of realism nor spiritual in an age of faith. So far from being the creation of its time it is usually in direct opposition to it, and the only history that it preserves for us is the history of its own progress.

People who mean well always do badly. They are like the ladies who wear clothes that don't fit them in order to show their piety. Good intentions are invariably ungrammatical.

Man can believe the impossible, but man can never believe the improbable.

When art is more varied nature will, no doubt, be more varied also.

If a man is sufficiently imaginative to produce evidence in support of a lie he might just as well speak the truth at once.

The ancient historians gave us delightful fiction in the form of fact; the modern novelist presents us with dull facts under the guise of fiction.

Nature is no great mother who has home us. She is our own creation. It is in our brain that she quickens to life. Things are because we see them, and what we see and how we see it depends on the arts that have influenced us. To look at a thing is very different from seeing a thing. One does not see anything until one sees its beauty.

The proper school to learn art in is not life but art.

I won't tell you that the world matters nothing, or the world's voice, or the voice of society. They matter a good deal. They matter far too much.

I wouldn't marry a man with a future before him for anything under the sun.

I am the only person in the world I should like to know thoroughly, but I don't see any chance of it just at present.

Modern memoirs are generally written by people who have entirely lost their memories and have never done anything worth recording.

Education is an admirable thing, but it is well to remember from time to time that nothing that is worth knowing can be taught.

Women are like minors, they live upon their expectations.

Twisted minds are as natural to some people as twisted bodies.

It is the very passions about whose origin we deceive ourselves that tyrannise most strongly over us. Our weakest motives are those of whose nature we are conscious. It often happens that when we think we are experimenting on others we are really experimenting on ourselves.

Whenever a man does a thoroughly stupid thing it is always from the noblest motives.

I thought I had no heart. I find I have, and a heart doesn't suit me. Somehow it doesn't go with modern dress. It makes one look old, and it spoils one's career at critical moments.

I don't play accurately—anyone can play accurately—but I play with wonderful expression. As far as the piano is concerned sentiment is my forte. I keep science for life.

I delight in men over seventy. They always offer one the devotion of a lifetime.

Everybody who is incapable of learning has taken to teaching—that is really what our enthusiasm for education has come to.

Nature hates mind.

From the point of view of form the type of all the arts is the art of the musician. From the point of view of feeling the actor's craft is the type.

Where we differ from each other is purely in accidentals—in dress, manner, tone of voice, religious opinions, personal appearance, tricks of habit, and the like.

The more we study art the less we care for Nature. What art really reveals to us is Nature's lack of design, her curious crudities, her extraordinary monotony, her absolutely unfinished condition.... It is fortunate for us, however, that nature is so imperfect, as otherwise we should have had no art at all. Art is our spirited protest, our gallant attempt to teach Nature her proper place. As for the infinite variety of nature, that is a pure myth. It is not to be found in Nature herself. It resides in the imagination or fancy or cultivated blindness of the man who looks at her.

Facts are not merely finding a footing-place in history but they are usurping the domain of fancy and have invaded the kingdom of romance. Their chilling touch is over everything. They are vulgarising mankind.

Ordinary people wait till life discloses to them its secrets, but to the few, to the elect, the mysteries of life are revealed before the veil is drawn away. Sometimes this is the effect of art, and chiefly of the art of literature which deals immediately with the passions and the intellect. But now and then a complex personality takes the place and assumes the office of art, is, indeed, in its way a real work of art, Life having its elaborate masterpieces just as poetry has, or sculpture, or painting.

Thinking is the most unhealthy thing in the world, and people die of it just as they die of any other disease.

A cigarette is the perfect type of a perfect pleasure. It is exquisite and it leaves one unsatisfied.

The aim of the liar is simply to charm, to delight, to give pleasure. He is the very basis of civilised society.

It is quite a mistake to believe, as many people do, that the mind shows itself in the face. Vice may sometimes write itself in lines and changes of contour, but that is all. Our faces are really masks given to us to conceal our minds with.

What on earth should we men do going about with purity and innocence? A carefully thought-out buttonhole is much more effective.

The only difference between a caprice and a lifelong passion is that the caprice lasts a little longer.

People say sometimes that beauty is only superficial. That may be so, but at least it is not so superficial as thought is.

It is the spectator and not life that art really mirrors.

Nowadays people know the price of everything and the value of nothing.

Conscience and cowardice are really the same things. Conscience is the trade name of the firm—that is all.

In every sphere of life form is the beginning of things. The rhythmic, harmonious gestures of dancing convey, Plato tells us, both rhythm and harmony into the mind. Forms are the food of faith, cried Newman, in one of those great moments of sincerity that make us admire and know the man. He was right, though he may not have known how terribly right he was. The creeds are believed not because they are rational but because they are repeated. Yes; form is everything. It is the secret of life. Find expression for a sorrow and it will become dear to you. Find expression for a joy and you intensify its ecstasy. Do you wish to love? Use love's litany and the words will create the yearning from which the world fancies that they spring. Have you a grief that corrodes your heart? Learn its utterance from Prince Hamlet and Queen Constance and you will find that mere expression is a mode of consolation and that form, which is the birth of passion, is also the death of pain. And so, to return to the sphere of art, it is form that creates not merely the critical temperament but also the æsthetic instinct that reveals to one all things under the condition of beauty. Start with the worship of form and there is no secret in art that will not be revealed to you.

It is only the intellectually lost who ever argue.

Nowadays most people die of a sort of creeping common-sense, and discover when it is too late that the only things one never regrets are one's mistakes.

Lady Henry Wotton was a curious woman, whose dresses always looked as if they had been designed in a rage and put on in a tempest. She was usually in love with somebody, and, as her passion was never returned, she had kept all her illusions. She tried to look picturesque but only succeeded in being untidy.

Those who go beneath the surface do so at their peril.

With an evening coat and a white tie anybody, even a stockbroker, can gain a reputation for being civilised.

There is nothing so interesting as telling a good man or woman how bad one has been. It is intellectually fascinating. One of the greatest pleasures of having been wicked is that one has so much to say to the good.

Laws are made in order that people in authority may not remember them, just as marriages are made in order that the divorce court may not play about idly.

To get back one's youth one has merely to repeat one's follies.

Never marry a woman with straw-coloured hair. They are so sentimental.

The reason we all like to think so well of others is that we are all afraid for ourselves. The basis of optimism is sheer terror. We think that we are generous because we credit our neighbours with the possession of those virtues that are likely to be a benefit to us. We praise the banker that we may overdraw our account, and find good qualities in the high-wayman in the hope that he may spare our pockets. I have the greatest contempt for optimism.

Art begins with abstract decoration, with purely imaginative and pleasureable work dealing with what is unreal and non-existent. This is the first stage. Then life becomes fascinated with this new wonder, and asks to be admitted into the charmed circle. Art takes life as part of her rough material, recreates it and refashions it in fresh form; is absolutely indifferent to facts; invents, imagines, dreams, and keeps between herself and reality the impenetrable barrier of beautiful style, of decorative or ideal treatment. The third stage is when Life gets the upper hand and drives Art out into the wilderness. This is the true decadence, and it is from this that we are now suffering.

Good intentions have been the ruin of the world. The only people who have achieved anything have been those who have had no intentions at all.

I never take any notice of what common people say, and I never interfere with what charming people do.

You know I am not a champion of marriage. The real drawback to marriage is that it makes one unselfish, and unselfish people are colourless— they lack individuality. Still there are certain temperaments that marriage makes more complex. They retain their egotism, and add to it many other egos. They are forced to have more than one life. They become more highly organised, and to be highly organised is, I should fancy, the object of man's existence. Besides, every experience is of value, and whatever one may say against marriage it is certainly an experience.

Those who read the symbol do so at their peril.

I never talk during music—at least not during good music. If anyone hears bad music it is one's duty to drown it in conversation.

When critics disagree the artist is in accord with himself.

Faith is the most plural thing I know. We are all supposed to believe in the same thing in different ways. It is like eating out of the same dish with different coloured spoons.

Experience is of no ethical value. It is merely the name men give to their mistakes. Moralists have, as a rule, regarded it as a mode of warning, have claimed for it a certain ethical efficacy in the formation of character, have praised it as something that teaches us what to follow and shows us what to avoid. But there is no motive power in experience. It is as little of an active cause as conscience itself. All that it really demonstrates is that our future will be the same as our past and that the sin we have done once, and with loathing, we shall do many times, and with joy.

Sensations are the details that build up the stories of our lives.

No artist has ethical sympathies. An ethical sympathy in an artist is an unpardonable mannerism of style.

She looks like an 'edition de luxe' of a wicked French novel meant specially for the English market.

I never knew what terror was before; I know it now. It is as if a hand of ice were laid upon one's heart. It is as if one's heart were beating itself to death in some empty hollow.

We can forgive a man for making a useful thing as long as he does not admire it. The only excuse for making a useless thing is that one admires it intensely.

No artist desires to prove anything. Even things that are true can be proved.

One knows so well the popular idea of health. The English country gentleman galloping along after a fox—the unspeakable in pursuit of the uneatable.

People seldom tell the truths that are worth telling. We ought to choose our truths as carefully as we choose our lies and to select our virtues with as much thought as we bestow upon the selection of our enemies.

Soul and body, body and soul—how mysterious they are! There is animalism in the soul, and the body has its moments of spirituality. The senses can refine and the intellect can degrade. Who can say where the fleshly impulse ceases or the psychical impulse begins? How shallow are the arbitrary definitions of ordinary psychologists! And yet how difficult to decide between the claims of the various schools! Is the soul a shadow seated in the house of sin? Or is the body really in the soul, as Giordano Bruno thought? The separation of spirit from matter is a mystery, and the unison of spirit with matter is a mystery also.

Those who find beautiful meanings in beautiful things are the cultivated. For these there is hope.

There is no such thing as a moral or an immoral book. Books are well written or badly written-that is all.

Marriage is a sort of forcing house. It brings strange sins to fruit, and sometimes strange renunciations.

The moral life of man forms part of the subject-matter of the artist, but the morality of art consists in the perfect use of an imperfect medium.

A sense of duty is like some horrible disease. It destroys the tissues of the mind, as certain complaints destroy the tissues of the body. The catechism has a great deal to answer for.

They are the elect to whom beautiful things mean only beauty.

Those who find ugly meanings in beautiful things are corrupt without being charming. This is a fault.

Few people have sufficient strength to resist the preposterous claims of orthodoxy.

She wore far too much rouge last night and not quite enough clothes. That is always a sign of despair in a woman.

A virtue is like a city set upon a hill—it cannot be hid. We can conceal our vices if we care to—for a time at least—but a virtue will out.

Can't make out how you stand London society. The thing has gone to the dogs: a lot of damned nobodies talking about nothing.

You don't know what an existence they lead down there. It is pure, unadulterated country life. They get up early because they have so much to do, and go to bed early because they have so little to think about.

Nothing is so fatal to a personality as the keeping of promises, unless it be telling the truth.

Who cares whether Mr Ruskin's views on Turner are sound or not? What does it matter? That mighty and majestic prose of his, so fervid and so fiery coloured in its noble eloquence, so rich in its elaborate symphonic music, so sure and certain, at its best, in subtle choice of word and epithet, is, at least, as great a work of art as any of those wonderful sunsets that bleach or rot on their corrupted canvases in England's gallery—greater, indeed, one is apt to think at times, not merely because its equal beauty is more enduring but on account of the fuller variety of its appeal—soul speaking to soul in those long, cadenced lines, not through form and colour alone, though through these, indeed, completely and without loss, but with intellectual and emotional utterance, with lofty passion and with loftier thought, with imaginative insight and with poetic aim—greater, I always think, even as literature is the greater art.

Laughter is not at all a bad beginning for a friendship, and it is far the best ending for one.

Mrs Cheveley is one of those very modern women of our time who find a new scandal as becoming as a new bonnet, and air them both in the Park every afternoon at 5.30. I am sure she adores scandals, and that the sorrow of her life at present is that she can't manage to have enough of them.

The world divides actions into three classes: good actions, bad actions that you may do, and bad actions that you may not do. If you stick to the good actions you are respected by the good. If you stick to the bad actions that you may do you are respected by the bad. But if you perform the bad actions that no one may do then the good and the bad set upon you and you are lost indeed.

I choose my friends for their good looks, my acquaintances for their good characters, and my enemies for their good intellects.

The artist is the creator of beautiful things.

To me the word 'natural' means all that is middle class, all that is of the essence of Jingoism, all that is colourless and without form and void. It might be a beautiful word, but it is the most debased coin in the currency of language.

I pity any woman who is married to a man called John. She would probably never be allowed to know the entrancing pleasure of a single moment's solitude.

It is only when we have learned to love forgetfulness that we have learned the art of living.

To reveal art and conceal the artist is art's aim.

The world taken 'en masse' is a monster, crammed with prejudices, packed with prepossessions, cankered with what it calls virtues, a Puritan, a prig. And the art of life is the art of defiance. To defy—that is what we ought to live for, instead of living, as we do, to acquiesce.

Some resemblance the creative work of the critic will have to the work that has stirred him to creation, but it will be such resemblance as exists, not between nature and the mirror that the painter of landscape or figure may be supposed to hold up to her, but between nature and the work of the decorative artist. Just as on the flowerless carpets of Persia tulip and rose blossom indeed, and are lovely to look on, though they are not reproduced in visible shape or line; just as the pearl and purple of the sea shell is echoed in the church of St Mark at Venice; just as the vaulted ceiling of the wondrous chapel at Ravenna is made gorgeous by the gold and green and sapphire of the peacock's tail, though the birds of Juno fly not across it; so the critic reproduces the work that he criticises in a mode that is never imitative, and part of whose charm may really consist in the rejection of resemblance, and shows us in this way not merely the meaning but also the mystery of beauty, and by transforming each art into literature solves once for all the problem of art's unity.

Diversity of opinion about a work of art shows that the work is new, complex, and vital.

Nothing is more painful to me than to come across virtue in a person in whom I have never suspected its existence. It is like finding a needle in a bundle of hay. It pricks you. If we have virtue we should warn people of it.

The critic is he who can translate into another manner or a new material his impression of beautiful things.

Hopper is one of nature's gentlemen—the worst type of gentleman I know.

If one intends to be good one must take it up as a profession. It is quite the most engrossing one in the world.

I like Wagner's music better than anybody's. It is so loud that one can talk the whole time without other people hearing what one says.

All art is at once surface and symbol.

Childhood is one long career of innocent eavesdropping, of hearing what one ought not to hear.

The highest as the lowest form of criticism is a mode of autobiography.

The only things worth saying are those that we forget, just as the only things worth doing are those that the world is surprised at.

Maturity is one long career of saying what one ought not to say. That is the art of conversation.

Virtue is generally merely a form of deficiency, just as vice is an assertion of intellect.

People teach in order to conceal their ignorance, as people smile in order to conceal their tears.

To be unnatural is often to be great. To be natural is generally to be stupid.

To lie finely is an art, to tell the truth is to act according to nature.

People who talk sense are like people who break stones in the road: they cover one with dust and splinters.

Jesus said to man: You have a wonderful personality. Develop it. Be yourself. Don't imagine that your perfection lies in accumulating or possessing external things. Your perfection is inside of you. If only you could realise that you would not want to be rich. Ordinary riches can be stolen from a man, real riches cannot. In the treasury-house of your soul there are infinitely precious things that may not be taken from you. Try to so shape your life that external things will not harm you, and try also to get rid of personal property. It involves sordid preoccupation, endless industry, continual wrong. Personal property hinders individualism at every step.

When Jesus talks about the poor He simply means personalities, just as when He talks about the rich He simply means people who have not developed their personalities.

An echo is often more beautiful than the voice it repeats.

THE SOUL OF MAN

The chief advantage that would result from the establishment of Socialism is, undoubtedly, the fact that Socialism would relieve us from that sordid necessity of living for others which, in the present condition of things, presses so hardly upon almost everybody. In fact, scarcely anyone at all escapes.

Now and then, in the course of the century, a great man of science, like Darwin; a great poet, like Keats; a fine critical spirit, like M, Renan; a supreme artist, like Flaubert, has been able to isolate himself, to keep himself out of reach of the clamorous claims of others, to stand 'under the shelter of the wall,' as Plato puts it, and so to realise the perfection of what was in him, to his own incomparable gain, and to the incomparable and lasting gain of the whole world. These, however, are exceptions. The majority of people spoil their lives by an unhealthy and exaggerated altruism—are forced, indeed, so to spoil them. They find themselves surrounded by hideous poverty, by hideous ugliness, by hideous starvation. It is inevitable that they should be strongly moved by all this. The emotions of man are stirred more quickly than man's intelligence; and, as I pointed out some time ago in an article on the function of criticism, it is much more easy to have sympathy with suffering than it is to have sympathy with thought. Accordingly, with admirable, though misdirected intentions, they very seriously and very sentimentally set themselves to the task of remedying the evils that they see. But their remedies do not cure the disease: they merely prolong it. Indeed, their remedies are part of the disease.

They try to solve the problem of poverty, for instance, by keeping the poor alive; or, in the case of a very advanced school, by amusing the poor.

But this is not a solution: it is an aggravation of the difficulty. The proper aim is to try and reconstruct society on such a basis that poverty will be impossible. And the altruistic virtues have really prevented the carrying out of this aim. Just as the worst slave-owners were those who were kind to their slaves, and so prevented the horror of the system being realised by those who suffered from it, and understood by those who contemplated it, so, in the present state of things in England, the people who do most harm are the people who try to do most good; and at last we have had the spectacle of men who have really studied the problem and know the life-educated men who live in the East End—coming forward and imploring the community to restrain its altruistic impulses of charity, benevolence, and the like. They do so on the ground that such charity degrades and demoralises. They are perfectly right. Charity creates a multitude of sins.

There is also this to be said. It is immoral to use private property in order to alleviate the horrible evils that result from the institution of private property. It is both immoral and unfair.

Under Socialism all this will, of course, be altered. There will be no people living in fetid dens and fetid rags, and bringing up unhealthy, hunger-pinched children in the midst of impossible and absolutely repulsive surroundings. The security of society will not depend, as it does now, on the state of the weather. If a frost comes we shall not have a hundred thousand men out of work, tramping about the streets in a state of disgusting misery, or whining to their neighbours for alms, or crowding round the doors of loathsome shelters to try and secure a hunch of bread and a night's unclean lodging. Each member of the society will share in the general prosperity and happiness of the society, and if a frost comes no one will practically be anything the worse.

Upon the other hand, Socialism itself will be of value simply because it will lead to Individualism.

Socialism, Communism, or whatever one chooses to call it, by converting private property into public wealth, and substituting co-operation for competition, will restore society to its proper condition of a thoroughly healthy organism, and insure the material well-being of each member of the community. It will, in fact, give Life it's proper basis and its proper environment. But for the full development of Life to its highest mode of perfection, something more is needed. What is needed is Individualism. If the

Socialism is Authoritarian; if there are Governments armed with economic power as they are now with political power; if, in a word, we are to have Industrial Tyrannies, then the last state of man will be worse than the first. At present, in consequence of the existence of private property, a great many people are enabled to develop a certain very limited amount of Individualism. They are either under no necessity to work for their living, or are enabled to choose the sphere of activity that is really congenial to them, and gives them pleasure. These are the poets, the philosophers, the men of science, the men of culture—in a word, the real men, the men who have realised themselves, and in whom all Humanity gains a partial realisation. Upon the other hand, there are a great many people who, having no private property of their own, and being always on the brink of sheer starvation, are compelled to do the work of beasts of burden, to do work that is quite uncongenial to them, and to which they are forced by the peremptory, unreasonable, degrading Tyranny of want. These are the poor, and amongst them there is no grace of manner, or charm of speech, or civilisation, or culture, or refinement in pleasures, or joy of life. From their collective force Humanity gains much in material prosperity. But it is only the material result that it gains, and the man who is poor is in himself absolutely of no importance. He is merely the infinitesimal atom of a force that, so far from regarding him, crushes him: indeed, prefers him crushed, as in that case he is far more obedient.

Of course, it might be said that the Individualism generated under conditions of private property is not always, or even as a rule, of a fine or wonderful type, and that the poor, if they have not culture and charm, have still many virtues. Both these statements would be quite true. The possession of private property is very often extremely demoralising, and that is, of course, one of the reasons why Socialism wants to get rid of the institution. In fact, property is really a nuisance. Some years ago people went about the country saying that property has duties. They said it so often and so tediously that, at last, the Church has begun to say it. One hears it now from every pulpit. It is perfectly true. Property not merely has duties, but has so many duties that its possession to any large extent is a bore. It involves endless claims upon one, endless attention to business, endless bother. If property had simply pleasures, we could stand it; but its duties make it unbearable. In the interest of the rich we must get rid of it. The virtues of the poor may be readily admitted, and are much to be regretted. We are often told that the poor are grateful for charity. Some of them are, no doubt, but the best amongst the poor are never grateful. They are ungrateful, discontented, disobedient, and rebellious. They are quite right to be so. Charity they feel to be a ridiculously inadequate mode of partial restitution, or a sentimental dole, usually accompanied by some impertinent attempt on the part of the sentimentalist to tyrannise over their private lives. Why should they be grateful for the crumbs that fall from the rich man's table? They should be seated at the board, and are beginning to know it. As for being discontented, a man who would not be discontented with such surroundings and such a low mode of life would be a perfect brute. Disobedience, in the eyes of anyone who has read history, is man's original virtue. It is through disobedience that progress has been made, through disobedience and through rebellion. Sometimes the poor are praised for being thrifty. But to recommend thrift to the poor is both grotesque and insulting. It is like advising a man who is starving to eat less. For a town or country labourer to practise thrift would be absolutely immoral. Man should not be ready to show that he can live like a badly-fed animal. He should decline to live like that, and should either steal or go on the rates, which is considered by many to be a form of stealing. As for begging, it is safer to beg than to take, but it is finer to take than to beg. No: a poor man who is ungrateful, unthrifty, discontented, and rebellious, is probably a real personality, and has much in him. He is at any rate a healthy protest. As for the virtuous poor, one can pity them, of course, but one cannot possibly admire them; They have made private terms with the enemy, and sold their birthright for very bad pottage. They must also be extraordinarily stupid. I can quite understand a man accepting laws that protect private property, and admit of its accumulation, as long as he himself is able under those conditions to realise some form of beautiful and intellectual life. But it is almost incredible to me how a man whose life is marred and made hideous by such laws can possibly acquiesce in their continuance.

However, the explanation is not really difficult to find. It is simply this. Misery and poverty are so absolutely degrading, and exercise such a paralysing effect over the nature of men, that no class is ever really conscious of its own suffering. They have to be told of it by other people, and they often entirely disbelieve them. What is said by great employers of labour against agitators is unquestionably true. Agitators are a set of interfering, meddling people, who come down to some perfectly contented class of the community, and sow the seeds of discontent amongst them. That is the reason why agitators are so absolutely necessary. Without them, in our incomplete state, there would be no advance towards civilisation. Slavery was put down in America, not in consequence of any action on the part of the slaves, or even any express desire on their part that they should be free. It was put down entirely through the grossly illegal conduct of certain agitators in Boston and elsewhere, who were not slaves themselves, nor owners of slaves, nor had anything to do with the question really. It was, undoubtedly, the Abolitionists who set the torch alight, who began the whole thing. And it is curious to note that from the slaves themselves they received, not merely very little assistance, but hardly any sympathy even; and when at the close of the war the slaves found themselves free, found themselves indeed so absolutely free that they were free to starve, many of them bitterly regretted the new state of things. To the thinker, the most tragic fact in the whole of the French Revolution is not that Marie Antoinette was killed for being a queen, but that the starved peasant of the Vendée voluntarily went out to die for the hideous cause of feudalism.

It is clear, then, that no Authoritarian Socialism will do. For while under the present system a very large number of people can lead lives of a certain amount of freedom and expression and happiness, under an industrial-barrack system, or a system of economic tyranny, nobody would be able to have any such freedom at all. It is to be regretted that a portion of our community should be practically in slavery, but to propose to solve the problem by enslaving the entire community is childish. Every man must be left quite free to choose his own work. No form of compulsion must be exercised over him. If there is, his work will not be good for him, will not be good in itself, and will not be good for others. And by work I simply mean activity of any kind.

I hardly think that any Socialist, nowadays, would seriously propose that an inspector should call every morning at each house to see that each citizen rose up and did manual labour for eight hours. Humanity has got beyond that stage, and reserves such a form of life for the people whom, in a very arbitrary manner, it chooses to call criminals. But I confess that many of the socialistic views that I have come across seem to me to be tainted with ideas of authority, if not of actual compulsion. Of course, authority and compulsion are out of the question. All association must be quite voluntary. It is only in voluntary associations that man is fine.

But it may be asked how Individualism, which is now more or less dependent on the existence of private property for its development, will benefit by the abolition of such private property. The answer is very simple. It is true that, under existing conditions, a few men who have had private means of their own, such as Byron, Shelley, Browning, Victor Hugo, Baudelaire, and others, have been able to realise their personality more or less completely. Not one of these men ever did a single day's work for hire. They were relieved from poverty. They had an immense advantage. The question is whether it would be for the good of Individualism that such an advantage should be taken away. Let us suppose that it is taken away. What happens then to Individualism? How will it benefit?

It will benefit in this way, under the new conditions Individualism will be far freer, far finer, and far more intensified than it is now. I am not talking of the great imaginatively-realised Individualism of such poets as I have mentioned, but of the great actual Individualism latent and potential in mankind generally. For the recognition of private property has really harmed Individualism, and obscured it, by confusing a man with what he possesses. It has led Individualism entirely astray. It has made gain not growth its aim. So that man thought that the important thing was to have, and did not know that the important thing is to be. The true perfection of man lies, not in what man has, but in what man is. Private property has crushed true Individualism, and set up an Individualism that is false. It has debarred one part of the community from being individual by starving them. It has debarred the other part of the community from being individual by putting them on the wrong road, and encumbering them. Indeed, so completely has man's personality been absorbed by his possessions that the English law has always treated offences against a man's property with far more severity than offences

76

against his person, and property is still the test of complete citizenship. The industry necessary for the making of money is also very demoralising. In a community like ours, where property confers immense distinction, social position, honour, respect, titles, and other pleasant things of the kind, man, being naturally ambitious, makes it his aim to accumulate this property, and goes on wearily and tediously accumulating it long after he has got far more than he wants, or can use, or enjoy, or perhaps even know of. Man will kill himself by overwork in order to secure property, and really, considering the enormous advantages that property brings, one is hardly surprised. One's regret is that society should be constructed on such a basis that man has been forced into a groove in which he cannot freely develop what is wonderful, and fascinating, and delightful in him—in which, in fact, he misses the true pleasure and joy of living. He is also, under existing conditions, very insecure. An enormously wealthy merchant may be—often is—at every moment of his life at the mercy of things that are not under his control. If the wind blows an extra point or so, or the weather suddenly changes, or some trivial thing happens, his ship may go down, his speculations may go wrong, and he finds himself a poor man, with his social position quite gone. Now, nothing should be able to harm a man except himself. Nothing should be able to rob a man at all. What a man really has, is what is in him. What is outside of him should be a matter of no importance.

With the abolition of private property, then, we shall have true, beautiful, healthy Individualism. Nobody will waste his life in accumulating things, and the symbols for things. One will live. To live is the rarest thing in the world. Most people exist, that is all.

It is a question whether we have ever seen the full expression of a personality, except on the imaginative plane of art. In action, we never have. Cæsar, says Mommsen, was the complete and perfect man. But how tragically insecure was Cæsar! Wherever there is a man who exercises authority, there is a man who resists authority. Cæsar was very perfect, but his perfection travelled by too dangerous a road. Marcus Aurelius was the perfect man, says Renan. Yes; the great emperor was a perfect man. But how intolerable were the endless claims upon him! He staggered under the burden of the empire.

He was conscious how inadequate one man was to bear the weight of that Titan and too vast orb. What I mean by a perfect man is one who develops under perfect conditions; one who is not wounded, or worried or maimed, or in danger. Most personalities have been obliged to be rebels. Half their strength has been wasted in friction. Byron's personality, for instance, was terribly wasted in its battle with the stupidity, and hypocrisy, and Philistinism of the English. Such battles do not always intensify strength: they often exaggerate weakness. Byron was never able to give us what he might have given us. Shelley escaped better. Like Byron, he got out of England as soon as possible. But he was not so well known. If the English had had any idea of what a great poet he really was, they would have fallen on him with tooth and nail, and made his life as unbearable to him as they possibly could. But he was not a remarkable figure in society, and consequently he escaped, to a certain degree. Still, even in Shelley the note of rebellion is sometimes too strong. The note of the perfect personality is not rebellion, but peace.

It will be a marvellous thing—the true personality of man—when we see it. It will grow naturally and simply, flowerlike, or as a tree grows. It will not be at discord. It will never argue or dispute. It will not prove things. It will know everything. And yet it will not busy itself about knowledge. It will have wisdom. Its value will not be measured by material things. It will have nothing. And yet it will have everything, and whatever one takes from it, it will still have, so rich will it he. It will not be always meddling with others, or asking them to be like itself. It will love them because they will be different. And yet while it will not meddle with others, it will help all, as a beautiful thing helps us, by being what it is. The personality of man will be very wonderful. It will be as wonderful as the personality of a child.

In its development it will be assisted by Christianity, if men desire that; but if men do not desire that, it will develop none the less surely. For it will not worry itself about the past, nor care whether things happened or did not happen. Nor will it admit any laws but its own laws; nor any authority but its own authority. Yet it will love those who sought to intensity it, and speak often of them. And of these Christ was one.

'Know thyself' was written over the portal of the antique world. Over

78

the portal of the new world, 'Be thyself' shall be written. And the message of Christ to man was simply 'Be thyself.' That is the secret of Christ.

When Jesus talks about the poor he simply means personalities, just as when he talks about the rich he simply means people who have not developed their personalities. Jesus moved in a community that allowed the accumulation of private property just as ours does, and the gospel that he preached was not that in such a community it is an advantage for a man to live on scanty, unwholesome food, to wear ragged, unwholesome clothes, to sleep in horrid, unwholesome dwellings, and a disadvantage for a man to live under healthy, pleasant, and decent conditions. Such a view would have been wrong there and then, and would, of course, be still more wrong now and in England; for as man moves northward the material necessities of life become of more vital importance, and our society is infinitely more complex, and displays far greater extremes of luxury and pauperism than any society of the antique world. What Jesus meant, was this. He said to man, 'You have a wonderful personality. Develop it. Be yourself. Don't imagine that your perfection lies in accumulating or possessing external things. Your perfection is inside of you. If only you could realise that, you would not want to be rich. Ordinary riches can be stolen from a man. Real riches cannot. In the treasury-house of your soul, there are infinitely precious things, that may not be taken from you. And so, try to so shape your life that external things will not harm you. And try also to get rid of personal property. It involves sordid preoccupation, endless industry, continual wrong. Personal property hinders Individualism at every step. It is to be noted that Jesus never says that impoverished people are necessarily good, or wealthy people necessarily bad. That would not have been true. Wealthy people are, as a class, better than impoverished people, more moral, more intellectual, more well-behaved. There is only one class in the community that thinks more about money than the rich, and that is the poor. The poor can think of nothing else. That is the misery of being poor. What Jesus does say is that man reaches his perfection, not through what he has, not even through what he does, but entirely through what he is. And so the wealthy young man who comes to Jesus is represented as a thoroughly good citizen, who has broken none of the laws of his state, none of the commandments of his religion. He is quite respectable, in the ordinary sense of that extraordinary word. Jesus says to him, 'You should give up private property. It hinders you from realising your perfection. It is a drag upon you. It is a burden. Your personality does not need it. It is within you, and not outside of you, that you will find what you really are, and what you really want.' To his own friends he says the same thing. He tells them to be themselves, and not to be always worrying about other things. What do other things matter? Man is complete in himself. When they go into the world, the world will disagree with them. That is inevitable. The world hates Individualism. But that is not to trouble them. They are to be calm and self-centred. If a man takes their cloak, they are to give him their coat, just to show that material things are of no importance. If people abuse them, they are not to answer back. What does it signify? The things people say of a man do not alter a man. He is what he is. Public opinion is of no value whatsoever. Even if people employ actual violence, they are not to be violent in turn. That would be to fall to the same low level. After all, even in prison, a man can be quite free. His soul can be free. His personality can be untroubled. He can be at peace. And, above all things, they are not to interfere with other people or judge them in any way. Personality is a very mysterious thing. A man cannot always be estimated by what he does. He may keep the law, and yet be worthless. He may break the law, and yet be fine. He may be bad, without ever doing anything bad. He may commit a sin against society, and yet realise through that sin his true perfection.

There was a woman who was taken in adultery. We are not told the history of her love, but that love must have been very great; for Jesus said that her sins were forgiven her, not because she repented, but because her love was so intense and wonderful. Later on, a short time before his death, as he sat at a feast, the woman came in and poured costly perfumes on his hair. His friends tried to interfere with her, and said that it was an extravagance, and that the money that the perfume cost should have been expended on charitable relief of people in want, or something of that kind. Jesus did not accept that view. He pointed out that the material needs of Man were great and very permanent, but that the spiritual needs of Man were greater still, and that in one divine moment, and by selecting its own mode of expression, a personality might make itself perfect. The world worships the woman, even now, as a saint.

Yes; there are suggestive things in Individualism. Socialism annihilates family life, for instance. With the abolition of private property, marriage in its present form must disappear. This is part of the programme. Individualism accepts this and makes it fine. It converts the abolition of legal restraint into a form of freedom that will help the full development of personality, and make the love of man and woman more wonderful, more beautiful, and more ennobling. Jesus knew this. He rejected the claims of family life, although they existed in his day and community in a very marked form. 'Who is my mother? Who are my brothers?' he said, when he was told that they wished to speak to him. When one of his followers asked leave to go and bury his father, 'Let the dead bury the dead,' was his terrible answer. He would allow no claim whatsoever to be made on personality.

And so he who would lead a Christ-like like life is he who is perfectly and absolutely himself. He may be a great poet, or a great man of science; or a young student at a University, or one who watches sheep upon a moor; or a maker of dramas, like Shakespeare, or a thinker about God, like Spinoza; or a child who plays in a garden, or a fisherman who throws his net into the sea. It does not matter what he is, as long as he realises the perfection of the soul that is within him. All imitation in morals and in life is wrong. Through the streets of Jerusalem at the present day crawls one who is mad and carries a wooden cross on his shoulders. He is a symbol of the lives that are marred by imitation. Father Damien was Christ-like when he went out to live with the lepers, because in such service he realised fully what was best in him. But he was not more Christ-like than Wagner when he realised his soul in music; or than Shelley, when he realised his soul in song. There is no one type for man. There are as many perfections as there are imperfect men. And while to the claims of charity a man may yield and yet be free, to the claims of conformity no man may yield and remain free at all.

Individualism, then, is what through Socialism we are to attain to. As a natural result the State must give up all idea of government. It must give it up because, as a wise man once said many centuries before Christ, there is such a thing as leaving mankind alone; there is no such thing as governing mankind. All modes of government are failures. Despotism is unjust to everybody, including the despot, who was probably made for better things. Oligarchies are unjust to the many, and ochlocracies are unjust to the few. High hopes were once formed of democracy; but democracy means simply the bludgeoning of the people by the people for the people. It has been found out. I must say that it was high time, for all authority is quite degrading. It degrades those who exercise it, and degrades those over whom it is exercised. When it is violently, grossly, and cruelly used, it produces a good effect, by creating, or at any rate bringing out, the spirit of revolt and Individualism that is to kill it. When it is used with a certain amount of kindness, and accompanied by prizes and rewards, it is dreadfully demoralising. People, in that case, are less conscious of the horrible pressure that is being put on them, and so go through their lives in a sort of coarse comfort, like petted animals, without ever realising that they are probably thinking other people's thoughts, living by other people's standards, wearing practically what one may call other people's second-hand clothes, and never being themselves for a single moment. 'He who would be free,' says a fine thinker, 'must not conform.' And authority, by bribing people to conform, produces a very gross kind of over-fed barbarism amongst us.

With authority, punishment will pass away. This will be a great gain—a gain, in fact, of incalculable value. As one reads history, not in the expurgated editions written for schoolboys and passmen, but in the original authorities of each time, one is absolutely sickened, not by the crimes that the wicked have committed, but by the punishments that the good have inflicted; and a community is infinitely more brutalised by the habitual employment of punishment, than it is by the occurrence of crime. It obviously follows that the more punishment is inflicted the more crime is produced, and most modern legislation has clearly recognised this, and has made it its task to diminish punishment as far as it thinks it can. Wherever it has really diminished it, the results have always been extremely good. The less punishment, the less crime. When there is no punishment at all, crime will either cease to exist, or, if it occurs, will be treated by physicians as a very distressing form of dementia, to be cured by care and kindness. For what are called criminals nowadays are not criminals at all. Starvation, and not sin, is the parent of modern crime. That indeed is the reason why our criminals are, as a class, so absolutely uninteresting from any psychological point of view. They are not marvellous Macbeths and terrible Vautrins. They are merely what ordinary, respectable, commonplace people would be if they had not got enough to eat. When private property is abolished there will be no necessity for crime, no demand for it; it will cease to exist. Of course, all crimes are not crimes against property, though such are the crimes that the English law, valuing what a man has more than what a man is, punishes with the harshest and most horrible severity, if we except the crime of murder, and regard death as worse than penal servitude, a point on which our criminals, I believe, disagree. But though a crime may not be against property, it may spring from the misery and rage and depression produced by our wrong system of property-holding, and so, when that system is abolished, will disappear. When each member of the community has sufficient for his wants, and is not interfered with by his neighbour, it will not be an object of any interest to him to interfere with anyone else. Jealousy, which is an extraordinary source of crime in modern life, is an emotion closely bound up with our conceptions of property, and under Socialism and Individualism will die out. It is remarkable that in communistic tribes jealousy is entirely unknown.

Now as the State is not to govern, it may be asked what the State is to do. The State is to be a voluntary association that will organise labour, and be the manufacturer and distributor of necessary commodities. The State is to make what is useful. The individual is to make what is beautiful. And as I have mentioned the word labour. I cannot help saying that a great deal of nonsense is being written and talked nowadays about the dignity of manual labour. There is nothing necessarily dignified about manual labour at all, and most of it is absolutely degrading. It is mentally and morally injurious to man to do anything in which he does not find pleasure, and many forms of labour are quite pleasureless activities, and should be regarded as such. To sweep a slushy crossing for eight hours on a day when the east wind is blowing is a disgusting occupation. To sweep it with mental, moral, or physical dignity seems to me to be impossible. To sweep it with joy would be appalling. Man is made for something better than disturbing dirt. All work of that kind should be done by a machine.

And I have no doubt that it will be so. Up to the present, man has been, to a certain extent, the slave of machinery, and there is something tragic in the fact that as soon as man had invented a machine to do his work he began to starve. This, however, is, of course, the result of our property system and our system of competition. One man owns a machine which does the work of five hundred men. Five hundred men are, in consequence, thrown out of employment, and, having no work to do, become hungry and take to thieving. The one man secures the produce of the machine and keeps it, and has five hundred times as much as he should have, and probably, which is of much more importance, a great deal more than he really wants. Were that machine the property of all, everyone would benefit by it. It would be an immense advantage to the community. All unintellectual labour, all monotonous, dull labour, all labour that deals with dreadful things, and involves unpleasant conditions, must be done by machinery. Machinery must work for us in coal mines, and do all sanitary services, and be the stoker of steamers, and clean the streets, and run messages on wet days, and do anything that is tedious or distressing. At present machinery competes against man. Under proper conditions machinery will serve man. There is no doubt at all that this is the future of machinery, and just as trees grow while the country gentleman is asleep, so while Humanity will be amusing itself, or enjoying cultivated leisure—which, and not labour, is the aim of man—or making beautiful things, or reading beautiful things, or simply contemplating the world with admiration and delight, machinery will he doing all the necessary and unpleasant work. The fact is, that civilisation requires slaves. The Greeks were quite right there. Unless there are slaves to do the ugly, horrible, uninteresting work, culture and contemplation become almost impossible. Human slavery is wrong, insecure, and demoralising. On mechanical slavery, on the slavery of the machine, the future of the world depends. And when scientific men are no longer called upon to go down to a depressing East End and distribute bad cocoa and worse blankets to starving people, they will have delightful leisure in which to devise wonderful and marvellous things for their own joy and the joy of everyone else. There will be great storages of force for every city, and for every house if required, and this force man will convert into heat, light, or motion, according to his needs. Is this Utopian? A map of the world that does not include Utopia is not worth even glancing at, for it leaves out the one country at which Humanity is always landing. And when Humanity lands there, it looks out, and, seeing a better country, sets sail. Progress is the realisation of Utopias.

Now, I have said that the community by means of organisation of machinery will supply the useful things, and that the beautiful things will be made by the individual. This is not merely necessary, but it is the only possible way by which we can get either the one or the other. An individual who has to make things for the use of others, and with reference to their wants and their wishes, does not work with interest, and consequently cannot put into his work what is best in him. Upon the other hand, whenever a community or a powerful section of a community, or a government of any kind, attempts to dictate to the artist what he is to do, Art either entirely vanishes, or becomes stereotyped, or degenerates into a low and ignoble form of craft. A work of art is the unique result of a unique temperament. Its beauty comes from the fact that the author is what he is. It has nothing to do with the fact that other people want what they want. Indeed, the moment that an artist takes notice of what other people want, and tries to supply the demand, he ceases to be an artist, and becomes a dull or an amusing craftsman, an honest or a dishonest tradesman. He has no further claim to be considered as an artist. Art is the most intense mode of Individualism that the world has known. I am inclined to say that it is the only real mode of Individualism that the world has known. Crime, which, under certain conditions, may seem to have created Individualism, must take cognisance of other people and interfere with them. It belongs to the sphere of action. But alone, without any reference to his neighbours, without any interference, the artist can fashion a beautiful thing; and if he does not do it solely for his own pleasure, he is not an artist at all.

And it is to be noted that it is the fact that Art is this intense form of Individualism that makes the public try to exercise over it an authority that is as immoral as it is ridiculous, and as corrupting as it is contemptible. It is not quite their fault. The public has always, and in every age, been badly brought up. They are continually asking Art to be popular, to please their want of taste, to flatter their absurd vanity, to tell them what they have been told before, to show them what they ought to be tired of seeing, to amuse them when they feel heavy after eating too much, and to distract their thoughts when they are wearied of their own stupidity. Now Art should never try to be popular. The public should try to make itself artistic. There is a very wide difference. If a man of science were told that the results of his experiments, and the conclusions that he arrived at, should be of such a character that they would not upset the received popular notions on the subject, or disturb popular prejudice, or hurt the sensibilities of people who knew nothing about science; if a philosopher were told that he had a perfect right to speculate in the highest spheres of thought, provided that he arrived at the same conclusions as were held by those who had never thought in any sphere at all—well, nowadays the man of science and the philosopher would be considerably amused. Yet it is really a very few years since both philosophy and science were subjected to brutal popular control, to authority in fact—the authority of either the general ignorance of the community, or the terror and greed for power of an ecclesiastical or governmental class. Of course, we have to a very great extent got rid of any attempt on the part of the community, or the Church, or the Government, to interfere with the individualism of speculative thought, but the attempt to interfere with the individualism of imaginative art still lingers. In fact, it does more than linger; it is aggressive, offensive, and brutalising.

In England, the arts that have escaped best are the arts in which the public take no interest. Poetry is an instance of what I mean. We have been able to have fine poetry in England because the public do not read it, and consequently do not influence it. The public like to insult poets because they are individual, but once they have insulted them, they leave them alone. In the case of the novel and the drama, arts in which the public do take an interest, the result of the exercise of popular authority has been absolutely ridiculous. No country produces such badly-written fiction, such tedious, common work in the novel form, such silly, vulgar plays as England. It must necessarily be so. The popular standard is of such a character that no artist can get to it. It is at once too easy and too difficult to be a popular novelist. It is too easy, because the requirements of the public as far as plot, style, psychology, treatment of life, and treatment of literature are concerned are within the reach of the very meanest capacity and the most uncultivated mind. It is too difficult, because to meet such requirements the artist would have to do violence to his temperament, would have to write not for the artistic joy of writing, but for the amusement of half-educated people, and so would have to suppress his individualism, forget his culture, annihilate his style, and surrender everything that is valuable in him. In the case of the drama, things are a little better: the theatre-going public like the obvious, it is true, but they do not like the tedious; and burlesque and farcical comedy, the two most popular forms, are distinct forms of art. Delightful work may be produced under burlesque and farcical conditions, and in work of this kind the artist in England is allowed very great freedom. It is when one comes to the higher forms of the drama that the result of popular control is seen. The one thing that the public dislike is novelty. Any attempt to extend the subject-matter of art is extremely distasteful to the public; and yet the vitality and progress of art depend in a large measure on the continual extension of subject-matter. The public dislike novelty because they are afraid of it. It represents to them a mode of Individualism, an assertion on the part of the artist that he selects his own subject, and treats it as he chooses. The public are quite right in their attitude. Art is Individualism, and Individualism is a disturbing and disintegrating force. Therein lies its immense value. For what it seeks to disturb is monotony of type, slavery of custom, tyranny of habit, and the reduction of man to the level of a machine. In Art, the public accept what has been, because they cannot alter it, not because they appreciate it. They swallow their classics whole, and never taste them. They endure them as the inevitable, and as they cannot mar them, they mouth about them. Strangely enough, or not strangely, according to one's own views, this acceptance of the classics does a great deal of harm. The uncritical admiration of the Bible and Shakespeare in England is an instance of what I mean. With regard to the Bible, considerations of ecclesiastical authority enter into the matter, so that I need not dwell upon the point.

But in the case of Shakespeare it is quite obvious that the public really see neither the beauties nor the defects of his plays. If they saw the beauties, they would not object to the development of the drama; and if they saw the defects, they would not object to the development of the drama either. The fact is, the public make use of the classics of a country as a means of checking the progress of Art. They degrade the classics into authorities. They use them as bludgeons for preventing the free expression of Beauty in new forms. They are always asking a writer why he does not write like somebody else, or a painter why he does not paint like somebody else, quite oblivious of the fact that if either of them did anything of the kind he would cease to be an artist. A fresh mode of Beauty is absolutely distasteful to them, and whenever it appears they get so angry and bewildered, that they always use two stupid expressions—one is that the work of art is grossly unintelligible; the other, that the work of art is grossly immoral. What they mean by these words seems to me to be this. When they say a work is grossly unintelligible, they mean that the artist has said or made a beautiful thing that is new; when they describe a work as grossly immoral, they mean that the artist has said or made a beautiful thing that is true. The former expression has reference to style; the latter to subject-matter. But they probably use the words very vaguely, as an ordinary mob will use ready-made paving-stones. There is not a single real poet or prose-writer of this century, for instance, on whom the British public have not solemnly conferred diplomas of immorality, and these diplomas practically take the place, with us, of what in France, is the formal recognition of an Academy of Letters, and fortunately make the establishment of such an institution quite unnecessary in England. Of course, the public are very reckless in their use of the word. That they should have called Wordsworth an immoral poet, was only to be expected. Wordsworth was a poet. But that they should have called Charles Kingsley an immoral novelist is extraordinary. Kingsley's prose was not of a very fine quality. Still, there is the word, and they use it as best they can. An artist is, of course, not disturbed by it. The true artist is a man who believes absolutely in himself, because he is absolutely himself. But I can fancy that if an artist produced a work of art in England that immediately on its appearance was recognised by the public, through their medium, which is the public press, as a work that was quite intelligible and highly moral, he would begin to seriously question whether in its creation he had really been himself at all, and consequently whether the work was not quite unworthy of him, and either of a thoroughly second-rate order, or of no artistic value whatsoever.

Perhaps, however, I have wronged the public in limiting them to such words as 'immoral,' 'unintelligible,' 'exotic,' and 'unhealthy.' There is one other word that they use. That word is 'morbid.' They do not use it often. The meaning of the word is so simple that they are afraid of using it. Still, they use it sometimes, and, now and then, one comes across it in popular newspapers. It is, of course, a ridiculous word to apply to a work of art. For what is morbidity but a mood of emotion or a mode of thought that one cannot express? The public are all morbid, because the public can never find expression for anything. The artist is never morbid. He expresses everything. He stands outside his subject, and through its medium produces incomparable and artistic effects. To call an artist morbid because he deals with morbidity as his subject-matter is as silly as if one called Shakespeare mad because he wrote 'King Lear.'

On the whole, an artist in England gains something by being attacked. His individuality is intensified. He becomes more completely himself. Of course, the attacks are very gross, very impertinent, and very contemptible. But then no artist expects grace from the vulgar mind, or style from the suburban intellect. Vulgarity and stupidity are two very vivid facts in modern life. One regrets them, naturally. But there they are. They are subjects for study, like everything else. And it is only fair to state, with regard to modern journalists, that they always apologise to one in private for what they have written against one in public.

Within the last few years two other adjectives, it may be mentioned, have been added to the very limited vocabulary of art-abuse that is at the disposal of the public. One is the word 'unhealthy,' the other is the word 'exotic.' The latter merely expresses the rage of the momentary mushroom against the immortal, entrancing, and exquisitely lovely orchid. It is a tribute, but a tribute of no importance. The word 'unhealthy,' however, admits of analysis. It is a rather interesting word. In fact, it is so interesting that the people who use it do not know what it means.

What does it mean? What is a healthy, or an unhealthy work of art? All terms that one applies to a work of art, provided that one applies them rationally, have reference to either its style or its subject, or to both together. From the point of view of style, a healthy work of art is one whose style recognises the beauty of the material it employs, be that material one of words or of bronze, of colour or of ivory, and uses that beauty as a factor in producing the æsthetic effect. From the point of view of subject, a healthy work of art is one the choice of whose subject is conditioned by the temperament of the artist, and comes directly out of it. In fine, a healthy work of art is one that has both perfection and personality. Of course, form and substance cannot be separated in a work of art; they are always one. But for purposes of analysis, and setting the wholeness of æsthetic impression aside for a moment, we can intellectually so separate them. An unhealthy work of art, on the other hand, is a work whose style is obvious, old-fashioned, and common, and whose subject is deliberately chosen, not because the artist has any pleasure in it, but because he thinks that the public will pay him for it. In fact, the popular novel that the public calls healthy is always a thoroughly unhealthy production; and what the public call an unhealthy novel is always a beautiful and healthy work of art.

I need hardly say that I am not, for a single moment, complaining that the public and the public press misuse these words. I do not see how, with their lack of comprehension of what Art is, they could possibly use them in the proper sense. I am merely pointing out the misuse; and as for the origin of the misuse and the meaning that lies behind it all, the explanation is very simple. It comes from the barbarous conception of authority. It comes from the natural inability of a community corrupted by authority to understand or appreciate Individualism. In a word, it comes from that monstrous and ignorant thing that is called Public Opinion, which, bad and well-meaning as it is when it tries to control action, is infamous and of evil meaning when it tries to control Thought or Art.

Indeed, there is much more to be said in favour of the physical force of the public than there is in favour of the public's opinion. The former may be fine. The latter must be foolish. It is often said that force is no argument. That, however, entirely depends on what one wants to prove. Many of the most important problems of the last few centuries, such as the continuance of personal government in England, or of feudalism in France, have been solved entirely by means of physical force. The very violence of a revolution may make the public grand and splendid for a moment. It was a fatal day when the public discovered that the pen is mightier than the paving-stone, and can be made as offensive as the brickbat. They at once sought for the journalist, found him, developed him, and made him their industrious and well-paid servant. It is greatly to be regretted, for both their sakes. Behind the barricade there may be much that is noble and heroic. But what is there behind the leading-article but prejudice, stupidity, cant, and twaddle? And when these four are joined together they make a terrible force, and constitute the new authority.

In old days men had the rack. Now they have the press. That is an improvement certainly. But still it is very bad, and wrong, and demoralising. Somebody—was it Burke?—called journalism the fourth estate. That was true at the time, no doubt. But at the present moment it really is the only estate. It has eaten up the other three. The Lords Temporal say nothing, the Lords Spiritual have nothing to say, and the House of Commons has nothing to say and says it. We are dominated by Journalism. In America the President reigns for four years, and Journalism governs for ever and ever. Fortunately in America Journalism has carried its authority to the grossest and most brutal extreme. As a natural consequence it has begun to create a spirit of revolt. People are amused by it, or disgusted by it, according to their temperaments. But it is no longer the real force it was. It is not seriously treated. In England, Journalism, not, except in a few well-known instances, having been carried to such excesses of brutality, is still a great factor, a really remarkable power. The tyranny that it proposes to exercise over people's private lives seems to me to be quite extraordinary. The fact is, that the public have an insatiable curiosity to know everything, except what is worth knowing. Journalism, conscious of this, and having tradesman-like habits, supplies their demands. In centuries before ours the public nailed the ears of journalists to the pump. That was quite hideous. In this century journalists have nailed their own ears to the keyhole. That is much worse. And what aggravates the mischief is that the journalists who are most to blame are not the amusing journalists who write for what are called Society papers. The harm is done by the serious, thoughtful, earnest journalists, who solemnly, as they are doing at present, will drag before the eyes of the public some incident in the private life of a great statesman, of a man who is a leader of political thought as he is a creator of political force, and invite the public to discuss the incident, to exercise authority in the matter, to give their views, and not merely to give their views, but to carry them into action, to dictate to the man upon all other points, to dictate to his party, to dictate to his country; in fact, to make themselves ridiculous, offensive, and harmful. The private lives of men and women should not be told to the public. The public have nothing to do with them at all. In Prance they manage these things better. There they do not allow the details of the trials that take place in the divorce courts to be published for the amusement or criticism of the public. All that the public are allowed to know is that the divorce has taken place and was granted on petition of one or other or both of the married parties concerned. In France, in fact, they limit the journalist, and allow the artist almost perfect freedom. Here we allow absolute freedom to the journalist, and entirely limit the artist. English public opinion, that is to say, tries to constrain and impede and warp the man who makes things that are beautiful in effect, and compels the journalist to retail things that are ugly, or disgusting, or revolting in fact, so that we have the most serious journalists in the world, and the most indecent newspapers. It is no exaggeration to talk of compulsion. There are possibly some journalists who take a real pleasure in publishing horrible things, or who, being poor, look to scandals as forming a sort of permanent basis for an income. But there are other journalists, I feel certain, men of education and cultivation, who really dislike publishing these things, who know that it is wrong to do so, and only do it because the unhealthy conditions under which their occupation is carried on oblige them to supply the public with what the public wants, and to compete with other journalists in making that supply as full and satisfying to the gross popular appetite as possible. It is a very degrading position for any body of educated men to be placed in, and I have no doubt that most of them feel it acutely.

However, let us leave what is really a very sordid side of the subject, and return to the question of popular control in the matter of Art, by which I mean Public Opinion dictating to the artist the form which he is to use, the mode in which he is to use it, and the materials with which he is to work. I have pointed out that the arts which have escaped best in England are the arts in which the public have not been interested. They are, however, interested in the drama, and as a certain advance has been made in the drama within the last ten or fifteen years, it is important to point out that this advance is entirely due to a few individual artists refusing to accept the popular want of taste as their standard, and refusing to regard Art as a mere matter of demand and supply. With his marvellous and vivid personality, with a style that has really a true colour-element in it, with his extraordinary power, not over mere mimicry but over imaginative and intellectual creation, Mr Irving, had his sole object been to give the public what they wanted, could have produced the commonest plays in the commonest manner, and made as much success and money as a man could possibly desire. But his object was not that. His object was to realise his own perfection as an artist, under certain conditions, and in certain forms of Art. At first he appealed to the few; now he has educated the many. He has created in the public both taste and temperament. The public appreciate his artistic success immensely. I often wonder, however, whether the public understand that that success is entirely due to the fact that he did not accept their standard, but realised his own. With their standard the Lyceum would have been a sort of second-rate booth, as some of the popular theatres in London are at present. Whether they understand it or not the fact however remains, that taste and temperament have, to a certain extent, been created in the public, and that the public is capable of developing these qualities. The problem then is, why do not the public become more civilised? They have the capacity. What stops them?

The thing that stops them, it must be said again, is their desire to exercise authority over the artist and over works of art. To certain theatres, such as the Lyceum and the Haymarket, the public seem to come in a proper mood. In both of these theatres there have been individual artists, who have succeeded in creating in their audiences—and every theatre in London has its own audience—the temperament to which Art appeals. And what is that temperament? It is the temperament of receptivity. That is all.

If a man approaches a work of art with any desire to exercise authority over it and the artist, he approaches it in such a spirit that he cannot receive any artistic impression from it at all. The work of art is to dominate the spectator: the spectator is not to dominate the work of art. The spectator is to be receptive. He is to be the violin on which the master is to play. And the more completely he can suppress his own silly views, his own foolish prejudices, his own absurd ideas of what Art should be, or should not be, the more likely he is to understand and appreciate the work of art in question. This is, of course, quite obvious in the case of the vulgar theatre-going public of English men and women. But it is equally true of what are called educated people. For an educated person's ideas of Art are drawn naturally from what Art has been, whereas the new work of art is beautiful by being what Art has never been; and to measure it by the standard of the past is to measure it by a standard on the rejection of which its real perfection depends. A temperament capable of receiving, through an imaginative medium, and under imaginative conditions, new and beautiful impressions, is the only temperament that can appreciate a work of art. And true as this is in the case of the appreciation of sculpture and painting, it is still more true of the appreciation of such arts as the drama. For a picture and a statue are not at war with Time. They take no count of its succession. In one moment their unity may be apprehended. In the case of literature it is different. Time must be traversed before the unity of effect is realised. And so, in the drama, there may occur in the first act of the play something whose real artistic value may not be evident to the spectator till the third or fourth act is reached. Is the silly fellow to get angry and call out, and disturb the play, and annoy the artists? No, the honest man is to sit quietly, and know the delightful emotions of wonder, curiosity, and suspense. He is not to go to the play to lose a vulgar temper. He is to go to the play to realise an artistic temperament. He is to go to the play to gain an artistic temperament. He is not the arbiter of the work of art. He is one who is admitted to contemplate the work of art, and, if the work be fine, to forget in its contemplation all, the egotism that mars him—the egotism of his ignorance, or the egotism of his information. This point about the drama is hardly, I think, sufficiently recognised. I can quite understand that were 'Macbeth' produced for the first time before a modern London audience, many of the people present would strongly and vigorously object to the introduction of the witches in the first act, with their grotesque phrases and their ridiculous words. But when the play is over one realises that the laughter of the witches in 'Macbeth' is as terrible as the laughter of madness in 'Lear,' more terrible than the daughter of Iago in the tragedy of the Moor. No spectator of art needs a more perfect mood of receptivity than the spectator of a play. The moment he seeks to exercise authority he becomes the avowed enemy of Art and of himself. Art does not mind. It is he who suffers.

With the novel it is the same thing. Popular authority and the recognition of popular authority are fatal. Thackeray's 'Esmond' is a beautiful work of art because he wrote it to please himself. In his other novels, in 'Pendennis,' in 'Philip,' in 'Vanity Fair' even, at times, he is too conscious of the public, and spoils his work by appealing directly to the sympathies of the public, or by directly mocking at them. A true artist takes no notice whatever of the public. The public are to him non-existent. He has no poppied or honeyed cakes through which to give the monster sleep or sustenance. He leaves that to the popular novelist. One incomparable novelist we have now in England, Mr George Meredith. There are better artists in France, but France has no one whose view of life is so large, so varied, so imaginatively true. There are tellers of stories in Russia who have a more vivid sense of what pain in fiction may be. But to him belongs philosophy in fiction. His people not merely live, but they live in thought. One can see them from myriad points of view. They are suggestive. There is soul in them and around them. They are interpretative and symbolic. And he who made them, those wonderful quickly-moving figures, made them for his own pleasure, and has never asked the public what they wanted, has never cared to know what they wanted, has never allowed the public to dictate to him or influence him in any way, but has gone on intensifying his own personality, and producing his own individual work. At first none came to him. That did not matter. Then the few came to him. That did not change him. The many have come now. He is still the same. He's an incomparable novelist.

With the decorative arts it is not different. The public clung with really pathetic tenacity to what I believe were the direct traditions of the Great Exhibition of international vulgarity, traditions that were so appalling that the houses in which people lived were only fit for blind people to live in. Beautiful things began to be made, beautiful colours came from the dyer's hand, beautiful patterns from the artist's brain, and the use of beautiful things and their value and importance were set forth. The public were really very indignant. They lost their temper. They said silly things. No one minded. No one was a whit the worse. No one accepted the authority of public opinion. And now it is almost impossible to enter any modern house without seeing some recognition of good taste, some recognition of the value of lovely surroundings, some sign of appreciation of beauty. In fact, people's houses are, as a rule, quite charming nowadays. People have been to a very great extent civilised. It is only fair to state, however, that the extraordinary success of the revolution in house-decoration and furniture and the like has not really been due to the majority of the public developing a very fine taste in such matters. It has been chiefly due to the fact that the craftsmen of things so appreciated the pleasure of making what was beautiful, and woke to such a vivid consciousness of the hideousness and vulgarity of what the public had previously wanted, that they simply starved the public out. It would be quite impossible at the present moment to furnish a room as rooms were furnished a few years ago, without going for everything to an auction of second-hand furniture from some third-rate lodging-house. The things are no longer made. However they may object to it, people must nowadays have something charming in their surroundings. Fortunately for them, their assumption of authority in these art-matters came to entire grief.

It is evident, then, that all authority in such things is bad. People sometimes inquire what form of government is most suitable for an artist to live under. To this question there is only one answer. The form of government that is most suitable to the artist is no government at all. Authority over him and his art is ridiculous. It has been stated that under despotisms artists have produced lovely work. This is not quite so. Artists have visited despots, not as subjects to be tyrannised over, but as wandering wonder-makers, as fascinating vagrant personalities, to be entertained and charmed and suffered to be at peace, and allowed to create. There is this to be said in favour of the despot, that he, being an individual, may have culture, while the mob, being a monster, has none. One who is an Emperor and King may stoop down to pick up a brush for a painter, but when the democracy stoops down it is merely to throw mud. And yet the democracy have not so far to stoop as the emperor. In fact, when they want to throw mud they have not to stoop at all. But there is no necessity to separate the monarch from the mob; all authority is equally bad.

There are three kinds of despots. There is the despot who tyrannises over the body. There is the despot who tyrannises over the soul. There is the despot who tyrannises over the soul and body alike. The first is called the Prince. The second is called the Pope The third is called the People. The Prince may be cultivated. Many Princes have been. Yet in the Prince there is danger. One thinks of Dante at the bitter feast in Verona, of Tasso in Ferrara's madman's cell. It is better for the artist not to live with Princes. The Pope may be cultivated. Many Popes have been; the bad Popes have been. The bad Popes loved Beauty, almost as passionately, nay, with as much passion as the good Popes hated Thought. To the wickedness of the Papacy humanity owes much. The goodness of the Papacy owes a terrible debt to humanity. Yet, though the Vatican has kept the rhetoric of its thunders, and lost the rod of its lightning, it is better for the artist not to live with Popes. It was a Pope who said of Cellini to a conclave of Cardinals that common laws and common authority were not made for men such as he; but it was a Pope who thrust Cellini into prison, and kept him there till he sickened with rage, and created unreal visions for himself, and saw the gilded sun enter his room, and grew so enamoured of it that he sought to escape, and crept out from tower to tower, and falling through dizzy air at dawn, maimed himself, and was by a vine-dresser covered with vine leaves, and carried in a cart to one who, loving beautiful things, had care of him. There is danger in Popes. And as for the People, what of them and their authority? Perhaps of them and their authority one has spoken enough. Their authority is a thing blind, deaf, hideous, grotesque, tragic, amusing, serious, and obscene. It is impossible for the artist to live with the People. All despots bribe. The people bribe and brutalise. Who told them to exercise authority? They were made to live, to listen, and to love. Someone has done them a great wrong. They have marred themselves by imitation of their inferiors. They have taken the sceptre of the Prince. How should they use it? They have taken the triple tiara of the Pope. How should they carry its burden? They are as a clown whose heart is broken. They are as a priest whose soul is not yet born. Let all who love Beauty pity

97

them. Though they themselves love not Beauty, yet let them pity themselves. Who taught them the trick of tyranny?

There are many other things that one might point out. One might point out how the Renaissance was great, because it sought to solve no social problem, and busied itself not about such things, but suffered the individual to develop freely, beautifully, and naturally, and so had great and individual artists, and great and individual men. One might point out how Louis XIV., by creating the modern state, destroyed the individualism of the artist, and made things monstrous in their monotony of repetition, and contemptible in their conformity to rule, and destroyed throughout all France all those fine freedoms of expression that had made tradition new in beauty, and new modes one with antique form. But the past is of no importance. The present is of no importance. It is with the future that we have to deal. For the past is what man should not have been. The present is what man ought not to be. The future is what artists are.

It will, of course, be said that such a scheme as is set forth here is quite unpractical, and goes against human nature. This is perfectly true. It is unpractical, and it goes against human nature. This is why it is worth carrying out, and that is why one proposes it. For what is a practical scheme? A practical scheme is either a scheme that is already in existence, or a scheme that could be carried out under existing conditions. But it is exactly the existing conditions that one objects to; and any scheme that could accept these conditions is wrong and foolish. The conditions will be done away with, and human nature will change. The only thing that one really knows about human nature is that it changes. Change is the one quality we can predicate of it. The systems that fail are those that rely on the permanency of human nature, and not on its growth and development. The error of Louis XIV. was that he thought human nature would always be the same. The result of his error was the French Revolution. It was an admirable result. All the results of the mistakes of governments are quite admirable.

It is to be noted also that Individualism does not come to man with any sickly cant about duty, which merely means doing what other people want because they want it; or any hideous cant about self-sacrifice, which is merely a survival of savage mutilation. In fact, it does not come to man with any claims upon him at all. It comes naturally and inevitably out of man. It is the point to which all development tends. It is the differentiation to which all organisms grow. It is the perfection that is inherent in every mode of life, and towards which every mode of life quickens. And so Individualism exercises no compulsion over man. On the contrary, it says to man that he should suffer no compulsion to be exercised over him. It does not try to force people to be good. It knows that people are good when they are let alone. Man will develop Individualism out of himself. Man is now so developing Individualism. To ask whether Individualism is practical is like asking whether Evolution is practical. Evolution is the law of life, and there is no evolution except towards Individualism. Where this tendency is not expressed, it is a case of artificially-arrested growth, or of disease, or of death.

Individualism will also be unselfish and unaffected. It has been pointed out that one of the results of the extraordinary tyranny of authority is that words are absolutely distorted from their proper and simple meaning, and are used to express the obverse of their right signification. What is true about Art is true about Life. A man is called affected, nowadays, if he dresses as he likes to dress. But in doing that he is acting in a perfectly natural manner. Affectation, in such matters, consists in dressing according to the views of one's neighbour, whose views, as they are the views of the majority, will probably be extremely stupid. Or a man is called selfish if he lives in the manner that seems to him most suitable for the full realisation of his own personality; if, in fact, the primary aim of his life is self-development. But this is the way in which everyone should live. Selfishness is not living as one wishes to live, it is asking others to live as one wishes to live. And unselfishness is letting other people's lives alone, not interfering with them. Selfishness always aims at creating around it an absolute uniformity of type. Unselfishness recognises infinite variety of type as a delightful thing, accepts it, acquiesces in it, enjoys it. It is not selfish to think for oneself. A man who does not think for himself does not think at all. It is grossly selfish to require of one's neighbour that he should think in the same way, and hold the same opinions. Why should he? If he can think, he will probably think differently. If he cannot think, it is monstrous to require thought of any kind from him. A red rose is not selfish because it wants to be a red rose. It would be horribly selfish if it wanted all the other flowers in the garden to be both red and roses. Under Individualism people will be quite natural and absolutely unselfish, and will know the meanings of the words, and realise them in their free, beautiful lives. Nor will men be egotistic as they are now. For the egotist is he who makes claims upon others, and the Individualist will not desire to do that. It will not give him pleasure. When man has realised Individualism, he will also realise sympathy and exercise it freely and spontaneously. Up to the present man has hardly cultivated sympathy at all. He has merely sympathy with pain, and sympathy with pain is not the highest form of sympathy. All sympathy is fine, but sympathy with suffering is the least fine mode. It is tainted with egotism. It is apt to become morbid. There is in it a certain element of terror for our own safety. We become afraid that we ourselves might be as the leper or as the blind, and that no man would have care of us. It is curiously limiting, too. One should sympathise with the entirety of life, not with life's sores and maladies merely, but with life's joy and beauty and energy and health and freedom. The wider sympathy is, of course, the more difficult. It requires more unselfishness. Anybody can sympathise with the sufferings of a friend, but it requires a very fine nature—it requires, in fact, the nature of a true Individualist—to sympathise with a friend's success.

In the modern stress of competition and struggle for place, such sympathy is naturally rare, and is also very much stifled by the immoral ideal of uniformity of type and conformity to rule which is so prevalent everywhere, and is perhaps most obnoxious in England.

Sympathy with pain there will, of course, always be. It is one of the first instincts of man. The animals which are individual, the higher animals, that is to say, share it with us. But it must be remembered that while sympathy with joy intensifies the sum of joy in the world, sympathy with pain does not really diminish the amount of pain. It may make man better able to endure evil, but the evil remains. Sympathy with consumption does not cure consumption; that is what Science does. And when Socialism has solved the problem of poverty, and Science solved the problem of disease, the area of the sentimentalists will be lessened, and the sympathy of man will be large, healthy, and spontaneous. Man will have joy in the contemplation of the joyous life of others.

For it is through joy that the Individualism of the future will develop itself. Christ made no attempt to reconstruct society, and consequently the Individualism that he preached to man could be realised only through pain or in solitude. The ideals that we owe to Christ are the ideals of the man who abandons society entirely, or of the man who resists society absolutely. But man is naturally social. Even the Thebaid became peopled at last. And though the cenobite realises his personality, it is often an impoverished personality that he so realises. Upon the other hand, the terrible truth that pain is a mode through which man may realise himself exercises a wonderful fascination over the world. Shallow speakers and shallow thinkers in pulpits and on platforms often talk about the world's worship of pleasure, and whine against it. But it is rarely in the world's history that its ideal has been one of joy and beauty. The worship of pain has far more often dominated the world. Mediævalism, with its saints and martyrs, its love of self-torture, its wild passion for wounding itself, its gashing with knives, and its whipping with rods—Mediævalism is real Christianity, and the mediæval Christ is the real Christ. When the Renaissance dawned upon the world, and brought with it the new ideals of the beauty of life and the joy of living, men could not understand Christ. Even Art shows us that. The painters of the Renaissance drew Christ as a little boy playing with another boy in a palace or a garden, or lying back in his mother's arms, smiling at her, or at a flower, or at a bright bird; or as a noble, stately figure moving nobly through the world; or as a wonderful figure rising in a sort of ecstasy from death to life. Even when they drew him crucified they drew him as a beautiful God on whom evil men had inflicted suffering. But he did not preoccupy them much. What delighted them was to paint the men and women whom they admired, and to show the loveliness of this lovely earth. They painted many religious pictures—in fact, they painted far too many, and the monotony of type and motive is wearisome, and was bad for art. It was the result of the authority of the public in art-matters, and is to be deplored. But their soul was not in the subject Raphael was a great artist when he painted his portrait of the Pope. When he painted his Madonnas and infant Christs, he is not a great artist at all. Christ had

101

no message for the Renaissance, which was wonderful because it brought an ideal at variance with his, and to find the presentation of the real Christ we must go to mediæval art. There he is one maimed and marred; one who is not comely to look on, because Beauty is a joy; one who is not in fair raiment, because that may be a joy also: he is a beggar who has a marvellous soul; he is a leper whose soul is divine; he needs neither property nor health; he is a God realising his perfection through pain.

The evolution of man is slow. The injustice of men is great. It was necessary that pain should be put forward as a mode of self-realisation. Even now, in some places in the world, the message of Christ is necessary. No one who lived in modern Russia could possibly realise his perfection except by pain. A few Russian artists have realised themselves in Art; in a fiction that is mediæval in character, hecauae its dominant note is the realisation of men through suffering. But for those who are not artists, and to whom there is no mode of life but the actual life of fact, pain is the only door to perfection. A Russian who lives happily under the present system of government in Russia must either believe that man has no soul, or that, if he has, it is not worth developing. A Nihilist who rejects all authority, because he knows authority to be evil, and welcomes all pain, because through that he realises his personality, is a real Christian. To him the Christian ideal is a true thing.

And yet, Christ did not revolt against authority. He accepted the imperial authority of the Roman Empire and paid tribute. He endured the ecclesiastical authority of the Jewish Church, and would not repel its violence by any violence of his own. He had, as I said before, no scheme for the reconstruction of society. But the modern world has schemes. It proposes to do away with poverty and the suffering that it entails. It desires to get rid of pain, and the suffering that pain entails. It trusts to Socialism and to Science as its methods. What it aims at is an Individualism expressing itself through joy. This Individualism will be larger, fuller, lovelier than any Individualism has ever been. Pain is not the ultimate mode of perfection. It is merely provisional and a protest. It has reference to wrong, unhealthy, unjust surroundings. When the wrong, and the disease, and the injustice are removed, it will have no further place. It will have done its work. It was a great work, but it is almost over. Its sphere lessens every day.

Nor will man miss it. For what man has sought for is, indeed, neither pain nor pleasure, but simply Life. Man has sought to live intensely, fully, perfectly. When he can do so without exercising restraint on others, or suffering it ever, and his activities are all pleasurable to him, he will be saner, healthier, more civilised, more himself. Pleasure is Nature's test, her sign of approval. When man is happy, he is in harmony with himself and his environment. The new Individualism, for whose service Socialism, whether it wills it or not, is working, will be perfect harmony. It will be what the Greeks sought for, but could not, except in Thought, realise completely, because they had slaves, and fed them; it will be what the Renaissance sought for, but could not realise completely except in Art, because they had slaves, and starved them. It will be complete, and through it each man will attain to his perfection. The new Individualism is the new Hellenism.

OSCAR WILDE
MISCELLANEOUS

PREFACE

*'As to my personal attitude towards criticism, I confess in brief the following:—"If my works are good and of any importance whatever for the further development of art, they will maintain their place in spite of all adverse criticism and in spite of all hateful suspicions attached to my artistic intentions. If my works are of no account, the most gratifying success of the moment and the most enthusiastic approval of as augurs cannot make them endure. The waste-paper press can devour them as it has devoured many others, and I will not shed a tear . . . and the world will move on just the same. "'—*RICHARD STRAUSS.

The contents of this volume require some explanation of an historical nature. It is scarcely realised by the present generation that Wilde's works on their first appearance, with the exception of De Profundis, were met with almost general condemnation and ridicule. The plays on their first production were grudgingly praised because their obvious success could not be ignored; but on their subsequent publication in book form they were violently assailed. That nearly all of them have held the stage is still a source of irritation among certain journalists. Salomé however enjoys a singular career. As every one knows, it was prohibited by the Censor when in rehearsal by Madame Bernhardt at the Palace Theatre in 1892. On its publication in 1893 it was greeted with greater abuse than any other of Wilde's works, and was consigned to the usual irrevocable oblivion. The accuracy of the French was freely canvassed, and of course it is obvious that the French is not that of a Frenchman. The play was passed for press, however, by no less a writer than Marcel Schwob whose letter to the Paris publisher, returning the proofs and mentioning two or three slight alterations, is still in my possession. Marcel Schwob told me some years afterwards that he thought it would have spoiled the spontaneity and character of Wilde's style if he had tried to harmonise it with the diction demanded by the French Academy. It was never composed with any idea of presentation. Madame Bernhardt happened to say she wished Wilde would write a play for her; he replied in jest that he had done so. She insisted on seeing the manuscript, and decided on its immediate production, ignorant or forgetful of the English law which prohibits the introduction of Scriptural characters on the stage. With his keen sense of the theatre Wilde would never have contrived the long speech of Salomé at the end in a drama intended for the stage, even in the days of long speeches. His threat to change his nationality shortly after the Censor's interference called forth a most delightful and good-natured caricature of him by Mr. Bernard Partridge in Punch.

Wilde was still in prison in 1896 when Salomé was produced by Lugne Poë at the Théâtre de L'Œuvre in Paris, but except for an account in the Daily Telegraph the incident was hardly mentioned in England. I gather that the performance was only a qualified success, though Lugne Poë's triumph as Herod was generally acknowledged. In 1901, within a year of the author's death, it was produced in Berlin; from that moment it has held the European stage. It has run for a longer consecutive period in Germany than any play by any Englishman, not excepting Shakespeare. Its popularity has extended to all countries where it is not prohibited. It is performed throughout Europe, Asia and America. It is played even in Yiddish. This is remarkable in view of the many dramas by French and German writers who treat of the same theme. To none of them, however, is Wilde indebted. Flaubert, Maeterlinck (some would add Ollendorff) and Scripture, are the obvious sources on which he has freely drawn for what I do not hesitate to call the most powerful and perfect of all his dramas. But on such a point a trustee and executor may be prejudiced because it is the most valuable asset in Wilde's literary estate. Aubrey Beardsley's illustrations are too well known to need more than a passing reference. In the world of art criticism they excited almost as much attention as Wilde's drama has excited in the world of intellect.

During May 1905 the play was produced in England for the first time at a private performance by the New Stage Club. No one present will have forgotten the extraordinary tension of the audience on that occasion, those who disliked the play and its author being hypnotised by the extraordinary power of Mr. Robert Farquharson's Herod, one of the finest pieces of acting ever seen in this country. My friends the dramatic critics (and many of them are personal friends) fell on Salomé with all the vigour of their predecessors twelve years before. Unaware of what was taking place in Germany, they spoke of the play as having been 'dragged from obscurity.' The Official Receiver in Bankruptcy and myself were, however, better informed. And much pleasure has been derived from reading those criticisms, all carefully preserved along with the list of receipts which were simultaneously pouring in from the German performances. To do the critics justice they never withdrew any of their printed opinions, which were all trotted out again when the play was produced privately for the second time in England by the Literary Theatre Society in 1906. In the Speaker of July 14th, 1906, however, some of the iterated misrepresentations of fact were corrected. No attempt was made to controvert the opinion of an ignorant critic: his veracity only was impugned. The powers of vaticination possessed by such judges of drama can be fairly tested in the career of Salomé on the European stage, apart from the opera. In an introduction to the English translation published by Mr. John Lane it is pointed out that Wilde's confusion of Herod Antipas (Matt. xiv. 1) with Herod the Great (Matt. ii. 1) and Herod Agrippa I. (Acts xii. 23) is intentional, and follows a mediæval convention. There is no attempt at historical accuracy or archæological exactness. Those who saw the marvellous décor of Mr. Charles Ricketts at the second English production can form a complete idea of what Wilde intended in that respect; although the stage management was clumsy and amateurish. The great opera of Richard Strauss does not fall within my province; but the fag ends of its popularity on the Continent have been imported here oddly enough through the agency of the Palace Theatre, where Salomé was originally to have been performed. Of a young lady's dancing, or of that of her rivals, I am not qualified to speak. I note merely that the critics who objected to the horror of one incident in the drama lost all self-control on seeing that incident repeated in dumb show and accompanied by fescennine corybantics. Except in 'name and borrowed notoriety' the music-hall sensation has no relation whatever to the drama which so profoundly moved the whole of Europe and the greatest living musician. The adjectives of contumely are easily transmuted into epithets of adulation, when a prominent ecclesiastic succumbs, like King Herod, to the fascination of a dancer.

It is not usually known in England that a young French naval officer, unaware that Dr. Strauss was composing an opera on the theme of Salomé, wrote another music drama to accompany Wilde's text. The exclusive musical rights having been already secured by Dr. Strauss, Lieutenant Marriotte's work cannot be performed regularly. One presentation, however, was permitted at Lyons, the composer's native town, where I am told it made an extraordinary impression. In order to give English readers some faint idea of the world-wide effect of Wilde's drama, my friend Mr. Walter Ledger has prepared a short bibliography of certain English and Continental translations.

At the time of Wilde's trial the nearly completed MS. of La Sainte Courtisane was entrusted to Mrs. Leverson, the well-known novelist, who in 1897 went to Paris on purpose to restore it to the author. Wilde immediately left the only copy in a cab. A few days later he laughingly informed me of the loss, and added that a cab was a very proper place for it. I have explained elsewhere that he looked on his works with disdain in his last years, though he was always full of schemes for writing others. All my attempts to recover the lost work failed. The passages here reprinted are from some odd leaves of a first draft. The play is, of course, not unlike Salomé, though it was written in English. It expanded Wilde's favourite theory that when you convert some one to an idea, you lose your faith in it; the same motive runs through Mr. W. H. Honorius the hermit, so far as I recollect the story, falls in love with the courtesan who has come to tempt him, and he reveals to her the secret of the love of God. She immediately becomes a Christian, and is murdered by robbers. Honorius the hermit goes back to Alexandria to pursue a life of pleasure. Two other similar plays Wilde invented in prison, Ahab and Isabel and Pharaoh; he would never write them down, though often importuned to do so. Pharaoh was intensely dramatic and perhaps more original than any of the group. None of these works must be confused with the manuscripts stolen from 16 Tite Street in 1895—namely, the enlarged version of Mr. W. H., the second draft of A Florentine Tragedy, and The Duchess of Padua (which, existing in a prompt copy, was of less importance than the others); nor with The Cardinal of Arragon, the manuscript of which I never saw. I scarcely think it ever existed, though Wilde used to recite proposed passages for it.

Some years after Wilde's death I was looking over the papers and letters rescued from Tite Street when I came across loose sheets of manuscript and typewriting, which I imagined were fragments of The Duchess of Padua; on putting them together in a coherent form I recognised that they belonged to the lost Florentine Tragedy. I assumed that the opening scene, though once extant, had disappeared. One day, however, Mr. Willard wrote that he possessed a typewritten fragment of a play which Wilde had submitted to him, and this he kindly forwarded for my inspection. It agreed in nearly every particular with what I had taken so much trouble to put together. This suggests that the opening scene had never been written, as Mr. Willard's version began where mine did. It was characteristic of the author to finish what he never began.

When the Literary Theatre Society produced Salomé in 1906 they asked me for some other short drama by Wilde to present at the same time, as Salomé does not take very long to play. I offered them the fragment of A Florentine Tragedy. By a fortunate coincidence the poet and dramatist, Mr. Thomas Sturge Moore, happened to be on the committee of this Society, and to him was entrusted the task of writing an opening scene to make the play complete. It is not for me to criticise his work, but there is justification for saying that Wilde himself would have envied, with an artist's envy, such lines as—

We will sup with the moon,

Like Persian princes that in Babylon

Sup in the hanging gardens of the King.

In a stylistic sense Mr. Sturge Moore has accomplished a feat in reconstruction, whatever opinions may be held of A Florentine Tragedy by Wilde's admirers or detractors. The achievement is particularly remarkable because Mr. Sturge Moore has nothing in common with Wilde other than what is shared by all real poets and dramatists: He is a landed proprietor on Parnassus, not a trespasser. In England we are more familiar with the poachers. Time and Death are of course necessary before there can come any adequate recognition of one of our most original and gifted singers.

Among his works are The Vinedresser and other Poems (1899), Absalom, A Chronicle Play (1903), and The Centaur's Booty (1903). Mr. Sturge Moore is also an art critic of distinction, and his learned works on Dürer (1905) and Correggio (1906) are more widely known (I am sorry to say) than his powerful and enthralling poems.

Once again I must express my obligations to Mr. Stuart Mason for revising and correcting the proofs of this new edition.

ROBERT ROSS

LA SAINTE COURTISANE

A FRAGMENT

LA SAINTE COURTISANE

OR, THE WOMAN COVERED WITH JEWELS

The scene represents the corner of a valley in the Thebaid. On the right hand of the stage is a cavern. In front of the cavern stands a great crucifix.

On the left [sand dunes].

The sky is blue like the inside of a cup of lapis lazuli. The hills are of red sand. Here and there on the hills there are clumps of thorns.

First Man. Who is she? She makes me afraid. She has a purple cloak and her hair is like threads of gold. I think she must be the daughter of the Emperor. I have heard the boatmen say that the Emperor has a daughter who wears a cloak of purple.

Second Man. She has birds' wings upon her sandals, and her tunic is of the colour of green corn. It is like corn in spring when she stands still. It is like young corn troubled by the shadows of hawks when she moves. The pearls on her tunic are like many moons.

First Man. They are like the moons one sees in the water when the wind blows from the hills.

Second Man. I think she is one of the gods. I think she comes from Nubia.

First Man. I am sure she is the daughter of the Emperor. Her nails are stained with henna. They are like the petals of a rose. She has come here to weep for Adonis.

Second Man. She is one of the gods. I do not know why she has left her temple. The gods should not leave their temples. If she speaks to us let us not answer, and she will pass by.

First Man. She will not speak to us. She is the daughter of the Emperor.

Myrrhina. Dwells he not here, the beautiful young hermit, he who will not look on the face of woman?

First Man. Of a truth it is here the hermit dwells.

Myrrhina. Why will he not look on the face of woman?

Second Man. We do not know.

Myrrhina. Why do ye yourselves not look at me?

First Man. You are covered with bright stones, and you dazzle our eyes.

Second Man. He who looks at the sun becomes blind. You are too bright to look at. It is not wise to look at things that are very bright. Many of the priests in the temples are blind, and have slaves to lead them.

Myrrhina. Where does he dwell, the beautiful young hermit who will not look on the face of woman? Has he a house of reeds or a house of burnt clay or does he lie on the hillside? Or does he make his bed in the rushes?

First Man. He dwells in that cavern yonder.

Myrrhina. What a curious place to dwell in!

First Man. Of old a centaur lived there. When the hermit came the centaur gave a shrill cry, wept and lamented, and galloped away.

Second Man. No. It was a white unicorn who lived in the cave. When it saw the hermit coming the unicorn knelt down and worshipped him. Many people saw it worshipping him.

First Man. I have talked with people who saw it.

. . . . .

Second Man. Some say he was a hewer of wood and worked for hire. But that may not be true.

. . . . .

Myrrhina. What gods then do ye worship? Or do ye worship any gods? There are those who have no gods to worship. The philosophers who wear long beards and brown cloaks have no gods to worship. They wrangle with each other in the porticoes. The [ ] laugh at them.

First Man. We worship seven gods. We may not tell their names. It is a very dangerous thing to tell the names of the gods. No one should ever tell the name of his god. Even the priests who praise the gods all day long, and eat of their food with them, do not call them by their right names.

Myrrhina. Where are these gods ye worship?

First Man. We hide them in the folds of our tunics. We do not show them to any one. If we showed them to any one they might leave us.

Myrrhina. Where did ye meet with them?

First Man. They were given to us by an embalmer of the dead who had found them in a tomb. We served him for seven years.

Myrrhina. The dead are terrible. I am afraid of Death.

First Man. Death is not a god. He is only the servant of the gods.

Myrrhina. He is the only god I am afraid of. Ye have seen many of the gods?

First Man. We have seen many of them. One sees them chiefly at night time. They pass one by very swiftly. Once we saw some of the gods at daybreak. They were walking across a plain.

Myrrhina. Once as I was passing through the market place I heard a sophist from Cilicia say that there is only one God. He said it before many people.

First Man. That cannot be true. We have ourselves seen many, though we are but common men and of no account. When I saw them I hid myself in a bush. They did me no harm.

. . . . .

Myrrhina. Tell me more about the beautiful young hermit. Talk to me about the beautiful young hermit who will not look on the face of woman. What is the story of his days? What mode of life has he?

First Man. We do not understand you.

Myrrhina. What does he do, the beautiful young hermit? Does he sow or reap? Does he plant a garden or catch fish in a net? Does he weave linen on a loom? Does he set his hand to the wooden plough and walk behind the oxen?

Second Man. He being a very holy man does nothing. We are common men and of no account. We toll all day long in the sun. Sometimes the ground is very hard.

Myrrhina. Do the birds of the air feed him? Do the jackals share their booty with him?

First Man. Every evening we bring him food. We do not think that the birds of the air feed him.

Myrrhina. Why do ye feed him? What profit have ye in so doing?

Second Man. He is a very holy man. One of the gods whom he has offended has made him mad. We think he has offended the moon.

Myrrhina. Go and tell him that one who has come from Alexandria desires to speak with him.

First Man. We dare not tell him. This hour he is praying to his God. We pray thee to pardon us for not doing thy bidding.

Myrrhina. Are ye afraid, of him?

First Man. We are afraid of him.

Myrrhina. Why are ye afraid of him?

First Man. We do not know.

Myrrhina. What is his name?

First Man. The voice that speaks to him at night time in the cavern calls to him by the name of Honorius. It was also by the name of Honorius that the three lepers who passed by once called to him. We think that his name is Honorius.

Myrrhina. Why did the three lepers call to him?

First Man. That he might heal them.

Myrrhina. Did he heal them?

Second Man. No. They had committed some sin: it was for that reason they were lepers. Their hands and faces were like salt. One of them wore a mask of linen. He was a king's son.

Myrrhina. What is the voice that speaks to him at night time in his cave?

First Man. We do not know whose voice it is. We think it is the voice of his God. For we have seen no man enter his cavern nor any come forth from it.

. . . . .

Myrrhina. Honorius.

Honorius (*from within*). Who calls Honorius?

Myrrhina. Come forth, Honorius.

. . . . .

My chamber is ceiled with cedar and odorous with myrrh. The pillars of my bed are of cedar and the hangings are of purple. My bed is strewn with purple and the steps are of silver. The hangings are sewn with silver pomegranates and the steps that are of silver are strewn with saffron and with myrrh. My lovers hang garlands round the pillars of my house. At night time they come with the flute players and the players of the harp. They woo me with apples and on the pavement of my courtyard they write my name in wine.

From the uttermost parts of the world my lovers come to me. The kings of the earth come to me and bring me presents.

When the Emperor of Byzantium heard of me he left his porphyry chamber and set sail in his galleys. His slaves bare no torches that none might know of his coming. When the King of Cyprus heard of me he sent me ambassadors. The two Kings of Libya who are brothers brought me gifts of amber.

I took the minion of Cæsar from Cæsar and made him my playfellow. He came to me at night in a litter. He was pale as a narcissus, and his body was like honey.

The son of the Præfect slew himself in my honour, and the Tetrarch of Cilicia scourged himself for my pleasure before my slaves.

The King of Hierapolis who is a priest and a robber set carpets for me to walk on.

Sometimes I sit in the circus and the gladiators fight beneath me. Once a Thracian who was my lover was caught in the net. I gave the signal for him to die and the whole theatre applauded. Sometimes I pass through the gymnasium and watch the young men wrestling or in the race. Their bodies are bright with oil and their brows are wreathed with willow sprays and with myrtle. They stamp their feet on the sand when they wrestle and when they run the sand follows them like a little cloud. He at whom I smile leaves his companions and follows me to my home. At other times I go down to the harbour and watch the merchants unloading their vessels. Those that come from Tyre have cloaks of silk and earrings of emerald. Those that come from Massilia have cloaks of fine wool and earrings of brass. When they see me coming they stand on the prows of their ships and call to me, but I do not answer them. I go to the little taverns where the sailors lie all day long drinking black wine and playing with dice and I sit down with them.

I made the Prince my slave, and his slave who was a Tyrian I made my lord for the space of a moon.

I put a figured ring on his finger and brought him to my house. I have wonderful things in my house.

The dust of the desert lies on your hair and your feet are scratched with thorns and your body is scorched by the sun. Come with me, Honorius, and I will clothe you in a tunic of silk. I will smear your body with myrrh and pour spikenard on your hair. I will clothe you in hyacinth and put honey in your mouth. Love—

Honorius. There is no love but the love of God.

Myrrhina. Who is He whose love is greater than that of mortal men?

Honorius. It is He whom thou seest on the cross, Myrrhina. He is the Son of God and was born of a virgin. Three wise men who were kings brought Him offerings, and the shepherds who were lying on the hills were wakened by a great light.

The Sibyls knew of His coming. The groves and the oracles spake of Him. David and the prophets announced Him. There is no love like the love of God nor any love that can be compared to it.

The body is vile, Myrrhina. God will raise thee up with a new body which will not know corruption, and thou shalt dwell in the Courts of the Lord and see Him whose hair is like fine wool and whose feet are of brass.

Myrrhina. The beauty . . .

Honorius. The beauty of the soul increases until it can see God. Therefore, Myrrhina, repent of thy sins. The robber who was crucified beside Him He brought into Paradise.

[*Exit.*

Myrrhina. How strangely he spake to me. And with what scorn did he regard me. I wonder why he spake to me so strangely.

. . . . .

Honorius. Myrrhina, the scales have fallen from my eyes and I see now clearly what I did not see before. Take me to Alexandria and let me taste of the seven sins.

Myrrhina. Do not mock me, Honorius, nor speak to me with such bitter words. For I have repented of my sins and I am seeking a cavern in this desert where I too may dwell so that my soul may become worthy to see God.

Honorius. The sun is setting, Myrrhina. Come with me to Alexandria.

Myrrhina. I will not go to Alexandria.

Honorius. Farewell, Myrrhina.

Myrrhina. Honorius, farewell. No, no, do not go.

. . . . .

I have cursed my beauty for what it has done, and cursed the wonder of my body for the evil that it has brought upon you.

Lord, this man brought me to Thy feet. He told me of Thy coming upon earth, and of the wonder of Thy birth, and the great wonder of Thy death also. By him, O Lord, Thou wast revealed to me.

Honorius. You talk as a child, Myrrhina, and without knowledge. Loosen your hands. Why didst thou come to this valley in thy beauty?

Myrrhina. The God whom thou worshippest led me here that I might repent of my iniquities and know Him as the Lord.

Honorius. Why didst thou tempt me with words?

Myrrhina. That thou shouldst see Sin in its painted mask and look on Death in its robe of Shame.

A FLORENTINE TRAGEDY

WITH OPENING SCENE BY T. STURGE MOORE

This play is only a fragment and was never completed. For the purposes of presentation, the well-known poet, Mr. T. Sturge Moore, has written an opening scene which is here included. Wilde's work begins with the entrance of Simone.

A private performance was given by the Literary Theatre Club in 1906. The first public presentation was given by the New English Players at the Cripplegate Institute, Golden Lane, E.C., in 1907. German, French and Hungarian translations have been presented on the Continental stage.

Dramatic and literary rights are the property of Robert Ross. The American literary and dramatic rights are vested in John Luce and Co., Boston, U.S.A.

CHARACTERS

GUIDO BARDI, A Florentine prince.

SIMONE, a merchant.

BIANNA, his wife.

MARIA, a tire-woman.

The action takes place at Florence in the early sixteenth century.

A FLORENTINE TRAGEDY

[The scene represents a tapestried upper room giving on to a balcony or loggia in an old house at Florence. A table laid for a frugal meal, a spinning-wheel, distaff, etc., chests, chairs and stools.]

As the Curtain rises enter Bianca, with her Servant, Maria.

Maria. Certain and sure, the sprig is Guido Bardi,

A lovely lord, a lord whose blood is blue!

Bianca. But where did he receive you?

Maria. Where, but there

In yonder palace, in a painted hall!—

Painted with naked women on the walls,—

Would make a common man or blush or smile

But he seemed not to heed them, being a lord.

Bianca. But how know you 'tis not a chamberlayne,

A lackey merely?

Maria. Why, how know I there is a God in heaven?

Because the angels have a master surely.

So to this lord they bowed, all others bowed,

And swept the marble flags, doffing their caps,

With the gay plumes. Because he stiffly said,

And seemed to see me as those folk are seen

That will be never seen again by you,

'Woman, your mistress then returns this purse

Of forty thousand crowns, is it fifty thousand?

Come name the sum will buy me grace of her.'

Bianca. What, were there forty thousand crowns therein?

Maria. I know it was all gold; heavy with gold.

Bianca. It must be he, none else could give so much.

Maria. 'Tis he, 'tis my lord Guido, Guido Bardi.

Bianca. What said you?

Maria. I, I said my mistress never

Looked at the gold, never opened the purse,

Never counted a coin. But asked again

What she had asked before, 'How young you looked?

How handsome your lordship looked? What doublet

Your majesty had on? What chains, what hose

Upon your revered legs?' And curtseyed

I, . . .

Bianca. What said he?

Maria. Curtseyed I, and he replied,

'Has she a lover then beside that old

Soured husband or is it him she loves, my God!

Is it him?'

Bianca. Well?

Maria. Curtseyed I low and said

'Not him, my lord, nor you, nor no man else.

Thou art rich, my lord, and honoured, my lord, and she

Though not so rich is honoured . . .'

Bianca. Fool, you fool,

I never bid you say a word of that.

Maria. Nor did I say a word of that you said;

I said, 'She loves him not, my lord, nor loves

Any man else. Yet she might like to love,

If she were loved by one who pleased her well;

For she is weary of spinning long alone.

She is not rich and yet she is not poor; but young

She is, my lord, and you are young.

[Pauses smiling.]

Bianca. Quick, quick!

Maria. There, there! 'Twas but to show you how I smiled

Saying the lord was young. It took him too;

For he said, 'This will do! If I should call

To-night to pay respect unto your lovely—

Our lovely mistress, tell her that I said,

Our lovely mistress, shall I be received?'

And I said, 'Yes.' 'Then say I come and if

All else is well let her throw down some favour

When as I pass below.' He should be there!

Look from the balcony; he should be there!—

And there he is, dost see?

Bianca. Some favour. Yes.

This ribbon weighted by this brooch will do.

Maria, be you busy near within, but, till

I call take care you enter not. Go down

And let the young lord in, for hark, he knocks.

[*Exit* Maria.]

Great ladies might he choose from and yet he

Is drawn . . . ah, there my fear is! Was he drawn

By love to me—by love's young strength alone?

That's where it is, if I were sure he loved,

I then might do what greater dames have done

And venge me on a husband blind to beauty.

But if! Ah if! he is a wandering bee,

Mere gallant taster, who befools poor flowers . . .

[Maria *opens the door for* Guido Bardi, *and then withdraws.*]

My lord, I learn that we have something here,

In this poor house, which thou dost wish to buy.

My husband is from home, but my poor fate

Has made me perfect in the price of velvets,

Of silks and gay brocades. I think you offered

Some forty thousand crowns, or fifty thousand,

For something we have here? And it must be

That wonder of the loom, which my Simone

Has lately home; it is a Lucca damask,

The web is silver over-wrought with roses.

125

Since you did offer fifty thousand crowns

It must be that. Pray wait, for I will fetch it.

Guido. Nay, nay, thou gracious wonder of a loom

More cunning far than those of Lucca, I

Had in my thought no damask silver cloth

By hunch-back weavers woven toilsomely,

If such are priced at fifty thousand crowns

It shames me, for I hoped to buy a fabric

For which a hundred thousand then were little.

Bianca. A hundred thousand was it that you said?

Nay, poor Simone for so great a sum

Would sell you everything the house contains.

The thought of such a sum doth daze the brains

Of merchant folk who live such lives as ours.

Guido. Would he sell everything this house contains?

And every one, would he sell every one?

Bianca. Oh, everything and every one, my lord,

Unless it were himself; he values not

A woman as a velvet, or a wife

At half the price of silver-threaded woof.

Guido. Then I would strike a bargain with him straight,

Bianca. He is from home; may be will sleep from home;

But I, my lord, can show you all we have;

Can measure ells and sum their price, my lord.

Guido. It is thyself, Bianca, I would buy.

Bianca. O, then, my lord, it must be with Simone

You strike your bargain; for to sell myself

Would be to do what I most truly loathe.

Good-night, my lord; it is with deep regret

I find myself unable to oblige

Your lordship.

Guido. Nay, I pray thee let me stay

And pardon me the sorry part I played,

As though I were a chapman and intent

To lower prices, cheapen honest wares.

Bianca. My lord, there is no reason you should stay.

Guido. Thou art my reason, peerless, perfect, thou,

The reason I am here and my life's goal,

For I was born to love the fairest things . . .

Bianca. To buy the fairest things that can be bought.

Guido. Cruel Bianca! Cover me with scorn,

I answer born to love thy priceless self,

That never to a market could be brought,

No more than winged souls that sail and soar

Among the planets or about the moon.

Bianca. It is so much thy habit to buy love,

Or that which is for sale and labelled love,

Hardly couldst thou conceive a priceless love.

But though my love has never been for sale

I have been in a market bought and sold.

Guido. This is some riddle which thy sweet wit reads

To baffle mine and mock me yet again.

Bianca. My marriage, sir, I speak of marriage now,

That common market where my husband went

And prides himself he made a bargain then.

Guido. The wretched chapman, how I hate his soul.

Bianca. He was a better bidder than thyself,

And knew with whom to deal . . . he did not speak

Of gold to me, but in my father's ear

He made it clink: to me he spoke of love,

Honest and free and open without price.

Guido. O white Bianca, lovely as the moon,

The light of thy pure soul and shining wit

Shows me my shame, and makes the thing I was

Slink like a shadow from the thing I am.

Bianca. Let that which casts the shadow act, my lord,

And waste no thought on what its shadow does

Or has done. Are youth, and strength, and love

Balked by mere shadows, so that they forget

Themselves so far they cannot be recalled?

Guido. Nobility is here, not in the court.

There are the tinsel stars, here is the moon,

Whose tranquil splendour makes a day of night.

I have been starved by ladies, specks of light,

And glory drowns me now I see the moon.

Bianca. I have refused round sums of solid gold

And shall not be by tinsel phrases bought.

Guido. Dispute no more, witty, divine Bianca;

Dispute no more. See I have brought my lute!

Close lock the door. We will sup with the moon

Like Persian princes, that, in Babylon

Sup in the hanging gardens of the king.

I know an air that can suspend the soul

As high in heaven as those towered-gardens hang.

Bianca. My husband may return, we are not safe.

Guido. Didst thou not say that he would sleep from home?

Bianca. He was not sure, he said it might be so.

He was not sure—and he would send my aunt

To sleep with me, if he did so decide,

And she has not yet come.

Guido [*starting*] Hark, what's that?

[*They listen, the sound of* Maria's *voice in anger with some one is faintly heard.*]

Bianca. It is Maria scolds some gossip crone.

Guido. I thought the other voice had been a man's.

Bianca. All still again, old crones are often gruff.

You should be gone, my lord.

Guido. O, sweet Bianca!

How can I leave thee now! Thy beauty made

Two captives of my eyes, and they were mad

To feast them on thy form, but now thy wit,

The liberated perfume of a bud,

Which while a bud seemed perfect, but now is

That which can make its former self forgot:

How can I leave the flower who loved the leaf?

Till now I was the richest prince in Florence,

I am a lover now would shun its throngs,

And put away all state and seek retreat

At Bellosguardo or Fiesole,

Where roses in their fin'st profusion hide

Some marble villa whose cool walls have rung

A laughing echo to Decameron,

And where thy laughter shall as gaily sound.

Say thou canst love or with a silent kiss

Instil that balmy knowledge on my soul.

Bianca. Canst tell me what love is?

Guido. It is consent,

The union of two minds, two souls, two hearts,

In all they think and hope and feel.

Bianca. Such lovers might as well be dumb, for those

Who think and hope and feel alike can never

Have anything for one another's ear.

Guido. Love is? Love is the meeting of two worlds

In never-ending change and counter-change.

Bianca. Thus will my husband praise the mercer's mart,

Where the two worlds of East and West exchange.

Guido. Come. Love is love, a kiss, a close embrace.

It is . . .

Bianca. My husband calls that love

When he hath slammed his weekly ledger to.

Guido. I find my wit no better match for thine
Than thou art match for an old crabbed man;
But I am sure my youth and strength and blood
Keep better tune with beauty gay and bright
As thine is, than lean age and miser toil.

Bianca. Well said, well said, I think he would not dare
To face thee, more than owls dare face the sun;
He's the bent shadow such a form as thine
Might cast upon a dung heap by the road,
Though should it fall upon a proper floor
Twould be at once a better man than he.

Guido. Your merchant living in the dread of loss
Becomes perforce a coward, eats his heart.
Dull souls they are, who, like caged prisoners watch
And envy others' joy; they taste no food
But what its cost is present to their thought.

Bianca. I am my father's daughter, in his eyes
A home-bred girl who has been taught to spin.
He never seems to think I have a face
Which makes you gallants turn where'er I pass.

Guido. Thy night is darker than I dreamed, bright Star.

Bianca. He waits, stands by, and mutters to himself,

And never enters with a frank address

To any company. His eyes meet mine

And with a shudder I am sure he counts

The cost of what I wear.

Guido. Forget him quite.

Come, come, escape from out this dismal life,

As a bright butterfly breaks spider's web,

And nest with me among those rosy bowers,

Where we will love, as though the lives we led

Till yesterday were ghoulish dreams dispersed

By the great dawn of limpid joyous life.

Bianca. Will I not come?

Guido. O, make no question, come.

They waste their time who ponder o'er bad dreams.

We will away to hills, red roses clothe,

And though the persons who did haunt that dream

Live on, they shall by distance dwindled, seem

No bigger than the smallest ear of corn

That cowers at the passing of a bird,

And silent shall they seem, out of ear-shot,

Those voices that could jar, while we gaze back

From rosy caves upon the hill-brow open,

And ask ourselves if what we see is not

A picture merely,—if dusty, dingy lives

Continue there to choke themselves with malice.

Wilt thou not come, Bianca? Wilt thou not?

[A sound on the stair.]

guido. What's that?

[The door opens, they separate guiltily, and the husband enters.]

Simone. My good wife, you come slowly; were it not better

To run to meet your lord? Here, take my cloak.

Take this pack first. 'Tis heavy. I have sold nothing:

Save a furred robe unto the Cardinal's son,

Who hopes to wear it when his father dies,

And hopes that will be soon.

But who is this?

Why you have here some friend. Some kinsman doubtless,

Newly returned from foreign lands and fallen

Upon a house without a host to greet him?

I crave your pardon, kinsman. For a house

Lacking a host is but an empty thing

And void of honour; a cup without its wine,

A scabbard without steel to keep it straight,

A flowerless garden widowed of the sun.

Again I crave your pardon, my sweet cousin.

Bianca. This is no kinsman and no cousin neither.

Simone. No kinsman, and no cousin! You amaze me.
Who is it then who with such courtly grace
Deigns to accept our hospitalities?

Guido. My name is Guido Bardi.

Simone. What! The son
Of that great Lord of Florence whose dim towers
Like shadows silvered by the wandering moon
I see from out my casement every night!
Sir Guido Bardi, you are welcome here,
Twice welcome. For I trust my honest wife,
Most honest if uncomely to the eye,
Hath not with foolish chatterings wearied you,
As is the wont of women.

Guido. Your gracious lady,
Whose beauty is a lamp that pales the stars
And robs Diana's quiver of her beams
Has welcomed me with such sweet courtesies
That if it be her pleasure, and your own,
I will come often to your simple house.
And when your business bids you walk abroad

I will sit here and charm her loneliness

Lest she might sorrow for you overmuch.

What say you, good Simone?

Simone. My noble Lord,

You bring me such high honour that my tongue

Like a slave's tongue is tied, and cannot say

The word it would. Yet not to give you thanks

Were to be too unmannerly. So, I thank you,

From my heart's core.

It is such things as these

That knit a state together, when a Prince

So nobly born and of such fair address,

Forgetting unjust Fortune's differences,

Comes to an honest burgher's honest home

As a most honest friend.

And yet, my Lord,

I fear I am too bold. Some other night

We trust that you will come here as a friend;

To-night you come to buy my merchandise.

Is it not so? Silks, velvets, what you will,

I doubt not but I have some dainty wares

Will woo your fancy. True, the hour is late,

But we poor merchants toil both night and day

To make our scanty gains. The tolls are high,

And every city levies its own toll,

And prentices are unskilful, and wives even

Lack sense and cunning, though Bianca here

Has brought me a rich customer to-night.

Is it not so, Bianca? But I waste time.

Where is my pack? Where is my pack, I say?

Open it, my good wife. Unloose the cords.

Kneel down upon the floor. You are better so.

Nay not that one, the other. Despatch, despatch!

Buyers will grow impatient oftentimes.

We dare not keep them waiting. Ay! 'tis that,

Give it to me; with care. It is most costly.

Touch it with care. And now, my noble Lord—

Nay, pardon, I have here a Lucca damask,

The very web of silver and the roses

So cunningly wrought that they lack perfume merely

To cheat the wanton sense. Touch it, my Lord.

Is it not soft as water, strong as steel?

And then the roses! Are they not finely woven?

I think the hillsides that best love the rose,

At Bellosguardo or at Fiesole,

Throw no such blossoms on the lap of spring,

Or if they do their blossoms droop and die.

Such is the fate of all the dainty things

That dance in wind and water. Nature herself

Makes war on her own loveliness and slays

Her children like Medea. Nay but, my Lord,

Look closer still. Why in this damask here

It is summer always, and no winter's tooth

Will ever blight these blossoms. For every ell

I paid a piece of gold. Red gold, and good,

The fruit of careful thrift.

Guido. Honest Simone,

Enough, I pray you. I am well content;

To-morrow I will send my servant to you,

Who will pay twice your price.

Simone. My generous Prince!

I kiss your hands. And now I do remember

Another treasure hidden in my house

Which you must see. It is a robe of state:

Woven by a Venetian: the stuff, cut-velvet:

The pattern, pomegranates: each separate seed

Wrought of a pearl: the collar all of pearls,

As thick as moths in summer streets at night,

And whiter than the moons that madmen see

Through prison bars at morning. A male ruby

Burns like a lighted coal within the clasp

The Holy Father has not such a stone,

Nor could the Indies show a brother to it.

The brooch itself is of most curious art,

Cellini never made a fairer thing

To please the great Lorenzo. You must wear it.

There is none worthier in our city here,

And it will suit you well. Upon one side

A slim and horned satyr leaps in gold

To catch some nymph of silver. Upon the other

Stands Silence with a crystal in her hand,

No bigger than the smallest ear of corn,

That wavers at the passing of a bird,

And yet so cunningly wrought that one would say,

It breathed, or held its breath.

Worthy Bianca,

Would not this noble and most costly robe

Suit young Lord Guido well?

Nay, but entreat him;

He will refuse you nothing, though the price

Be as a prince's ransom. And your profit

Shall not be less than mine.

Bianca. Am I your prentice?

Why should I chaffer for your velvet robe?

Guido. Nay, fair Bianca, I will buy the robe,

And all things that the honest merchant has

I will buy also. Princes must be ransomed,

And fortunate are all high lords who fall

Into the white hands of so fair a foe.

Simone. I stand rebuked. But you will buy my wares?

Will you not buy them? Fifty thousand crowns

Would scarce repay me. But you, my Lord, shall have them

For forty thousand. Is that price too high?

Name your own price. I have a curious fancy

To see you in this wonder of the loom

Amidst the noble ladies of the court,

A flower among flowers.

They say, my lord,

These highborn dames do so affect your Grace

That where you go they throng like flies around you,

Each seeking for your favour.

I have heard also

Of husbands that wear horns, and wear them bravely,

A fashion most fantastical.

Guido. Simone,

Your reckless tongue needs curbing; and besides,

You do forget this gracious lady here

Whose delicate ears are surely not attuned

To such coarse music.

Simone. True: I had forgotten,

Nor will offend again. Yet, my sweet Lord,

You'll buy the robe of state. Will you not buy it?

But forty thousand crowns—'tis but a trifle,

To one who is Giovanni Bardi's heir.

Guido. Settle this thing to-morrow with my steward,

Antonio Costa. He will come to you.

And you shall have a hundred thousand crowns

If that will serve your purpose.

Simone. A hundred thousand!

Said you a hundred thousand? Oh! be sure

That will for all time and in everything

Make me your debtor. Ay! from this time forth

My house, with everything my house contains

Is yours, and only yours.

A hundred thousand!

My brain is dazed. I shall be richer far

Than all the other merchants. I will buy

Vineyards and lands and gardens. Every loom

From Milan down to Sicily shall be mine,

And mine the pearls that the Arabian seas

Store in their silent caverns.

Generous Prince,

This night shall prove the herald of my love,

Which is so great that whatsoe'er you ask

It will not be denied you.

Guido. What if I asked

For white Bianca here?

Simone. You jest, my Lord;

She is not worthy of so great a Prince.

She is but made to keep the house and spin.

Is it not so, good wife? It is so. Look!

Your distaff waits for you. Sit down and spin.

Women should not be idle in their homes,

For idle fingers make a thoughtless heart.

Sit down, I say.

Bianca. What shall I spin?

Simone. Oh! spin

Some robe which, dyed in purple, sorrow might wear

For her own comforting: or some long-fringed cloth

In which a new-born and unwelcome babe

Might wail unheeded; or a dainty sheet

Which, delicately perfumed with sweet herbs,

Might serve to wrap a dead man. Spin what you will;

I care not, I.

Bianca. The brittle thread is broken,

The dull wheel wearies of its ceaseless round,

The duller distaff sickens of its load;

I will not spin to-night.

Simone. It matters not.

To-morrow you shall spin, and every day

Shall find you at your distaff. So Lucretia

Was found by Tarquin. So, perchance, Lucretia

Waited for Tarquin. Who knows? I have heard

Strange things about men's wives. And now, my lord,

What news abroad? I heard to-day at Pisa

That certain of the English merchants there

Would sell their woollens at a lower rate

Than the just laws allow, and have entreated

The Signory to hear them.

Is this well?

Should merchant be to merchant as a wolf?

And should the stranger living in our land

Seek by enforced privilege or craft

To rob us of our profits?

Guido. What should I do

With merchants or their profits? Shall I go

And wrangle with the Signory on your count?

And wear the gown in which you buy from fools,

Or sell to sillier bidders? Honest Simone,

Wool-selling or wool-gathering is for you.

My wits have other quarries.

Bianca. Noble Lord,

I pray you pardon my good husband here,

His soul stands ever in the market-place,

And his heart beats but at the price of wool.

Yet he is honest in his common way.

[To SIMONE]

And you, have you no shame? A gracious Prince

Comes to our house, and you must weary him

With most misplaced assurance. Ask his pardon.

Simone. I ask it humbly. We will talk to-night

Of other things. I hear the Holy Father

Has sent a letter to the King of France

Bidding him cross that shield of snow, the Alps,

And make a peace in Italy, which will be

Worse than a war of brothers, and more bloody

Than civil rapine or intestine feuds.

Guido. Oh! we are weary of that King of France,

Who never comes, but ever talks of coming.

What are these things to me? There are other things

Closer, and of more import, good Simone.

Bianca [*To Simone*]. I think you tire our most gracious guest.

What is the King of France to us? As much

As are your English merchants with their wool.

* * * * *

Simone. Is it so then? Is all this mighty world

Narrowed into the confines of this room

With but three souls for poor inhabitants?

Ay! there are times when the great universe,

Like cloth in some unskilful dyer's vat,

Shrivels into a handbreadth, and perchance

That time is now! Well! let that time be now.

Let this mean room be as that mighty stage

Whereon kings die, and our ignoble lives

Become the stakes God plays for.

I do not know

Why I speak thus. My ride has wearied me.

And my horse stumbled thrice, which is an omen

That bodes not good to any.

Alas! my lord,

How poor a bargain is this life of man,

And in how mean a market are we sold!

When we are born our mothers weep, but when

We die there is none weeps for us. No, not one.

[*Passes to back of stage.*]

Bianca. How like a common chapman does he speak!

I hate him, soul and body. Cowardice

Has set her pale seal on his brow. His hands

Whiter than poplar leaves in windy springs,

Shake with some palsy; and his stammering mouth

Blurts out a foolish froth of empty words

Like water from a conduit.

Guido. Sweet Bianca,

He is not worthy of your thought or mine.

The man is but a very honest knave

Full of fine phrases for life's merchandise,

Selling most dear what he must hold most cheap,

A windy brawler in a world of words.

I never met so eloquent a fool.

146

Bianca. Oh, would that Death might take him where he stands!

Simone [*turning round*]. Who spake of Death? Let no one speak of Death.

What should Death do in such a merry house,

With but a wife, a husband, and a friend

To give it greeting? Let Death go to houses

Where there are vile, adulterous things, chaste wives

Who growing weary of their noble lords

Draw back the curtains of their marriage beds,

And in polluted and dishonoured sheets

Feed some unlawful lust. Ay! 'tis so

Strange, and yet so. You do not know the world.

You are too single and too honourable.

I know it well. And would it were not so,

But wisdom comes with winters. My hair grows grey,

And youth has left my body. Enough of that.

To-night is ripe for pleasure, and indeed,

I would be merry as beseems a host

Who finds a gracious and unlooked-for guest

Waiting to greet him. [*Takes up a lute.*]

But what is this, my lord?

Why, you have brought a lute to play to us.

Oh! play, sweet Prince. And, if I am too bold,

Pardon, but play.

Guido. I will not play to-night.

Some other night, Simone.

[To BIANCA] You and I

Together, with no listeners but the stars,

Or the more jealous moon.

Simone. Nay, but my lord!

Nay, but I do beseech you. For I have heard

That by the simple fingering of a string,

Or delicate breath breathed along hollowed reeds,

Or blown into cold mouths of cunning bronze,

Those who are curious in this art can draw

Poor souls from prison-houses. I have heard also

How such strange magic lurks within these shells

That at their bidding casements open wide

And Innocence puts vine-leaves in her hair,

And wantons like a mænad. Let that pass.

Your lute I know is chaste. And therefore play:

Ravish my ears with some sweet melody;

My soul is in a prison-house, and needs

Music to cure its madness. Good Bianca,

Entreat our guest to play.

Bianca. Be not afraid,

Our well-loved guest will choose his place and moment:

That moment is not now. You weary him

With your uncouth insistence.

Guido. Honest Simone,

Some other night. To-night I am content

With the low music of Bianca's voice,

Who, when she speaks, charms the too amorous air,

And makes the reeling earth stand still, or fix

His cycle round her beauty.

Simone. You flatter her.

She has her virtues as most women have,

But beauty in a gem she may not wear.

It is better so, perchance.

Well, my dear lord,

If you will not draw melodies from your lute

To charm my moody and o'er-troubled soul

You'll drink with me at least?

[*Motioning* Guido *to his own place.*]

Your place is laid.

Fetch me a stool, Bianca. Close the shutters.

Set the great bar across. I would not have

The curious world with its small prying eyes

To peer upon our pleasure.

Now, my lord,

Give us a toast from a full brimming cup.

[*Starts back.*]

What is this stain upon the cloth? It looks

As purple as a wound upon Christ's side.

Wine merely is it? I have heard it said

When wine is spilt blood is spilt also,

But that's a foolish tale.

My lord, I trust

My grape is to your liking? The wine of Naples

Is fiery like its mountains. Our Tuscan vineyards

Yield a more wholesome juice.

Guido. I like it well,

Honest Simone; and, with your good leave,

Will toast the fair Bianca when her lips

Have like red rose-leaves floated on this cup

And left its vintage sweeter. Taste, Bianca.

[Bianca *drinks.*]

Oh, all the honey of Hyblean bees,

Matched with this draught were bitter!

Good Simone,

You do not share the feast.

Simone. It is strange, my lord,

I cannot eat or drink with you, to-night.

Some humour, or some fever in my blood,

At other seasons temperate, or some thought

That like an adder creeps from point to point,

That like a madman crawls from cell to cell,

Poisons my palate and makes appetite

A loathing, not a longing.

[Goes aside.]

Guido. Sweet Bianca,

This common chapman wearies me with words.

I must go hence. To-morrow I will come.

Tell me the hour.

Bianca. Come with the youngest dawn!

Until I see you all my life is vain.

Guido. Ah! loose the falling midnight of your hair,

And in those stars, your eyes, let me behold

Mine image, as in mirrors. Dear Bianca,

Though it be but a shadow, keep me there,

Nor gaze at anything that does not show

Some symbol of my semblance. I am jealous

Of what your vision feasts on.

Bianca. Oh! be sure

Your image will be with me always. Dear

Love can translate the very meanest thing

Into a sign of sweet remembrances.

But come before the lark with its shrill song

Has waked a world of dreamers. I will stand

Upon the balcony.

Guido. And by a ladder

Wrought out of scarlet silk and sewn with pearls

Will come to meet me. White foot after foot,

Like snow upon a rose-tree.

Bianca. As you will.

You know that I am yours for love or Death.

Guido. Simone, I must go to mine own house.

Simone. So soon? Why should you? The great Duomo's bell

Has not yet tolled its midnight, and the watchmen

Who with their hollow horns mock the pale moon,

Lie drowsy in their towers. Stay awhile.

I fear we may not see you here again,

And that fear saddens my too simple heart.

Guido. Be not afraid, Simone. I will stand

Most constant in my friendship, But to-night

I go to mine own home, and that at once.

152

To-morrow, sweet Bianca.

Simone.   Well, well, so be it.

I would have wished for fuller converse with you,

My new friend, my honourable guest,

But that it seems may not be.

And besides

I do not doubt your father waits for you,

Wearying for voice or footstep. You, I think,

Are his one child? He has no other child.

You are the gracious pillar of his house,

The flower of a garden full of weeds.

Your father's nephews do not love him well

So run folks' tongues in Florence. I meant but that.

Men say they envy your inheritance

And look upon your vineyards with fierce eyes

As Ahab looked on Naboth's goodly field.

But that is but the chatter of a town

Where women talk too much.

Good-night, my lord.

Fetch a pine torch, Bianca. The old staircase

Is full of pitfalls, and the churlish moon

Grows, like a miser, niggard of her beams,

And hides her face behind a muslin mask

As harlots do when they go forth to snare

Some wretched soul in sin. Now, I will get

Your cloak and sword. Nay, pardon, my good Lord,

It is but meet that I should wait on you

Who have so honoured my poor burgher's house,

Drunk of my wine, and broken bread, and made

Yourself a sweet familiar. Oftentimes

My wife and I will talk of this fair night

And its great issues.

Why, what a sword is this.

Ferrara's temper, pliant as a snake,

And deadlier, I doubt not. With such steel,

One need fear nothing in the moil of life.

I never touched so delicate a blade.

I have a sword too, somewhat rusted now.

We men of peace are taught humility,

And to bear many burdens on our backs,

And not to murmur at an unjust world,

And to endure unjust indignities.

We are taught that, and like the patient Jew

Find profit in our pain.

Yet I remember

How once upon the road to Padua

A robber sought to take my pack-horse from me,

I slit his throat and left him.   I can bear

Dishonour, public insult, many shames,

Shrill scorn, and open contumely, but he

Who filches from me something that is mine,

Ay! though it be the meanest trencher-plate

From which I feed mine appetite—oh! he

Perils his soul and body in the theft

And dies for his small sin.   From what strange clay

We men are moulded!

Guido.   Why do you speak like this?

Simone.   I wonder, my Lord Guido, if my sword

Is better tempered than this steel of yours?

Shall we make trial?   Or is my state too low

For you to cross your rapier against mine,

In jest, or earnest?

Guido.   Naught would please me better

Than to stand fronting you with naked blade

In jest, or earnest.   Give me mine own sword.

Fetch yours.   To-night will settle the great issue

Whether the Prince's or the merchant's steel

Is better tempered. Was not that your word?

Fetch your own sword. Why do you tarry, sir?

Simone. My lord, of all the gracious courtesies

That you have showered on my barren house

This is the highest.

Bianca, fetch my sword.

Thrust back that stool and table. We must have

An open circle for our match at arms,

And good Bianca here shall hold the torch

Lest what is but a jest grow serious.

Bianca [*To Guido*]. Oh! kill him, kill him!

Simone. Hold the torch, Bianca.

[*They begin to fight.*]

Simone. Have at you! Ah! Ha! would you?

[*He is wounded by* Guido.]

A scratch, no more. The torch was in mine eyes.

Do not look sad, Bianca. It is nothing.

Your husband bleeds, 'tis nothing. Take a cloth,

Bind it about mine arm. Nay, not so tight.

More softly, my good wife. And be not sad,

I pray you be not sad. No; take it off.

What matter if I bleed?

[*Tears bandage off.*]

Again! again!

[Simone *disarms* Guido]

My gentle Lord, you see that I was right

My sword is better tempered, finer steel,

But let us match our daggers.

Bianca [*to Guido*]

Kill him! kill him!

Simone. Put out the torch, Bianca.

[Bianca *puts out torch.*]

Now, my good Lord,

Now to the death of one, or both of us,

Or all three it may be. [*They fight.*]

There and there.

Ah, devil! do I hold thee in my grip?

[Simone *overpowers* Guido *and throws him down over table.*]

Guido. Fool! take your strangling fingers from my throat.

I am my father's only son; the State

Has but one heir, and that false enemy France

Waits for the ending of my father's line

To fall upon our city.

Simone. Hush! your father

When he is childless will be happier.

As for the State, I think our state of Florence

Needs no adulterous pilot at its helm.

Your life would soil its lilies.

Guido. Take off your hands

Take off your damned hands. Loose me, I say!

Simone. Nay, you are caught in such a cunning vice

That nothing will avail you, and your life

Narrowed into a single point of shame

Ends with that shame and ends most shamefully.

Guido. Oh! let me have a priest before I die!

Simone. What wouldst thou have a priest for? Tell thy sins

To God, whom thou shalt see this very night

And then no more for ever. Tell thy sins

To Him who is most just, being pitiless,

Most pitiful being just. As for myself. . .

Guido. Oh! help me, sweet Bianca! help me, Bianca,

Thou knowest I am innocent of harm.

Simone. What, is there life yet in those lying lips?

Die like a dog with lolling tongue! Die! Die!

And the dumb river shall receive your corse

And wash it all unheeded to the sea.

Guido. Lord Christ receive my wretched soul to-night!

Simone. Amen to that. Now for the other.

[*He dies.* Simone *rises and looks at* Bianca. *She comes towards him as one dazed with wonder and with outstretched arms.*]

Bianca. Why

Did you not tell me you were so strong?

Simone. Why

Did you not tell me you were beautiful?

[*He kisses her on the mouth.*]

CURTAIN

.

POEMS, WITH THE BALLAD
OF READING GAOL

NOTE

This collection of Wilde's Poems contains the volume of 1881 in its entirety, 'The Sphinx', 'The Ballad of Reading Gaol,' and 'Ravenna.' Of the Uncollected Poems published in the Uniform Edition of 1908, a few, including the Translations from the Greek and the Polish, are omitted. Two new poems, 'Désespoir' and 'Pan,' which I have recently discovered in manuscript, are now printed for the first time. Particulars as to the original publication of each poem will be found in 'A Bibliography of the Poems of Oscar Wilde,' by Stuart Mason, London 1907.

ROBERT ROSS.

HÉLAS!

To drift with every passion till my soul

Is a stringed lute on which all winds can play,

Is it for this that I have given away

Mine ancient wisdom, and austere control?

Methinks my life is a twice-written scroll

Scrawled over on some boyish holiday

With idle songs for pipe and virelay,

Which do but mar the secret of the whole.

Surely there was a time I might have trod

The sunlit heights, and from life's dissonance

Struck one clear chord to reach the ears of God:

Is that time dead? lo! with a little rod

I did but touch the honey of romance—

And must I lose a soul's inheritance?

ELEUTHERIA

SONNET TO LIBERTY

Not that I love thy children, whose dull eyes

See nothing save their own unlovely woe,

Whose minds know nothing, nothing care to know,—

But that the roar of thy Democracies,

Thy reigns of Terror, thy great Anarchies,

Mirror my wildest passions like the sea

And give my rage a brother—! Liberty!

For this sake only do thy dissonant cries

Delight my discreet soul, else might all kings

By bloody knout or treacherous cannonades

Rob nations of their rights inviolate

And I remain unmoved—and yet, and yet,

These Christs that die upon the barricades,

God knows it I am with them, in some things.

AVE IMPERATRIX

Set in this stormy Northern sea,

   Queen of these restless fields of tide,

England! what shall men say of thee,

Before whose feet the worlds divide?

The earth, a brittle globe of glass,

   Lies in the hollow of thy hand,

And through its heart of crystal pass,

   Like shadows through a twilight land,

The spears of crimson-suited war,

   The long white-crested waves of fight,

And all the deadly fires which are

   The torches of the lords of Night.

The yellow leopards, strained and lean,

   The treacherous Russian knows so well,

With gaping blackened jaws are seen

   Leap through the hail of screaming shell.

The strong sea-lion of England's wars

   Hath left his sapphire cave of sea,

To battle with the storm that mars

   The stars of England's chivalry.

The brazen-throated clarion blows

Across the Pathan's reedy fen,

And the high steeps of Indian snows

Shake to the tread of armèd men.

And many an Afghan chief, who lies

Beneath his cool pomegranate-trees,

Clutches his sword in fierce surmise

When on the mountain-side he sees

The fleet-foot Marri scout, who comes

To tell how he hath heard afar

The measured roll of English drums

Beat at the gates of Kandahar.

For southern wind and east wind meet

Where, girt and crowned by sword and fire,

England with bare and bloody feet

Climbs the steep road of wide empire.

O lonely Himalayan height,

Grey pillar of the Indian sky,

Where saw'st thou last in clanging flight

Our wingèd dogs of Victory?

The almond-groves of Samarcand,
  Bokhara, where red lilies blow,
And Oxus, by whose yellow sand
  The grave white-turbaned merchants go:

And on from thence to Ispahan,
  The gilded garden of the sun,
Whence the long dusty caravan
  Brings cedar wood and vermilion;

And that dread city of Cabool
  Set at the mountain's scarpèd feet,
Whose marble tanks are ever full
  With water for the noonday heat:

Where through the narrow straight Bazaar
  A little maid Circassian
Is led, a present from the Czar
  Unto some old and bearded khan,—

Here have our wild war-eagles flown,
  And flapped wide wings in fiery fight;

But the sad dove, that sits alone

In England—she hath no delight.

In vain the laughing girl will lean

To greet her love with love-lit eyes:

Down in some treacherous black ravine,

Clutching his flag, the dead boy lies.

And many a moon and sun will see

The lingering wistful children wait

To climb upon their father's knee;

And in each house made desolate

Pale women who have lost their lord

Will kiss the relics of the slain—

Some tarnished epaulette—some sword—

Poor toys to soothe such anguished pain.

For not in quiet English fields

Are these, our brothers, lain to rest,

Where we might deck their broken shields

With all the flowers the dead love best.

For some are by the Delhi walls,

And many in the Afghan land,

And many where the Ganges falls

   Through seven mouths of shifting sand.

And some in Russian waters lie,

   And others in the seas which are

The portals to the East, or by

   The wind-swept heights of Trafalgar.

O wandering graves! O restless sleep!

   O silence of the sunless day!

O still ravine! O stormy deep!

   Give up your prey! Give up your prey!

And thou whose wounds are never healed,

   Whose weary race is never won,

O Cromwell's England! must thou yield

   For every inch of ground a son?

Go! crown with thorns thy gold-crowned head,

   Change thy glad song to song of pain;

Wind and wild wave have got thy dead,

   And will not yield them back again.

Wave and wild wind and foreign shore

    Possess the flower of English land—

Lips that thy lips shall kiss no more,

    Hands that shall never clasp thy hand.

What profit now that we have bound

    The whole round world with nets of gold,

If hidden in our heart is found

    The care that groweth never old?

What profit that our galleys ride,

    Pine-forest-like, on every main?

Ruin and wreck are at our side,

    Grim warders of the House of Pain.

Where are the brave, the strong, the fleet?

    Where is our English chivalry?

Wild grasses are their burial-sheet,

    And sobbing waves their threnody.

O loved ones lying far away,

    What word of love can dead lips send!

O wasted dust! O senseless clay!

   Is this the end! is this the end!

Peace, peace! we wrong the noble dead

   To vex their solemn slumber so;

Though childless, and with thorn-crowned head,

   Up the steep road must England go,

Yet when this fiery web is spun,

   Her watchmen shall descry from far

The young Republic like a sun

   Rise from these crimson seas of war.

TO MILTON

Milton! I think thy spirit hath passed away

From these white cliffs and high-embattled towers;

   This gorgeous fiery-coloured world of ours

Seems fallen into ashes dull and grey,

And the age changed unto a mimic play

   Wherein we waste our else too-crowded hours:

   For all our pomp and pageantry and powers

We are but fit to delve the common clay,

Seeing this little isle on which we stand,

   This England, this sea-lion of the sea,

By ignorant demagogues is held in fee,

Who love her not: Dear God! is this the land

Which bare a triple empire in her hand

When Cromwell spake the word Democracy!

LOUIS NAPOLEON

Eagle of Austerlitz! where were thy wings

When far away upon a barbarous strand,

In fight unequal, by an obscure hand,

Fell the last scion of thy brood of Kings!

Poor boy! thou shalt not flaunt thy cloak of red,

Or ride in state through Paris in the van

Of thy returning legions, but instead

Thy mother France, free and republican,

Shall on thy dead and crownless forehead place

The better laurels of a soldier's crown,

That not dishonoured should thy soul go down

To tell the mighty Sire of thy race

That France hath kissed the mouth of Liberty,

And found it sweeter than his honied bees,

And that the giant wave Democracy

Breaks on the shores where Kings lay couched at ease.

SONNET ON THE MASSACRE OF THE CHRISTIANS IN BULGARIA

Christ, dost Thou live indeed? or are Thy bones

Still straitened in their rock-hewn sepulchre?

And was Thy Rising only dreamed by her

Whose love of Thee for all her sin atones?

For here the air is horrid with men's groans,

The priests who call upon Thy name are slain,

Dost Thou not hear the bitter wail of pain

From those whose children lie upon the stones?

Come down, O Son of God! incestuous gloom

Curtains the land, and through the starless night

Over Thy Cross a Crescent moon I see!

If Thou in very truth didst burst the tomb

Come down, O Son of Man! and show Thy might

Lest Mahomet be crowned instead of Thee!

QUANTUM MUTATA

There was a time in Europe long ago

When no man died for freedom anywhere,

But England's lion leaping from its lair

Laid hands on the oppressor! it was so

While England could a great Republic show.

Witness the men of Piedmont, chiefest care

Of Cromwell, when with impotent despair

The Pontiff in his painted portico

Trembled before our stern ambassadors.

How comes it then that from such high estate

We have thus fallen, save that Luxury

With barren merchandise piles up the gate

Where noble thoughts and deeds should enter by:

Else might we still be Milton's heritors.

LIBERTATIS SACRA FAMES

Albeit nurtured in democracy,

And liking best that state republican

Where every man is Kinglike and no man

Is crowned above his fellows, yet I see,

Spite of this modern fret for Liberty,

Better the rule of One, whom all obey,

Than to let clamorous demagogues betray

Our freedom with the kiss of anarchy.

Wherefore I love them not whose hands profane

Plant the red flag upon the piled-up street

For no right cause, beneath whose ignorant reign

Arts, Culture, Reverence, Honour, all things fade,

Save Treason and the dagger of her trade,

Or Murder with his silent bloody feet.

THEORETIKOS

This mighty empire hath but feet of clay:

Of all its ancient chivalry and might

Our little island is forsaken quite:

Some enemy hath stolen its crown of bay,

And from its hills that voice hath passed away

Which spake of Freedom: O come out of it,

Come out of it, my Soul, thou art not fit

For this vile traffic-house, where day by day

Wisdom and reverence are sold at mart,

And the rude people rage with ignorant cries

Against an heritage of centuries.

It mars my calm: wherefore in dreams of Art

And loftiest culture I would stand apart,

Neither for God, nor for his enemies.

THE GARDEN OF EROS

It is full summer now, the heart of June;

    Not yet the sunburnt reapers are astir

Upon the upland meadow where too soon

    Rich autumn time, the season's usurer,

Will lend his hoarded gold to all the trees,

And see his treasure scattered by the wild and spendthrift breeze.

Too soon indeed! yet here the daffodil,

    That love-child of the Spring, has lingered on

To vex the rose with jealousy, and still

    The harebell spreads her azure pavilion,

And like a strayed and wandering reveller

Abandoned of its brothers, whom long since June's messenger

The missel-thrush has frighted from the glade,

    One pale narcissus loiters fearfully

Close to a shadowy nook, where half afraid

    Of their own loveliness some violets lie

That will not look the gold sun in the face

For fear of too much splendour,—ah! methinks it is a place

Which should be trodden by Persephone

    When wearied of the flowerless fields of Dis!

Or danced on by the lads of Arcady!

    The hidden secret of eternal bliss

Known to the Grecian here a man might find,

Ah! you and I may find it now if Love and Sleep be kind.

There are the flowers which mourning Herakles

    Strewed on the tomb of Hylas, columbine,

Its white doves all a-flutter where the breeze

    Kissed them too harshly, the small celandine,

That yellow-kirtled chorister of eve,

And lilac lady's-smock,—but let them bloom alone, and leave

Yon spirèd hollyhock red-crocketed

    To sway its silent chimes, else must the bee,

Its little bellringer, go seek instead

    Some other pleasaunce; the anemone

That weeps at daybreak, like a silly girl

Before her love, and hardly lets the butterflies unfurl

Their painted wings beside it,—bid it pine

In pale virginity; the winter snow

Will suit it better than those lips of thine

   Whose fires would but scorch it, rather go

And pluck that amorous flower which blooms alone,

Fed by the pander wind with dust of kisses not its own.

The trumpet-mouths of red convolvulus

   So dear to maidens, creamy meadow-sweet

Whiter than Juno's throat and odorous

   As all Arabia, hyacinths the feet

Of Huntress Dian would be loth to mar

For any dappled fawn,—pluck these, and those fond flowers which are

Fairer than what Queen Venus trod upon

   Beneath the pines of Ida, eucharis,

That morning star which does not dread the sun,

   And budding marjoram which but to kiss

Would sweeten Cytheræa's lips and make

Adonis jealous,—these for thy head,—and for thy girdle take

Yon curving spray of purple clematis

   Whose gorgeous dye outflames the Tyrian King,

And foxgloves with their nodding chalices,

But that one narciss which the startled Spring

Let from her kirtle fall when first she heard

In her own woods the wild tempestuous song of summer's bird,

Ah! leave it for a subtle memory

 Of those sweet tremulous days of rain and sun,

When April laughed between her tears to see

 The early primrose with shy footsteps run

From the gnarled oak-tree roots till all the wold,

 Spite of its brown and trampled leaves, grew bright with shimmering gold.

Nay, pluck it too, it is not half so sweet

 As thou thyself, my soul's idolatry!

And when thou art a-wearied at thy feet

 Shall oxlips weave their brightest tapestry,

For thee the woodbine shall forget its pride

And veil its tangled whorls, and thou shalt walk on daisies pied.

And I will cut a reed by yonder spring

 And make the wood-gods jealous, and old Pan

Wonder what young intruder dares to sing

 In these still haunts, where never foot of man

Should tread at evening, lest he chance to spy

The marble limbs of Artemis and all her company.

And I will tell thee why the jacinth wears

   Such dread embroidery of dolorous moan,

And why the hapless nightingale forbears

   To sing her song at noon, but weeps alone

When the fleet swallow sleeps, and rich men feast,

And why the laurel trembles when she sees the lightening east.

And I will sing how sad Proserpina

   Unto a grave and gloomy Lord was wed,

And lure the silver-breasted Helena

   Back from the lotus meadows of the dead,

So shalt thou see that awful loveliness

For which two mighty Hosts met fearfully in war's abyss!

And then I'll pipe to thee that Grecian tale

   How Cynthia loves the lad Endymion,

And hidden in a grey and misty veil

   Hies to the cliffs of Latmos once the Sun

Leaps from his ocean bed in fruitless chase

Of those pale flying feet which fade away in his embrace.

And if my flute can breathe sweet melody,

We may behold Her face who long ago

Dwelt among men by the Ægean sea,

   And whose sad house with pillaged portico

And friezeless wall and columns toppled down

Looms o'er the ruins of that fair and violet cinctured town.

Spirit of Beauty! tarry still awhile,

   They are not dead, thine ancient votaries;

Some few there are to whom thy radiant smile

   Is better than a thousand victories,

Though all the nobly slain of Waterloo

Rise up in wrath against them! tarry still, there are a few

Who for thy sake would give their manlihood

   And consecrate their being; I at least

Have done so, made thy lips my daily food,

   And in thy temples found a goodlier feast

Than this starved age can give me, spite of all

Its new-found creeds so sceptical and so dogmatical.

Here not Cephissos, not Ilissos flows,

   The woods of white Colonos are not here,

On our bleak hills the olive never blows,

No simple priest conducts his lowing steer

Up the steep marble way, nor through the town

Do laughing maidens bear to thee the crocus-flowered gown.

Yet tarry! for the boy who loved thee best,

    Whose very name should be a memory

To make thee linger, sleeps in silent rest

    Beneath the Roman walls, and melody

Still mourns her sweetest lyre; none can play

The lute of Adonais: with his lips Song passed away.

Nay, when Keats died the Muses still had left

    One silver voice to sing his threnody,

But ah! too soon of it we were bereft

    When on that riven night and stormy sea

Panthea claimed her singer as her own,

And slew the mouth that praised her; since which time we walk alone,

Save for that fiery heart, that morning star

    Of re-arisen England, whose clear eye

Saw from our tottering throne and waste of war

    The grand Greek limbs of young Democracy

Rise mightily like Hesperus and bring

The great Republic! him at least thy love hath taught to sing,

And he hath been with thee at Thessaly,

   And seen white Atalanta fleet of foot

In passionless and fierce virginity

   Hunting the tuskèd boar, his honied lute

Hath pierced the cavern of the hollow hill,

And Venus laughs to know one knee will bow before her still.

And he hath kissed the lips of Proserpine,

   And sung the Galilæan's requiem,

That wounded forehead dashed with blood and wine

   He hath discrowned, the Ancient Gods in him

Have found their last, most ardent worshipper,

And the new Sign grows grey and dim before its conqueror.

Spirit of Beauty! tarry with us still,

   It is not quenched the torch of poesy,

The star that shook above the Eastern hill

   Holds unassailed its argent armoury

From all the gathering gloom and fretful fight—

O tarry with us still! for through the long and common night,

Morris, our sweet and simple Chaucer's child,

Dear heritor of Spenser's tuneful reed,

With soft and sylvan pipe has oft beguiled

The weary soul of man in troublous need,

And from the far and flowerless fields of ice

Has brought fair flowers to make an earthly paradise.

We know them all, Gudrun the strong men's bride,

Aslaug and Olafson we know them all,

How giant Grettir fought and Sigurd died,

And what enchantment held the king in thrall

When lonely Brynhild wrestled with the powers

That war against all passion, ah! how oft through summer hours,

Long listless summer hours when the noon

Being enamoured of a damask rose

Forgets to journey westward, till the moon

The pale usurper of its tribute grows

From a thin sickle to a silver shield

And chides its loitering car—how oft, in some cool grassy field

Far from the cricket-ground and noisy eight,

At Bagley, where the rustling bluebells come

Almost before the blackbird finds a mate

And overstay the swallow, and the hum

Of many murmuring bees flits through the leaves,

Have I lain poring on the dreamy tales his fancy weaves,

And through their unreal woes and mimic pain

 Wept for myself, and so was purified,

And in their simple mirth grew glad again;

 For as I sailed upon that pictured tide

The strength and splendour of the storm was mine

Without the storm's red ruin, for the singer is divine;

The little laugh of water falling down

 Is not so musical, the clammy gold

Close hoarded in the tiny waxen town

 Has less of sweetness in it, and the old

Half-withered reeds that waved in Arcady

Touched by his lips break forth again to fresher harmony.

Spirit of Beauty, tarry yet awhile!

 Although the cheating merchants of the mart

With iron roads profane our lovely isle,

 And break on whirling wheels the limbs of Art,

Ay! though the crowded factories beget

The blindworm Ignorance that slays the soul, O tarry yet!

For One at least there is,—He bears his name

   From Dante and the seraph Gabriel,—

Whose double laurels burn with deathless flame

   To light thine altar; He too loves thee well,

Who saw old Merlin lured in Vivien's snare,

And the white feet of angels coming down the golden stair,

Loves thee so well, that all the World for him

   A gorgeous-coloured vestiture must wear,

And Sorrow take a purple diadem,

   Or else be no more Sorrow, and Despair

Gild its own thorns, and Pain, like Adon, be

Even in anguish beautiful;—such is the empery

Which Painters hold, and such the heritage

   This gentle solemn Spirit doth possess,

Being a better mirror of his age

   In all his pity, love, and weariness,

Than those who can but copy common things,

And leave the Soul unpainted with its mighty questionings.

But they are few, and all romance has flown,

And men can prophesy about the sun,

And lecture on his arrows—how, alone,

   Through a waste void the soulless atoms run,

How from each tree its weeping nymph has fled,

And that no more 'mid English reeds a Naiad shows her head.

Methinks these new Actæons boast too soon

   That they have spied on beauty; what if we

Have analysed the rainbow, robbed the moon

   Of her most ancient, chastest mystery,

Shall I, the last Endymion, lose all hope

Because rude eyes peer at my mistress through a telescope!

What profit if this scientific age

   Burst through our gates with all its retinue

Of modern miracles! Can it assuage

   One lover's breaking heart? what can it do

To make one life more beautiful, one day

More godlike in its period? but now the Age of Clay

Returns in horrid cycle, and the earth

   Hath borne again a noisy progeny

Of ignorant Titans, whose ungodly birth

Hurls them against the august hierarchy

Which sat upon Olympus; to the Dust

They have appealed, and to that barren arbiter they must

Repair for judgment; let them, if they can,

From Natural Warfare and insensate Chance,

Create the new Ideal rule for man!

Methinks that was not my inheritance;

For I was nurtured otherwise, my soul

Passes from higher heights of life to a more supreme goal.

Lo! while we spake the earth did turn away

Her visage from the God, and Hecate's boat

Rose silver-laden, till the jealous day

Blew all its torches out: I did not note

The waning hours, to young Endymions

Time's palsied fingers count in vain his rosary of suns!

Mark how the yellow iris wearily

Leans back its throat, as though it would be kissed

By its false chamberer, the dragon-fly,

Who, like a blue vein on a girl's white wrist,

Sleeps on that snowy primrose of the night,

Which 'gins to flush with crimson shame, and die beneath the light.

Come let us go, against the pallid shield

  Of the wan sky the almond blossoms gleam,

The corncrake nested in the unmown field

  Answers its mate, across the misty stream

On fitful wing the startled curlews fly,

And in his sedgy bed the lark, for joy that Day is nigh,

Scatters the pearlèd dew from off the grass,

  In tremulous ecstasy to greet the sun,

Who soon in gilded panoply will pass

  Forth from yon orange-curtained pavilion

Hung in the burning east: see, the red rim

O'ertops the expectant hills! it is the God! for love of him

Already the shrill lark is out of sight,

  Flooding with waves of song this silent dell,—

Ah! there is something more in that bird's flight

  Than could be tested in a crucible!—

But the air freshens, let us go, why soon

The woodmen will be here; how we have lived this night of June!

ROSA MYSTICA

REQUIESCAT

Tread lightly, she is near
  Under the snow,
Speak gently, she can hear
  The daisies grow.

All her bright golden hair
  Tarnished with rust,
She that was young and fair
  Fallen to dust.

Lily-like, white as snow,
  She hardly knew
She was a woman, so
  Sweetly she grew.

Coffin-board, heavy stone,
  Lie on her breast,
I vex my heart alone,

She is at rest.

Peace, Peace, she cannot hear

Lyre or sonnet,

All my life's buried here,

Heap earth upon it.

Avignon.

SONNET ON APPROACHING ITALY

I reached the Alps: the soul within me burned,

Italia, my Italia, at thy name:

And when from out the mountain's heart I came

And saw the land for which my life had yearned,

I laughed as one who some great prize had earned:

And musing on the marvel of thy fame

I watched the day, till marked with wounds of flame

The turquoise sky to burnished gold was turned.

The pine-trees waved as waves a woman's hair,

And in the orchards every twining spray

Was breaking into flakes of blossoming foam:

But when I knew that far away at Rome

In evil bonds a second Peter lay,

I wept to see the land so very fair.

Turin.

SAN MINIATO

See, I have climbed the mountain side

Up to this holy house of God,

Where once that Angel-Painter trod

Who saw the heavens opened wide,

And throned upon the crescent moon

The Virginal white Queen of Grace,—

Mary! could I but see thy face

Death could not come at all too soon.

O crowned by God with thorns and pain!

Mother of Christ! O mystic wife!

My heart is weary of this life

And over-sad to sing again.

O crowned by God with love and flame!

O crowned by Christ the Holy One!

O listen ere the searching sun

Show to the world my sin and shame.

194

AVE MARIA GRATIA PLENA

Was this His coming! I had hoped to see

   A scene of wondrous glory, as was told

   Of some great God who in a rain of gold

Broke open bars and fell on Danae:

Or a dread vision as when Semele

   Sickening for love and unappeased desire

   Prayed to see God's clear body, and the fire

Caught her brown limbs and slew her utterly:

With such glad dreams I sought this holy place,

   And now with wondering eyes and heart I stand

   Before this supreme mystery of Love:

Some kneeling girl with passionless pale face,

   An angel with a lily in his hand,

   And over both the white wings of a Dove.

FLORENCE.

ITALIA

Italia! thou art fallen, though with sheen

   Of battle-spears thy clamorous armies stride

   From the north Alps to the Sicilian tide!

Ay! fallen, though the nations hail thee Queen

Because rich gold in every town is seen,

    And on thy sapphire-lake in tossing pride

    Of wind-filled vans thy myriad galleys ride

Beneath one flag of red and white and green.

O Fair and Strong! O Strong and Fair in vain!

    Look southward where Rome's desecrated town

    Lies mourning for her God-anointed King!

Look heaven-ward! shall God allow this thing?

    Nay! but some flame-girt Raphael shall come down,

    And smite the Spoiler with the sword of pain.

VENICE.

SONNET WRITTEN IN HOLY WEEK AT GENOA

I wandered through Scoglietto's far retreat,

    The oranges on each o'erhanging spray

    Burned as bright lamps of gold to shame the day;

Some startled bird with fluttering wings and fleet

Made snow of all the blossoms; at my feet

    Like silver moons the pale narcissi lay:

    And the curved waves that streaked the great green bay

Laughed i' the sun, and life seemed very sweet.

Outside the young boy-priest passed singing clear,

'Jesus the son of Mary has been slain,

O come and fill His sepulchre with flowers.'

Ah, God! Ah, God! those dear Hellenic hours

Had drowned all memory of Thy bitter pain,

The Cross, the Crown, the Soldiers and the Spear.

ROME UNVISITED

I.

The corn has turned from grey to red,

Since first my spirit wandered forth

From the drear cities of the north,

And to Italia's mountains fled.

And here I set my face towards home,

For all my pilgrimage is done,

Although, methinks, yon blood-red sun

Marshals the way to Holy Rome.

O Blessed Lady, who dost hold

Upon the seven hills thy reign!

O Mother without blot or stain,

Crowned with bright crowns of triple gold!

O Roma, Roma, at thy feet

    I lay this barren gift of song!

    For, ah! the way is steep and long

That leads unto thy sacred street.

II.

And yet what joy it were for me

    To turn my feet unto the south,

    And journeying towards the Tiber mouth

To kneel again at Fiesole!

And wandering through the tangled pines

    That break the gold of Arno's stream,

    To see the purple mist and gleam

Of morning on the Apennines

By many a vineyard-hidden home,

    Orchard and olive-garden grey,

    Till from the drear Campagna's way

The seven hills bear up the dome!

III.

A pilgrim from the northern seas—

What joy for me to seek alone

The wondrous temple and the throne

Of him who holds the awful keys!

When, bright with purple and with gold

Come priest and holy cardinal,

And borne above the heads of all

The gentle Shepherd of the Fold.

O joy to see before I die

The only God-anointed king,

And hear the silver trumpets ring

A triumph as he passes by!

Or at the brazen-pillared shrine

Holds high the mystic sacrifice,

And shows his God to human eyes

Beneath the veil of bread and wine.

IV.

For lo, what changes time can bring!

The cycles of revolving years

May free my heart from all its fears,

And teach my lips a song to sing.

Before yon field of trembling gold

Is garnered into dusty sheaves,

Or ere the autumn's scarlet leaves

Flutter as birds adown the wold,

I may have run the glorious race,

And caught the torch while yet aflame,

And called upon the holy name

Of Him who now doth hide His face.

ARONA.

URBS SACRA ÆTERNA

Rome! what a scroll of History thine has been;

In the first days thy sword republican

Ruled the whole world for many an age's span:

Then of the peoples wert thou royal Queen,

Till in thy streets the bearded Goth was seen;

And now upon thy walls the breezes fan

(Ah, city crowned by God, discrowned by man!)

The hated flag of red and white and green.

When was thy glory! when in search for power

 Thine eagles flew to greet the double sun,

 And the wild nations shuddered at thy rod?

Nay, but thy glory tarried for this hour,

 When pilgrims kneel before the Holy One,

 The prisoned shepherd of the Church of God.

Montre Mario.

SONNET ON HEARING THE DIES IRÆ SUNG IN THE SISTINE CHAPEL

Nay, Lord, not thus! white lilies in the spring,

Sad olive-groves, or silver-breasted dove,

 Teach me more clearly of Thy life and love

Than terrors of red flame and thundering.

The hillside vines dear memories of Thee bring:

 A bird at evening flying to its nest

 Tells me of One who had no place of rest:

I think it is of Thee the sparrows sing.

Come rather on some autumn afternoon,

 When red and brown are burnished on the leaves,

 And the fields echo to the gleaner's song,

Come when the splendid fulness of the moon

Looks down upon the rows of golden sheaves,

And reap Thy harvest: we have waited long.

EASTER DAY

The silver trumpets rang across the Dome:

The people knelt upon the ground with awe:

And borne upon the necks of men I saw,

Like some great God, the Holy Lord of Rome.

Priest-like, he wore a robe more white than foam,

And, king-like, swathed himself in royal red,

Three crowns of gold rose high upon his head:

In splendour and in light the Pope passed home.

My heart stole back across wide wastes of years

To One who wandered by a lonely sea,

And sought in vain for any place of rest:

'Foxes have holes, and every bird its nest.

I, only I, must wander wearily,

And bruise my feet, and drink wine salt with tears.'

E TENEBRIS

Come down, O Christ, and help me! reach Thy hand,

For I am drowning in a stormier sea

Than Simon on Thy lake of Galilee:

The wine of life is spilt upon the sand,

My heart is as some famine-murdered land

Whence all good things have perished utterly,

And well I know my soul in Hell must lie

If I this night before God's throne should stand.

'He sleeps perchance, or rideth to the chase,

Like Baal, when his prophets howled that name

From morn to noon on Carmel's smitten height.'

Nay, peace, I shall behold, before the night,

The feet of brass, the robe more white than flame,

The wounded hands, the weary human face.

VITA NUOVA

I stood by the unvintageable sea

Till the wet waves drenched face and hair with spray;

The long red fires of the dying day

Burned in the west; the wind piped drearily;

And to the land the clamorous gulls did flee:

'Alas!' I cried, 'my life is full of pain,

And who can garner fruit or golden grain

From these waste fields which travail ceaselessly!'

My nets gaped wide with many a break and flaw,

Nathless I threw them as my final cast

Into the sea, and waited for the end.

When lo! a sudden glory! and I saw

From the black waters of my tortured past

The argent splendour of white limbs ascend!

MADONNA MIA

A lily-girl, not made for this world's pain,

    With brown, soft hair close braided by her ears,

    And longing eyes half veiled by slumberous tears

Like bluest water seen through mists of rain:

Pale cheeks whereon no love hath left its stain,

    Red underlip drawn in for fear of love,

    And white throat, whiter than the silvered dove,

Through whose wan marble creeps one purple vein.

Yet, though my lips shall praise her without cease,

    Even to kiss her feet I am not bold,

    Being o'ershadowed by the wings of awe,

Like Dante, when he stood with Beatrice

    Beneath the flaming Lion's breast, and saw

    The seventh Crystal, and the Stair of Gold.

THE NEW HELEN

Where hast thou been since round the walls of Troy

    The sons of God fought in that great emprise?

    Why dost thou walk our common earth again?

Hast thou forgotten that impassioned boy,

His purple galley and his Tyrian men

And treacherous Aphrodite's mocking eyes?

For surely it was thou, who, like a star

Hung in the silver silence of the night,

Didst lure the Old World's chivalry and might

Into the clamorous crimson waves of war!

Or didst thou rule the fire-laden moon?

In amorous Sidon was thy temple built

Over the light and laughter of the sea

Where, behind lattice scarlet-wrought and gilt,

Some brown-limbed girl did weave thee tapestry,

All through the waste and wearied hours of noon;

Till her wan cheek with flame of passion burned,

And she rose up the sea-washed lips to kiss

Of some glad Cyprian sailor, safe returned

From Calpé and the cliffs of Herakles!

No! thou art Helen, and none other one!

It was for thee that young Sarpedôn died,

And Memnôn's manhood was untimely spent;

It was for thee gold-crested Hector tried

With Thetis' child that evil race to run,

In the last year of thy beleaguerment;

Ay! even now the glory of thy fame

Burns in those fields of trampled asphodel,

Where the high lords whom Ilion knew so well

Clash ghostly shields, and call upon thy name.

Where hast thou been? in that enchanted land

Whose slumbering vales forlorn Calypso knew,

Where never mower rose at break of day

But all unswathed the trammelling grasses grew,

And the sad shepherd saw the tall corn stand

Till summer's red had changed to withered grey?

Didst thou lie there by some Lethæan stream

Deep brooding on thine ancient memory,

The crash of broken spears, the fiery gleam

From shivered helm, the Grecian battle-cry?

Nay, thou wert hidden in that hollow hill

With one who is forgotten utterly,

That discrowned Queen men call the Erycine;

Hidden away that never mightst thou see

The face of Her, before whose mouldering shrine

To-day at Rome the silent nations kneel;

Who gat from Love no joyous gladdening,

But only Love's intolerable pain,

Only a sword to pierce her heart in twain,

Only the bitterness of child-bearing.

The lotus-leaves which heal the wounds of Death

Lie in thy hand; O, be thou kind to me,

While yet I know the summer of my days;

For hardly can my tremulous lips draw breath

To fill the silver trumpet with thy praise,

So bowed am I before thy mystery;

So bowed and broken on Love's terrible wheel,

That I have lost all hope and heart to sing,

Yet care I not what ruin time may bring

If in thy temple thou wilt let me kneel.

Alas, alas, thou wilt not tarry here,

But, like that bird, the servant of the sun,

Who flies before the north wind and the night,

So wilt thou fly our evil land and drear,

Back to the tower of thine old delight,

And the red lips of young Euphorion;

Nor shall I ever see thy face again,

But in this poisonous garden-close must stay,

Crowning my brows with the thorn-crown of pain,

Till all my loveless life shall pass away.

O Helen! Helen! Helen! yet a while,

Yet for a little while, O, tarry here,

Till the dawn cometh and the shadows flee!

For in the gladsome sunlight of thy smile

Of heaven or hell I have no thought or fear,

Seeing I know no other god but thee:

No other god save him, before whose feet

In nets of gold the tired planets move,

The incarnate spirit of spiritual love

Who in thy body holds his joyous seat.

Thou wert not born as common women are!

But, girt with silver splendour of the foam,

Didst from the depths of sapphire seas arise!

And at thy coming some immortal star,

Bearded with flame, blazed in the Eastern skies,

And waked the shepherds on thine island-home.

Thou shalt not die: no asps of Egypt creep

Close at thy heels to taint the delicate air;

No sullen-blooming poppies stain thy hair,

Those scarlet heralds of eternal sleep.

Lily of love, pure and inviolate!

Tower of ivory! red rose of fire!

Thou hast come down our darkness to illume:

For we, close-caught in the wide nets of Fate,

Wearied with waiting for the World's Desire,

Aimlessly wandered in the House of gloom,

Aimlessly sought some slumberous anodyne

For wasted lives, for lingering wretchedness,

Till we beheld thy re-arisen shrine,

And the white glory of thy loveliness.

THE BURDEN OF ITYS

This English Thames is holier far than Rome,

    Those harebells like a sudden flush of sea

Breaking across the woodland, with the foam

    Of meadow-sweet and white anemone

To fleck their blue waves,—God is likelier there

Than hidden in that crystal-hearted star the pale monks bear!

Those violet-gleaming butterflies that take

    Yon creamy lily for their pavilion

Are monsignores, and where the rushes shake

    A lazy pike lies basking in the sun,

His eyes half shut,—he is some mitred old

Bishop in partibus! look at those gaudy scales all green and gold.

The wind the restless prisoner of the trees

    Does well for Palæstrina, one would say

The mighty master's hands were on the keys

    Of the Maria organ, which they play

When early on some sapphire Easter morn

In a high litter red as blood or sin the Pope is borne

From his dark House out to the Balcony

  Above the bronze gates and the crowded square,

Whose very fountains seem for ecstasy

  To toss their silver lances in the air,

And stretching out weak hands to East and West

In vain sends peace to peaceless lands, to restless nations rest.

Is not yon lingering orange after-glow

  That stays to vex the moon more fair than all

Rome's lordliest pageants! strange, a year ago

  I knelt before some crimson Cardinal

Who bare the Host across the Esquiline,

And now—those common poppies in the wheat seem twice as fine.

The blue-green beanfields yonder, tremulous

  With the last shower, sweeter perfume bring

Through this cool evening than the odorous

  Flame-jewelled censers the young deacons swing,

When the grey priest unlocks the curtained shrine,

And makes God's body from the common fruit of corn and vine.

Poor Fra Giovanni bawling at the mass

Were out of tune now, for a small brown bird

Sings overhead, and through the long cool grass

   I see that throbbing throat which once I heard

On starlit hills of flower-starred Arcady,

Once where the white and crescent sand of Salamis meets sea.

Sweet is the swallow twittering on the eaves

   At daybreak, when the mower whets his scythe,

And stock-doves murmur, and the milkmaid leaves

   Her little lonely bed, and carols blithe

To see the heavy-lowing cattle wait

Stretching their huge and dripping mouths across the farmyard gate.

And sweet the hops upon the Kentish leas,

   And sweet the wind that lifts the new-mown hay,

And sweet the fretful swarms of grumbling bees

   That round and round the linden blossoms play;

And sweet the heifer breathing in the stall,

And the green bursting figs that hang upon the red-brick wall,

And sweet to hear the cuckoo mock the spring

   While the last violet loiters by the well,

And sweet to hear the shepherd Daphnis sing

The song of Linus through a sunny dell

Of warm Arcadia where the corn is gold

And the slight lithe-limbed reapers dance about the wattled fold.

And sweet with young Lycoris to recline

   In some Illyrian valley far away,

Where canopied on herbs amaracine

   We too might waste the summer-trancèd day

Matching our reeds in sportive rivalry,

   While far beneath us frets the troubled purple of the sea.

But sweeter far if silver-sandalled foot

   Of some long-hidden God should ever tread

The Nuneham meadows, if with reeded flute

   Pressed to his lips some Faun might raise his head

By the green water-flags, ah! sweet indeed

To see the heavenly herdsman call his white-fleeced flock to feed.

Then sing to me thou tuneful chorister,

   Though what thou sing'st be thine own requiem!

Tell me thy tale thou hapless chronicler

   Of thine own tragedies! do not contemn

These unfamiliar haunts, this English field,

For many a lovely coronal our northern isle can yield

Which Grecian meadows know not, many a rose
   Which all day long in vales Æolian
A lad might seek in vain for over-grows
   Our hedges like a wanton courtesan
Unthrifty of its beauty; lilies too
Ilissos never mirrored star our streams, and cockles blue

Dot the green wheat which, though they are the signs
   For swallows going south, would never spread
Their azure tents between the Attic vines;
   Even that little weed of ragged red,
Which bids the robin pipe, in Arcady
Would be a trespasser, and many an unsung elegy

Sleeps in the reeds that fringe our winding Thames
   Which to awake were sweeter ravishment
Than ever Syrinx wept for; diadems
   Of brown bee-studded orchids which were meant
For Cytheræa's brows are hidden here
Unknown to Cytheræa, and by yonder pasturing steer

There is a tiny yellow daffodil,

The butterfly can see it from afar,

Although one summer evening's dew could fill

   Its little cup twice over ere the star

Had called the lazy shepherd to his fold

And be no prodigal; each leaf is flecked with spotted gold

As if Jove's gorgeous leman Danae

   Hot from his gilded arms had stooped to kiss

The trembling petals, or young Mercury

   Low-flying to the dusky ford of Dis

Had with one feather of his pinions

Just brushed them! the slight stem which bears the burden of its suns

Is hardly thicker than the gossamer,

   Or poor Arachne's silver tapestry,—

Men say it bloomed upon the sepulchre

   Of One I sometime worshipped, but to me

It seems to bring diviner memories

Of faun-loved Heliconian glades and blue nymph-haunted seas,

Of an untrodden vale at Tempe where

   On the clear river's marge Narcissus lies,

The tangle of the forest in his hair,

The silence of the woodland in his eyes,

Wooing that drifting imagery which is

No sooner kissed than broken; memories of Salmacis

Who is not boy nor girl and yet is both,

    Fed by two fires and unsatisfied

Through their excess, each passion being loth

    For love's own sake to leave the other's side

Yet killing love by staying; memories

Of Oreads peeping through the leaves of silent moonlit trees,

Of lonely Ariadne on the wharf

    At Naxos, when she saw the treacherous crew

Far out at sea, and waved her crimson scarf

    And called false Theseus back again nor knew

That Dionysos on an amber pard

Was close behind her; memories of what Mæonia's bard

With sightless eyes beheld, the wall of Troy,

    Queen Helen lying in the ivory room,

And at her side an amorous red-lipped boy

    Trimming with dainty hand his helmet's plume,

And far away the moil, the shout, the groan,

As Hector shielded off the spear and Ajax hurled the stone;

Of wingèd Perseus with his flawless sword
   Cleaving the snaky tresses of the witch,
And all those tales imperishably stored
   In little Grecian urns, freightage more rich
Than any gaudy galleon of Spain
Bare from the Indies ever! these at least bring back again,

For well I know they are not dead at all,
   The ancient Gods of Grecian poesy:
They are asleep, and when they hear thee call
   Will wake and think 't is very Thessaly,
This Thames the Daulian waters, this cool glade
The yellow-irised mead where once young Itys laughed and played.

If it was thou dear jasmine-cradled bird
   Who from the leafy stillness of thy throne
Sang to the wondrous boy, until he heard
   The horn of Atalanta faintly blown
Across the Cumnor hills, and wandering
Through Bagley wood at evening found the Attic poets' spring,—

Ah! tiny sober-suited advocate

That pleadest for the moon against the day!

If thou didst make the shepherd seek his mate

  On that sweet questing, when Proserpina

Forgot it was not Sicily and leant

Across the mossy Sandford stile in ravished wonderment,—

Light-winged and bright-eyed miracle of the wood!

  If ever thou didst soothe with melody

One of that little clan, that brotherhood

  Which loved the morning-star of Tuscany

More than the perfect sun of Raphael

And is immortal, sing to me! for I too love thee well.

Sing on! sing on! let the dull world grow young,

  Let elemental things take form again,

And the old shapes of Beauty walk among

  The simple garths and open crofts, as when

The son of Leto bare the willow rod,

And the soft sheep and shaggy goats followed the boyish God.

Sing on! sing on! and Bacchus will be here

  Astride upon his gorgeous Indian throne,

And over whimpering tigers shake the spear

With yellow ivy crowned and gummy cone,

While at his side the wanton Bassarid

Will throw the lion by the mane and catch the mountain kid!

Sing on! and I will wear the leopard skin,

   And steal the moonèd wings of Ashtaroth,

Upon whose icy chariot we could win

   Cithæron in an hour ere the froth

Has over-brimmed the wine-vat or the Faun

Ceased from the treading! ay, before the flickering lamp of dawn

Has scared the hooting owlet to its nest,

   And warned the bat to close its filmy vans,

Some Mænad girl with vine-leaves on her breast

   Will filch their beech-nuts from the sleeping Pans

So softly that the little nested thrush

Will never wake, and then with shrilly laugh and leap will rush

Down the green valley where the fallen dew

   Lies thick beneath the elm and count her store,

Till the brown Satyrs in a jolly crew

   Trample the loosestrife down along the shore,

And where their hornèd master sits in state

Bring strawberries and bloomy plums upon a wicker crate!

Sing on! and soon with passion-wearied face

   Through the cool leaves Apollo's lad will come,

The Tyrian prince his bristled boar will chase

   Adown the chestnut-copses all a-bloom,

And ivory-limbed, grey-eyed, with look of pride,

After yon velvet-coated deer the virgin maid will ride.

Sing on! and I the dying boy will see

   Stain with his purple blood the waxen bell

That overweighs the jacinth, and to me

   The wretched Cyprian her woe will tell,

And I will kiss her mouth and streaming eyes,

And lead her to the myrtle-hidden grove where Adon lies!

Cry out aloud on Itys! memory

   That foster-brother of remorse and pain

Drops poison in mine ear,—O to be free,

   To burn one's old ships! and to launch again

Into the white-plumed battle of the waves

And fight old Proteus for the spoil of coral-flowered caves!

O for Medea with her poppied spell!

O for the secret of the Colchian shrine!

O for one leaf of that pale asphodel

   Which binds the tired brows of Proserpine,

And sheds such wondrous dews at eve that she

Dreams of the fields of Enna, by the far Sicilian sea,

Where oft the golden-girdled bee she chased

   From lily to lily on the level mead,

Ere yet her sombre Lord had bid her taste

   The deadly fruit of that pomegranate seed,

Ere the black steeds had harried her away

Down to the faint and flowerless land, the sick and sunless day.

O for one midnight and as paramour

   The Venus of the little Melian farm!

O that some antique statue for one hour

   Might wake to passion, and that I could charm

The Dawn at Florence from its dumb despair,

Mix with those mighty limbs and make that giant breast my lair!

Sing on! sing on! I would be drunk with life,

   Drunk with the trampled vintage of my youth,

I would forget the wearying wasted strife,

The riven veil, the Gorgon eyes of Truth,

The prayerless vigil and the cry for prayer,

The barren gifts, the lifted arms, the dull insensate air!

Sing on! sing on! O feathered Niobe,

   Thou canst make sorrow beautiful, and steal

From joy its sweetest music, not as we

   Who by dead voiceless silence strive to heal

Our too untented wounds, and do but keep

Pain barricadoed in our hearts, and murder pillowed sleep.

Sing louder yet, why must I still behold

   The wan white face of that deserted Christ,

Whose bleeding hands my hands did once enfold,

   Whose smitten lips my lips so oft have kissed,

And now in mute and marble misery

Sits in his lone dishonoured House and weeps, perchance for me?

O Memory cast down thy wreathèd shell!

   Break thy hoarse lute O sad Melpomene!

O Sorrow, Sorrow keep thy cloistered cell

   Nor dim with tears this limpid Castaly!

Cease, Philomel, thou dost the forest wrong

To vex its sylvan quiet with such wild impassioned song!

Cease, cease, or if 't is anguish to be dumb
  Take from the pastoral thrush her simpler air,
Whose jocund carelessness doth more become
  This English woodland than thy keen despair,
Ah! cease and let the north wind bear thy lay
Back to the rocky hills of Thrace, the stormy Daulian bay.

A moment more, the startled leaves had stirred,
  Endymion would have passed across the mead
Moonstruck with love, and this still Thames had heard
  Pan plash and paddle groping for some reed
To lure from her blue cave that Naiad maid
Who for such piping listens half in joy and half afraid.

A moment more, the waking dove had cooed,
  The silver daughter of the silver sea
With the fond gyves of clinging hands had wooed
  Her wanton from the chase, and Dryope
Had thrust aside the branches of her oak
To see the lusty gold-haired lad rein in his snorting yoke.

A moment more, the trees had stooped to kiss

Pale Daphne just awakening from the swoon

Of tremulous laurels, lonely Salmacis

Had bared his barren beauty to the moon,

And through the vale with sad voluptuous smile

Antinous had wandered, the red lotus of the Nile

Down leaning from his black and clustering hair,

To shade those slumberous eyelids' caverned bliss,

Or else on yonder grassy slope with bare

High-tuniced limbs unravished Artemis

Had bade her hounds give tongue, and roused the deer

From his green ambuscade with shrill halloo and pricking spear.

Lie still, lie still, O passionate heart, lie still!

O Melancholy, fold thy raven wing!

O sobbing Dryad, from thy hollow hill

Come not with such despondent answering!

No more thou wingèd Marsyas complain,

Apollo loveth not to hear such troubled songs of pain!

It was a dream, the glade is tenantless,

No soft Ionian laughter moves the air,

The Thames creeps on in sluggish leadenness,

And from the copse left desolate and bare

Fled is young Bacchus with his revelry,

Yet still from Nuneham wood there comes that thrilling melody

So sad, that one might think a human heart

  Brake in each separate note, a quality

Which music sometimes has, being the Art

  Which is most nigh to tears and memory;

Poor mourning Philomel, what dost thou fear?

  Thy sister doth not haunt these fields, Pandion is not here,

Here is no cruel Lord with murderous blade,

  No woven web of bloody heraldries,

But mossy dells for roving comrades made,

  Warm valleys where the tired student lies

With half-shut book, and many a winding walk

Where rustic lovers stray at eve in happy simple talk.

The harmless rabbit gambols with its young

  Across the trampled towing-path, where late

A troop of laughing boys in jostling throng

  Cheered with their noisy cries the racing eight;

The gossamer, with ravelled silver threads,

Works at its little loom, and from the dusky red-eaved sheds

Of the lone Farm a flickering light shines out
   Where the swinked shepherd drives his bleating flock
Back to their wattled sheep-cotes, a faint shout
   Comes from some Oxford boat at Sandford lock,
And starts the moor-hen from the sedgy rill,
And the dim lengthening shadows flit like swallows up the hill.

The heron passes homeward to the mere,
   The blue mist creeps among the shivering trees,
Gold world by world the silent stars appear,
   And like a blossom blown before the breeze
A white moon drifts across the shimmering sky,
Mute arbitress of all thy sad, thy rapturous threnody.

She does not heed thee, wherefore should she heed,
   She knows Endymion is not far away;
'Tis I, 'tis I, whose soul is as the reed
   Which has no message of its own to play,
So pipes another's bidding, it is I,
Drifting with every wind on the wide sea of misery.

Ah! the brown bird has ceased: one exquisite trill

About the sombre woodland seems to cling

Dying in music, else the air is still,

So still that one might hear the bat's small wing

Wander and wheel above the pines, or tell

Each tiny dew-drop dripping from the bluebell's brimming cell.

And far away across the lengthening wold,

Across the willowy flats and thickets brown,

Magdalen's tall tower tipped with tremulous gold

Marks the long High Street of the little town,

And warns me to return; I must not wait,

Hark! 't is the curfew booming from the bell at Christ Church gate.

WIND FLOWERS

IMPRESSION DU MATIN

The Thames nocturne of blue and gold
  Changed to a Harmony in grey:
  A barge with ochre-coloured hay
Dropt from the wharf: and chill and cold

The yellow fog came creeping down
  The bridges, till the houses' walls
  Seemed changed to shadows and St. Paul's
Loomed like a bubble o'er the town.

Then suddenly arose the clang
  Of waking life; the streets were stirred
  With country waggons: and a bird
Flew to the glistening roofs and sang.

But one pale woman all alone,
  The daylight kissing her wan hair,
  Loitered beneath the gas lamps' flare,
With lips of flame and heart of stone.

MAGDALEN WALKS

The little white clouds are racing over the sky,

    And the fields are strewn with the gold of the flower of March,

    The daffodil breaks under foot, and the tasselled larch

Sways and swings as the thrush goes hurrying by.

A delicate odour is borne on the wings of the morning breeze,

    The odour of deep wet grass, and of brown new-furrowed earth,

    The birds are singing for joy of the Spring's glad birth,

Hopping from branch to branch on the rocking trees.

And all the woods are alive with the murmur and sound of Spring,

    And the rose-bud breaks into pink on the climbing briar,

    And the crocus-bed is a quivering moon of fire

Girdled round with the belt of an amethyst ring.

And the plane to the pine-tree is whispering some tale of love

    Till it rustles with laughter and tosses its mantle of green,

    And the gloom of the wych-elm's hollow is lit with the iris sheen

Of the burnished rainbow throat and the silver breast of a dove.

See! the lark starts up from his bed in the meadow there,

    Breaking the gossamer threads and the nets of dew,

And flashing adown the river, a flame of blue!

The kingfisher flies like an arrow, and wounds the air.

ATHANASIA

To that gaunt House of Art which lacks for naught

Of all the great things men have saved from Time,

The withered body of a girl was brought

Dead ere the world's glad youth had touched its prime,

And seen by lonely Arabs lying hid

In the dim womb of some black pyramid.

But when they had unloosed the linen band

Which swathed the Egyptian's body,—lo! was found

Closed in the wasted hollow of her hand

A little seed, which sown in English ground

Did wondrous snow of starry blossoms bear

And spread rich odours through our spring-tide air.

With such strange arts this flower did allure

That all forgotten was the asphodel,

And the brown bee, the lily's paramour,

Forsook the cup where he was wont to dwell,

For not a thing of earth it seemed to be,

But stolen from some heavenly Arcady.

In vain the sad narcissus, wan and white

    At its own beauty, hung across the stream,

The purple dragon-fly had no delight

    With its gold dust to make his wings a-gleam,

Ah! no delight the jasmine-bloom to kiss,

Or brush the rain-pearls from the eucharis.

For love of it the passionate nightingale

    Forgot the hills of Thrace, the cruel king,

And the pale dove no longer cared to sail

    Through the wet woods at time of blossoming,

But round this flower of Egypt sought to float,

With silvered wing and amethystine throat.

While the hot sun blazed in his tower of blue

    A cooling wind crept from the land of snows,

And the warm south with tender tears of dew

    Drenched its white leaves when Hesperos up-rose

Amid those sea-green meadows of the sky

On which the scarlet bars of sunset lie.

But when o'er wastes of lily-haunted field

The tired birds had stayed their amorous tune,

And broad and glittering like an argent shield

   High in the sapphire heavens hung the moon,

Did no strange dream or evil memory make

Each tremulous petal of its blossoms shake?

Ah no! to this bright flower a thousand years

   Seemed but the lingering of a summer's day,

It never knew the tide of cankering fears

   Which turn a boy's gold hair to withered grey,

The dread desire of death it never knew,

Or how all folk that they were born must rue.

For we to death with pipe and dancing go,

   Nor would we pass the ivory gate again,

As some sad river wearied of its flow

   Through the dull plains, the haunts of common men,

Leaps lover-like into the terrible sea!

And counts it gain to die so gloriously.

We mar our lordly strength in barren strife

   With the world's legions led by clamorous care,

It never feels decay but gathers life

From the pure sunlight and the supreme air,

We live beneath Time's wasting sovereignty,

It is the child of all eternity.

SERENADE
(FOR MUSIC)

The western wind is blowing fair

  Across the dark Ægean sea,

And at the secret marble stair

  My Tyrian galley waits for thee.

Come down! the purple sail is spread,

  The watchman sleeps within the town,

O leave thy lily-flowered bed,

  O Lady mine come down, come down!

She will not come, I know her well,

  Of lover's vows she hath no care,

And little good a man can tell

  Of one so cruel and so fair.

True love is but a woman's toy,

  They never know the lover's pain,

And I who loved as loves a boy

  Must love in vain, must love in vain.

O noble pilot, tell me true,

 Is that the sheen of golden hair?

Or is it but the tangled dew

 That binds the passion-flowers there?

Good sailor come and tell me now

 Is that my Lady's lily hand?

Or is it but the gleaming prow,

 Or is it but the silver sand?

No! no! 'tis not the tangled dew,

 'Tis not the silver-fretted sand,

It is my own dear Lady true

 With golden hair and lily hand!

O noble pilot, steer for Troy,

 Good sailor, ply the labouring oar,

This is the Queen of life and joy

 Whom we must bear from Grecian shore!

The waning sky grows faint and blue,

 It wants an hour still of day,

Aboard! aboard! my gallant crew,

 O Lady mine, away! away!

234

O noble pilot, steer for Troy,

  Good sailor, ply the labouring oar,

O loved as only loves a boy!

  O loved for ever evermore!

ENDYMION

(FOR MUSIC)

The apple trees are hung with gold,

  And birds are loud in Arcady,

The sheep lie bleating in the fold,

The wild goat runs across the wold,

But yesterday his love he told,

  I know he will come back to me.

O rising moon! O Lady moon!

  Be you my lover's sentinel,

  You cannot choose but know him well,

For he is shod with purple shoon,

You cannot choose but know my love,

  For he a shepherd's crook doth bear,

And he is soft as any dove,

  And brown and curly is his hair.

The turtle now has ceased to call

Upon her crimson-footed groom,

The grey wolf prowls about the stall,

The lily's singing seneschal

Sleeps in the lily-bell, and all

The violet hills are lost in gloom.

O risen moon! O holy moon!

Stand on the top of Helice,

And if my own true love you see,

Ah! if you see the purple shoon,

The hazel crook, the lad's brown hair,

The goat-skin wrapped about his arm,

Tell him that I am waiting where

The rushlight glimmers in the Farm.

The falling dew is cold and chill,

And no bird sings in Arcady,

The little fauns have left the hill,

Even the tired daffodil

Has closed its gilded doors, and still

My lover comes not back to me.

False moon! False moon! O waning moon!

Where is my own true lover gone,

Where are the lips vermilion,

The shepherd's crook, the purple shoon?

Why spread that silver pavilion,

    Why wear that veil of drifting mist?

Ah! thou hast young Endymion,

    Thou hast the lips that should be kissed!

LA BELLA DONNA DELLA MIA MENTE

My limbs are wasted with a flame,

    My feet are sore with travelling,

For, calling on my Lady's name,

    My lips have now forgot to sing.

O Linnet in the wild-rose brake

    Strain for my Love thy melody,

O Lark sing louder for love's sake,

    My gentle Lady passeth by.

She is too fair for any man

    To see or hold his heart's delight,

Fairer than Queen or courtesan

    Or moonlit water in the night.

Her hair is bound with myrtle leaves,

    (Green leaves upon her golden hair!)

Green grasses through the yellow sheaves

    Of autumn corn are not more fair.

Her little lips, more made to kiss

    Than to cry bitterly for pain,

Are tremulous as brook-water is,

    Or roses after evening rain.

Her neck is like white melilote

    Flushing for pleasure of the sun,

The throbbing of the linnet's throat

    Is not so sweet to look upon.

As a pomegranate, cut in twain,

    White-seeded, is her crimson mouth,

Her cheeks are as the fading stain

    Where the peach reddens to the south.

O twining hands! O delicate

    White body made for love and pain!

O House of love! O desolate

    Pale flower beaten by the rain!

CHANSON

A ring of gold and a milk-white dove

Are goodly gifts for thee,

And a hempen rope for your own love

To hang upon a tree.

For you a House of Ivory,

(Roses are white in the rose-bower)!

A narrow bed for me to lie,

(White, O white, is the hemlock flower)!

Myrtle and jessamine for you,

(O the red rose is fair to see)!

For me the cypress and the rue,

(Finest of all is rosemary)!

For you three lovers of your hand,

(Green grass where a man lies dead)!

For me three paces on the sand,

(Plant lilies at my head)!

CHARMIDES

I.

He was a Grecian lad, who coming home
  With pulpy figs and wine from Sicily
Stood at his galley's prow, and let the foam
  Blow through his crisp brown curls unconsciously,
And holding wave and wind in boy's despite
Peered from his dripping seat across the wet and stormy night.

Till with the dawn he saw a burnished spear
  Like a thin thread of gold against the sky,
And hoisted sail, and strained the creaking gear,
  And bade the pilot head her lustily
Against the nor'west gale, and all day long
Held on his way, and marked the rowers' time with measured song.

And when the faint Corinthian hills were red
  Dropped anchor in a little sandy bay,
And with fresh boughs of olive crowned his head,
  And brushed from cheek and throat the hoary spray,
And washed his limbs with oil, and from the hold

Brought out his linen tunic and his sandals brazen-soled,

And a rich robe stained with the fishers' juice
  Which of some swarthy trader he had bought
Upon the sunny quay at Syracuse,
  And was with Tyrian broideries inwrought,
And by the questioning merchants made his way
Up through the soft and silver woods, and when the labouring day

Had spun its tangled web of crimson cloud,
  Clomb the high hill, and with swift silent feet
Crept to the fane unnoticed by the crowd
  Of busy priests, and from some dark retreat
Watched the young swains his frolic playmates bring
The firstling of their little flock, and the shy shepherd fling

The crackling salt upon the flame, or hang
  His studded crook against the temple wall
To Her who keeps away the ravenous fang
  Of the base wolf from homestead and from stall;
And then the clear-voiced maidens 'gan to sing,
And to the altar each man brought some goodly offering,

A beechen cup brimming with milky foam,

A fair cloth wrought with cunning imagery

Of hounds in chase, a waxen honey-comb

Dripping with oozy gold which scarce the bee

Had ceased from building, a black skin of oil

Meet for the wrestlers, a great boar the fierce and white-tusked spoil

Stolen from Artemis that jealous maid

To please Athena, and the dappled hide

Of a tall stag who in some mountain glade

Had met the shaft; and then the herald cried,

And from the pillared precinct one by one

Went the glad Greeks well pleased that they their simple vows had done.

And the old priest put out the waning fires

Save that one lamp whose restless ruby glowed

For ever in the cell, and the shrill lyres

Came fainter on the wind, as down the road

In joyous dance these country folk did pass,

And with stout hands the warder closed the gates of polished brass.

Long time he lay and hardly dared to breathe,

And heard the cadenced drip of spilt-out wine,

And the rose-petals falling from the wreath

As the night breezes wandered through the shrine,

And seemed to be in some entrancèd swoon

Till through the open roof above the full and brimming moon

Flooded with sheeny waves the marble floor,

When from his nook up leapt the venturous lad,

And flinging wide the cedar-carven door

Beheld an awful image saffron-clad

And armed for battle! the gaunt Griffin glared

From the huge helm, and the long lance of wreck and ruin flared

Like a red rod of flame, stony and steeled

The Gorgon's head its leaden eyeballs rolled,

And writhed its snaky horrors through the shield,

And gaped aghast with bloodless lips and cold

In passion impotent, while with blind gaze

The blinking owl between the feet hooted in shrill amaze.

The lonely fisher as he trimmed his lamp

Far out at sea off Sunium, or cast

The net for tunnies, heard a brazen tramp

Of horses smite the waves, and a wild blast

Divide the folded curtains of the night,

And knelt upon the little poop, and prayed in holy fright.

And guilty lovers in their venery

    Forgat a little while their stolen sweets,

Deeming they heard dread Dian's bitter cry;

    And the grim watchmen on their lofty seats

Ran to their shields in haste precipitate,

    Or strained black-bearded throats across the dusky parapet.

For round the temple rolled the clang of arms,

    And the twelve Gods leapt up in marble fear,

And the air quaked with dissonant alarums

    Till huge Poseidon shook his mighty spear,

And on the frieze the prancing horses neighed,

And the low tread of hurrying feet rang from the cavalcade.

Ready for death with parted lips he stood,

    And well content at such a price to see

That calm wide brow, that terrible maidenhood,

    The marvel of that pitiless chastity,

Ah! well content indeed, for never wight

Since Troy's young shepherd prince had seen so wonderful a sight.

Ready for death he stood, but lo! the air

Grew silent, and the horses ceased to neigh,

And off his brow he tossed the clustering hair,

And from his limbs he throw the cloak away;

For whom would not such love make desperate?

And nigher came, and touched her throat, and with hands violate

Undid the cuirass, and the crocus gown,

And bared the breasts of polished ivory,

Till from the waist the peplos falling down

Left visible the secret mystery

Which to no lover will Athena show,

The grand cool flanks, the crescent thighs, the bossy hills of snow.

Those who have never known a lover's sin

Let them not read my ditty, it will be

To their dull ears so musicless and thin

That they will have no joy of it, but ye

To whose wan cheeks now creeps the lingering smile,

Ye who have learned who Eros is,—O listen yet awhile.

A little space he let his greedy eyes

Rest on the burnished image, till mere sight

Half swooned for surfeit of such luxuries,

And then his lips in hungering delight

Fed on her lips, and round the towered neck

He flung his arms, nor cared at all his passion's will to check.

Never I ween did lover hold such tryst,

    For all night long he murmured honeyed word,

And saw her sweet unravished limbs, and kissed

    Her pale and argent body undisturbed,

And paddled with the polished throat, and pressed

His hot and beating heart upon her chill and icy breast.

It was as if Numidian javelins

    Pierced through and through his wild and whirling brain,

And his nerves thrilled like throbbing violins

    In exquisite pulsation, and the pain

Was such sweet anguish that he never drew

His lips from hers till overhead the lark of warning flew.

They who have never seen the daylight peer

    Into a darkened room, and drawn the curtain,

And with dull eyes and wearied from some dear

    And worshipped body risen, they for certain

Will never know of what I try to sing,

How long the last kiss was, how fond and late his lingering.

The moon was girdled with a crystal rim,

    The sign which shipmen say is ominous

Of wrath in heaven, the wan stars were dim,

    And the low lightening east was tremulous

With the faint fluttering wings of flying dawn,

Ere from the silent sombre shrine his lover had withdrawn.

Down the steep rock with hurried feet and fast

    Clomb the brave lad, and reached the cave of Pan,

And heard the goat-foot snoring as he passed,

    And leapt upon a grassy knoll and ran

Like a young fawn unto an olive wood

Which in a shady valley by the well-built city stood;

And sought a little stream, which well he knew,

    For oftentimes with boyish careless shout

The green and crested grebe he would pursue,

    Or snare in woven net the silver trout,

And down amid the startled reeds he lay

Panting in breathless sweet affright, and waited for the day.

On the green bank he lay, and let one hand

Dip in the cool dark eddies listlessly,

And soon the breath of morning came and fanned

His hot flushed cheeks, or lifted wantonly

The tangled curls from off his forehead, while

He on the running water gazed with strange and secret smile.

And soon the shepherd in rough woollen cloak

   With his long crook undid the wattled cotes,

And from the stack a thin blue wreath of smoke

   Curled through the air across the ripening oats,

And on the hill the yellow house-dog bayed

As through the crisp and rustling fern the heavy cattle strayed.

And when the light-foot mower went afield

   Across the meadows laced with threaded dew,

And the sheep bleated on the misty weald,

   And from its nest the waking corncrake flew,

Some woodmen saw him lying by the stream

And marvelled much that any lad so beautiful could seem,

Nor deemed him born of mortals, and one said,

   'It is young Hylas, that false runaway

Who with a Naiad now would make his bed

Forgetting Herakles,' but others, 'Nay,

It is Narcissus, his own paramour,

Those are the fond and crimson lips no woman can allure.'

And when they nearer came a third one cried,

 'It is young Dionysos who has hid

His spear and fawnskin by the river side

 Weary of hunting with the Bassarid,

And wise indeed were we away to fly:

They live not long who on the gods immortal come to spy.'

So turned they back, and feared to look behind,

 And told the timid swain how they had seen

Amid the reeds some woodland god reclined,

 And no man dared to cross the open green,

And on that day no olive-tree was slain,

Nor rushes cut, but all deserted was the fair domain,

Save when the neat-herd's lad, his empty pail

 Well slung upon his back, with leap and bound

Raced on the other side, and stopped to hail,

 Hoping that he some comrade new had found,

And gat no answer, and then half afraid

Passed on his simple way, or down the still and silent glade

A little girl ran laughing from the farm,

   Not thinking of love's secret mysteries,

And when she saw the white and gleaming arm

   And all his manlihood, with longing eyes

Whose passion mocked her sweet virginity

Watched him awhile, and then stole back sadly and wearily.

Far off he heard the city's hum and noise,

   And now and then the shriller laughter where

The passionate purity of brown-limbed boys

   Wrestled or raced in the clear healthful air,

And now and then a little tinkling bell

As the shorn wether led the sheep down to the mossy well.

Through the grey willows danced the fretful gnat,

   The grasshopper chirped idly from the tree,

In sleek and oily coat the water-rat

   Breasting the little ripples manfully

Made for the wild-duck's nest, from bough to bough

Hopped the shy finch, and the huge tortoise crept across the slough.

On the faint wind floated the silky seeds

As the bright scythe swept through the waving grass,

The ouzel-cock splashed circles in the reeds

And flecked with silver whorls the forest's glass,

Which scarce had caught again its imagery

Ere from its bed the dusky tench leapt at the dragon-fly.

But little care had he for any thing

Though up and down the beech the squirrel played,

And from the copse the linnet 'gan to sing

To its brown mate its sweetest serenade;

Ah! little care indeed, for he had seen

The breasts of Pallas and the naked wonder of the Queen.

But when the herdsman called his straggling goats

With whistling pipe across the rocky road,

And the shard-beetle with its trumpet-notes

Boomed through the darkening woods, and seemed to bode

Of coming storm, and the belated crane

Passed homeward like a shadow, and the dull big drops of rain

Fell on the pattering fig-leaves, up he rose,

And from the gloomy forest went his way

Past sombre homestead and wet orchard-close,

And came at last unto a little quay,

And called his mates aboard, and took his seat

On the high poop, and pushed from land, and loosed the dripping sheet,

And steered across the bay, and when nine suns

    Passed down the long and laddered way of gold,

And nine pale moons had breathed their orisons

    To the chaste stars their confessors, or told

Their dearest secret to the downy moth

That will not fly at noonday, through the foam and surging froth

Came a great owl with yellow sulphurous eyes

    And lit upon the ship, whose timbers creaked

As though the lading of three argosies

    Were in the hold, and flapped its wings and shrieked,

And darkness straightway stole across the deep,

Sheathed was Orion's sword, dread Mars himself fled down the steep,

And the moon hid behind a tawny mask

    Of drifting cloud, and from the ocean's marge

Rose the red plume, the huge and hornèd casque,

    The seven-cubit spear, the brazen targe!

And clad in bright and burnished panoply

Athena strode across the stretch of sick and shivering sea!

To the dull sailors' sight her loosened looks
   Seemed like the jagged storm-rack, and her feet
Only the spume that floats on hidden rocks,
   And, marking how the rising waters beat
Against the rolling ship, the pilot cried
To the young helmsman at the stern to luff to windward side

But he, the overbold adulterer,
   A dear profaner of great mysteries,
An ardent amorous idolater,
   When he beheld those grand relentless eyes
Laughed loud for joy, and crying out 'I come'
Leapt from the lofty poop into the chill and churning foam.

Then fell from the high heaven one bright star,
   One dancer left the circling galaxy,
And back to Athens on her clattering car
   In all the pride of venged divinity
Pale Pallas swept with shrill and steely clank,
And a few gurgling bubbles rose where her boy lover sank.

And the mast shuddered as the gaunt owl flew

With mocking hoots after the wrathful Queen,

And the old pilot bade the trembling crew

   Hoist the big sail, and told how he had seen

Close to the stern a dim and giant form,

And like a dipping swallow the stout ship dashed through the storm.

And no man dared to speak of Charmides

   Deeming that he some evil thing had wrought,

And when they reached the strait Symplegades

   They beached their galley on the shore, and sought

The toll-gate of the city hastily,

And in the market showed their brown and pictured pottery.

II.

But some good Triton-god had ruth, and bare

   The boy's drowned body back to Grecian land,

And mermaids combed his dank and dripping hair

   And smoothed his brow, and loosed his clenching hand;

Some brought sweet spices from far Araby,

And others bade the halcyon sing her softest lullaby.

And when he neared his old Athenian home,

   A mighty billow rose up suddenly

Upon whose oily back the clotted foam

  Lay diapered in some strange fantasy,

And clasping him unto its glassy breast

Swept landward, like a white-maned steed upon a venturous quest!

Now where Colonos leans unto the sea

  There lies a long and level stretch of lawn;

The rabbit knows it, and the mountain bee

  For it deserts Hymettus, and the Faun

Is not afraid, for never through the day

Comes a cry ruder than the shout of shepherd lads at play.

But often from the thorny labyrinth

  And tangled branches of the circling wood

The stealthy hunter sees young Hyacinth

  Hurling the polished disk, and draws his hood

Over his guilty gaze, and creeps away,

Nor dares to wind his horn, or—else at the first break of day

The Dryads come and throw the leathern ball

  Along the reedy shore, and circumvent

Some goat-eared Pan to be their seneschal

  For fear of bold Poseidon's ravishment,

And loose their girdles, with shy timorous eyes,

Lest from the surf his azure arms and purple beard should rise.

On this side and on that a rocky cave,

   Hung with the yellow-belled laburnum, stands

Smooth is the beach, save where some ebbing wave

   Leaves its faint outline etched upon the sands,

As though it feared to be too soon forgot

By the green rush, its playfellow,—and yet, it is a spot

So small, that the inconstant butterfly

   Could steal the hoarded money from each flower

Ere it was noon, and still not satisfy

   Its over-greedy love,—within an hour

A sailor boy, were he but rude enow

To land and pluck a garland for his galley's painted prow,

Would almost leave the little meadow bare,

   For it knows nothing of great pageantry,

Only a few narcissi here and there

   Stand separate in sweet austerity,

Dotting the unmown grass with silver stars,

And here and there a daffodil waves tiny scimitars.

Hither the billow brought him, and was glad

Of such dear servitude, and where the land

Was virgin of all waters laid the lad

Upon the golden margent of the strand,

And like a lingering lover oft returned

To kiss those pallid limbs which once with intense fire burned,

Ere the wet seas had quenched that holocaust,

That self-fed flame, that passionate lustihead,

Ere grisly death with chill and nipping frost

Had withered up those lilies white and red

Which, while the boy would through the forest range,

Answered each other in a sweet antiphonal counter-change.

And when at dawn the wood-nymphs, hand-in-hand,

Threaded the bosky dell, their satyr spied

The boy's pale body stretched upon the sand,

And feared Poseidon's treachery, and cried,

And like bright sunbeams flitting through a glade

Each startled Dryad sought some safe and leafy ambuscade.

Save one white girl, who deemed it would not be

So dread a thing to feel a sea-god's arms

Crushing her breasts in amorous tyranny,

And longed to listen to those subtle charms

Insidious lovers weave when they would win

Some fencèd fortress, and stole back again, nor thought it sin

To yield her treasure unto one so fair,

And lay beside him, thirsty with love's drouth,

Called him soft names, played with his tangled hair,

And with hot lips made havoc of his mouth

Afraid he might not wake, and then afraid

Lest he might wake too soon, fled back, and then, fond renegade,

Returned to fresh assault, and all day long

Sat at his side, and laughed at her new toy,

And held his hand, and sang her sweetest song,

Then frowned to see how froward was the boy

Who would not with her maidenhood entwine,

Nor knew that three days since his eyes had looked on Proserpine;

Nor knew what sacrilege his lips had done,

But said, 'He will awake, I know him well,

He will awake at evening when the sun

Hangs his red shield on Corinth's citadel;

This sleep is but a cruel treachery

To make me love him more, and in some cavern of the sea

Deeper than ever falls the fisher's line

    Already a huge Triton blows his horn,

And weaves a garland from the crystalline

    And drifting ocean-tendrils to adorn

The emerald pillars of our bridal bed,

For sphered in foaming silver, and with coral crownèd head,

We two will sit upon a throne of pearl,

    And a blue wave will be our canopy,

And at our feet the water-snakes will curl

    In all their amethystine panoply

Of diamonded mail, and we will mark

The mullets swimming by the mast of some storm-foundered bark,

Vermilion-finned with eyes of bossy gold

    Like flakes of crimson light, and the great deep

His glassy-portaled chamber will unfold,

    And we will see the painted dolphins sleep

Cradled by murmuring halcyons on the rocks

Where Proteus in quaint suit of green pastures his monstrous flocks.

And tremulous opal-hued anemones
   Will wave their purple fringes where we tread
Upon the mirrored floor, and argosies
   Of fishes flecked with tawny scales will thread
The drifting cordage of the shattered wreck,
And honey-coloured amber beads our twining limbs will deck.'

But when that baffled Lord of War the Sun
   With gaudy pennon flying passed away
Into his brazen House, and one by one
   The little yellow stars began to stray
Across the field of heaven, ah! then indeed
She feared his lips upon her lips would never care to feed,

And cried, 'Awake, already the pale moon
   Washes the trees with silver, and the wave
Creeps grey and chilly up this sandy dune,
   The croaking frogs are out, and from the cave
The nightjar shrieks, the fluttering bats repass,
And the brown stoat with hollow flanks creeps through the dusky grass.

Nay, though thou art a god, be not so coy,

For in yon stream there is a little reed

That often whispers how a lovely boy

   Lay with her once upon a grassy mead,

Who when his cruel pleasure he had done

Spread wings of rustling gold and soared aloft into the sun.

Be not so coy, the laurel trembles still

   With great Apollo's kisses, and the fir

Whose clustering sisters fringe the seaward hill

   Hath many a tale of that bold ravisher

Whom men call Boreas, and I have seen

The mocking eyes of Hermes through the poplar's silvery sheen.

Even the jealous Naiads call me fair,

   And every morn a young and ruddy swain

Woos me with apples and with locks of hair,

   And seeks to soothe my virginal disdain

By all the gifts the gentle wood-nymphs love;

But yesterday he brought to me an iris-plumaged dove

With little crimson feet, which with its store

   Of seven spotted eggs the cruel lad

Had stolen from the lofty sycamore

At daybreak, when her amorous comrade had

Flown off in search of berried juniper

Which most they love; the fretful wasp, that earliest vintager

Of the blue grapes, hath not persistency

So constant as this simple shepherd-boy

For my poor lips, his joyous purity

And laughing sunny eyes might well decoy

A Dryad from her oath to Artemis;

For very beautiful is he, his mouth was made to kiss;

His argent forehead, like a rising moon

Over the dusky hills of meeting brows,

Is crescent shaped, the hot and Tyrian noon

Leads from the myrtle-grove no goodlier spouse

For Cytheræa, the first silky down

Fringes his blushing cheeks, and his young limbs are strong and brown;

And he is rich, and fat and fleecy herds

Of bleating sheep upon his meadows lie,

And many an earthen bowl of yellow curds

Is in his homestead for the thievish fly

To swim and drown in, the pink clover mead

Keeps its sweet store for him, and he can pipe on oaten reed.

And yet I love him not; it was for thee

I kept my love; I knew that thou would'st come

To rid me of this pallid chastity,

Thou fairest flower of the flowerless foam

Of all the wide Ægean, brightest star

Of ocean's azure heavens where the mirrored planets are!

I knew that thou would'st come, for when at first

The dry wood burgeoned, and the sap of spring

Swelled in my green and tender bark or burst

To myriad multitudinous blossoming

Which mocked the midnight with its mimic moons

That did not dread the dawn, and first the thrushes' rapturous tunes

Startled the squirrel from its granary,

And cuckoo flowers fringed the narrow lane,

Through my young leaves a sensuous ecstasy

Crept like new wine, and every mossy vein

Throbbed with the fitful pulse of amorous blood,

And the wild winds of passion shook my slim stem's maidenhood.

The trooping fawns at evening came and laid

Their cool black noses on my lowest boughs,

And on my topmost branch the blackbird made

  A little nest of grasses for his spouse,

And now and then a twittering wren would light

On a thin twig which hardly bare the weight of such delight.

I was the Attic shepherd's trysting place,

  Beneath my shadow Amaryllis lay,

And round my trunk would laughing Daphnis chase

  The timorous girl, till tired out with play

She felt his hot breath stir her tangled hair,

And turned, and looked, and fled no more from such delightful snare.

Then come away unto my ambuscade

  Where clustering woodbine weaves a canopy

For amorous pleasaunce, and the rustling shade

  Of Paphian myrtles seems to sanctify

The dearest rites of love; there in the cool

And green recesses of its farthest depth there is pool,

The ouzel's haunt, the wild bee's pasturage,

  For round its rim great creamy lilies float

Through their flat leaves in verdant anchorage,

Each cup a white-sailed golden-laden boat

Steered by a dragon-fly,—be not afraid

To leave this wan and wave-kissed shore, surely the place was made

For lovers such as we; the Cyprian Queen,

   One arm around her boyish paramour,

Strays often there at eve, and I have seen

   The moon strip off her misty vestiture

For young Endymion's eyes; be not afraid,

The panther feet of Dian never tread that secret glade.

Nay if thou will'st, back to the beating brine,

   Back to the boisterous billow let us go,

And walk all day beneath the hyaline

   Huge vault of Neptune's watery portico,

And watch the purple monsters of the deep

Sport in ungainly play, and from his lair keen Xiphias leap.

For if my mistress find me lying here

   She will not ruth or gentle pity show,

But lay her boar-spear down, and with austere

   Relentless fingers string the cornel bow,

And draw the feathered notch against her breast,

And loose the archèd cord; aye, even now upon the quest

I hear her hurrying feet,—awake, awake,

Thou laggard in love's battle! once at least

Let me drink deep of passion's wine, and slake

My parchèd being with the nectarous feast

Which even gods affect! O come, Love, come,

Still we have time to reach the cavern of thine azure home.'

Scarce had she spoken when the shuddering trees

Shook, and the leaves divided, and the air

Grew conscious of a god, and the grey seas

Crawled backward, and a long and dismal blare

Blew from some tasselled horn, a sleuth-hound bayed,

And like a flame a barbèd reed flew whizzing down the glade.

And where the little flowers of her breast

Just brake into their milky blossoming,

This murderous paramour, this unbidden guest,

Pierced and struck deep in horrid chambering,

And ploughed a bloody furrow with its dart,

And dug a long red road, and cleft with wingèd death her heart.

Sobbing her life out with a bitter cry

On the boy's body fell the Dryad maid,

Sobbing for incomplete virginity,

   And raptures unenjoyed, and pleasures dead,

And all the pain of things unsatisfied,

And the bright drops of crimson youth crept down her throbbing side.

Ah! pitiful it was to hear her moan,

   And very pitiful to see her die

Ere she had yielded up her sweets, or known

   The joy of passion, that dread mystery

Which not to know is not to live at all,

And yet to know is to be held in death's most deadly thrall.

But as it hapt the Queen of Cythere,

   Who with Adonis all night long had lain

Within some shepherd's hut in Arcady,

   On team of silver doves and gilded wain

Was journeying Paphos-ward, high up afar

From mortal ken between the mountains and the morning star,

And when low down she spied the hapless pair,

   And heard the Oread's faint despairing cry,

Whose cadence seemed to play upon the air

As though it were a viol, hastily

She bade her pigeons fold each straining plume,

And dropt to earth, and reached the strand, and saw their dolorous doom.

For as a gardener turning back his head

    To catch the last notes of the linnet, mows

With careless scythe too near some flower bed,

    And cuts the thorny pillar of the rose,

And with the flower's loosened loneliness

Strews the brown mould; or as some shepherd lad in wantonness

Driving his little flock along the mead

    Treads down two daffodils, which side by aide

Have lured the lady-bird with yellow brede

    And made the gaudy moth forget its pride,

Treads down their brimming golden chalices

Under light feet which were not made for such rude ravages;

Or as a schoolboy tired of his book

    Flings himself down upon the reedy grass

And plucks two water-lilies from the brook,

    And for a time forgets the hour glass,

Then wearies of their sweets, and goes his way,

And lets the hot sun kill them, even go these lovers lay.

And Venus cried, 'It is dread Artemis

  Whose bitter hand hath wrought this cruelty,

Or else that mightier maid whose care it is

  To guard her strong and stainless majesty

Upon the hill Athenian,—alas!

That they who loved so well unloved into Death's house should pass.'

So with soft hands she laid the boy and girl

  In the great golden waggon tenderly

(Her white throat whiter than a moony pearl

  Just threaded with a blue vein's tapestry

Had not yet ceased to throb, and still her breast

Swayed like a wind-stirred lily in ambiguous unrest)

And then each pigeon spread its milky van,

  The bright car soared into the dawning sky,

And like a cloud the aerial caravan

  Passed over the Ægean silently,

Till the faint air was troubled with the song

From the wan mouths that call on bleeding Thammuz all night long.

But when the doves had reached their wonted goal

Where the wide stair of orbèd marble dips

Its snows into the sea, her fluttering soul

   Just shook the trembling petals of her lips

And passed into the void, and Venus knew

That one fair maid the less would walk amid her retinue,

And bade her servants carve a cedar chest

   With all the wonder of this history,

Within whose scented womb their limbs should rest

   Where olive-trees make tender the blue sky

On the low hills of Paphos, and the Faun

Pipes in the noonday, and the nightingale sings on till dawn.

Nor failed they to obey her hest, and ere

   The morning bee had stung the daffodil

With tiny fretful spear, or from its lair

   The waking stag had leapt across the rill

And roused the ouzel, or the lizard crept

Athwart the sunny rock, beneath the grass their bodies slept.

And when day brake, within that silver shrine

   Fed by the flames of cressets tremulous,

Queen Venus knelt and prayed to Proserpine

That she whose beauty made Death amorous

Should beg a guerdon from her pallid Lord,

And let Desire pass across dread Charon's icy ford.

III

In melancholy moonless Acheron,

   Farm for the goodly earth and joyous day

Where no spring ever buds, nor ripening sun

   Weighs down the apple trees, nor flowery May

Chequers with chestnut blooms the grassy floor,

Where thrushes never sing, and piping linnets mate no more,

There by a dim and dark Lethæan well

   Young Charmides was lying; wearily

He plucked the blossoms from the asphodel,

   And with its little rifled treasury

Strewed the dull waters of the dusky stream,

And watched the white stars founder, and the land was like a dream,

When as he gazed into the watery glass

   And through his brown hair's curly tangles scanned

His own wan face, a shadow seemed to pass

   Across the mirror, and a little hand

271

Stole into his, and warm lips timidly

Brushed his pale cheeks, and breathed their secret forth into a sigh.

Then turned he round his weary eyes and saw,

　And ever nigher still their faces came,

And nigher ever did their young mouths draw

　Until they seemed one perfect rose of flame,

And longing arms around her neck he cast,

And felt her throbbing bosom, and his breath came hot and fast,

And all his hoarded sweets were hers to kiss,

　And all her maidenhood was his to slay,

And limb to limb in long and rapturous bliss

　Their passion waxed and waned,—O why essay

To pipe again of love, too venturous reed!

Enough, enough that Eros laughed upon that flowerless mead.

Too venturous poesy, O why essay

　To pipe again of passion! fold thy wings

O'er daring Icarus and bid thy lay

　Sleep hidden in the lyre's silent strings

Till thou hast found the old Castalian rill,

　Or from the Lesbian waters plucked drowned Sappho's golden quid!

Enough, enough that he whose life had been

   A fiery pulse of sin, a splendid shame,

Could in the loveless land of Hades glean

   One scorching harvest from those fields of flame

Where passion walks with naked unshod feet

And is not wounded,—ah! enough that once their lips could meet

In that wild throb when all existences

   Seemed narrowed to one single ecstasy

Which dies through its own sweetness and the stress

   Of too much pleasure, ere Persephone

Had bade them serve her by the ebon throne

Of the pale God who in the fields of Enna loosed her zone.

FLOWERS OF GOLD

IMPRESSIONS

I

LES SILHOUETTES

The sea is flecked with bars of grey,
The dull dead wind is out of tune,
And like a withered leaf the moon
Is blown across the stormy bay.

Etched clear upon the pallid sand
Lies the black boat: a sailor boy
Clambers aboard in careless joy
With laughing face and gleaming hand.

And overhead the curlews cry,
Where through the dusky upland grass
The young brown-throated reapers pass,
Like silhouettes against the sky.

II

LA FUITE DE LA LUNE

To outer senses there is peace,

A dreamy peace on either hand

Deep silence in the shadowy land,

Deep silence where the shadows cease.

Save for a cry that echoes shrill

From some lone bird disconsolate;

A corncrake calling to its mate;

The answer from the misty hill.

And suddenly the moon withdraws

Her sickle from the lightening skies,

And to her sombre cavern flies,

Wrapped in a veil of yellow gauze.

THE GRAVE OF KEATS

Rid of the world's injustice, and his pain,

He rests at last beneath God's veil of blue:

Taken from life when life and love were new

The youngest of the martyrs here is lain,

Fair as Sebastian, and as early slain.

No cypress shades his grave, no funeral yew,

But gentle violets weeping with the dew

Weave on his bones an ever-blossoming chain.

O proudest heart that broke for misery!

O sweetest lips since those of Mitylene!

O poet-painter of our English Land!

Thy name was writ in water—it shall stand:

And tears like mine will keep thy memory green,

As Isabella did her Basil-tree.

ROME.

THEOCRITUS:A VILLANELLE

O singer of Persephone!

In the dim meadows desolate

Dost thou remember Sicily?

Still through the ivy flits the bee

Where Amaryllis lies in state;

O Singer of Persephone!

Simætha calls on Hecate

And hears the wild dogs at the gate;

Dost thou remember Sicily?

Still by the light and laughing sea

Poor Polypheme bemoans his fate;

O Singer of Persephone!

And still in boyish rivalry
  Young Daphnis challenges his mate;
Dost thou remember Sicily?

Slim Lacon keeps a goat for thee,
  For thee the jocund shepherds wait;
O Singer of Persephone!
Dost thou remember Sicily?

IN THE GOLD ROOM: A HARMONY

Her ivory hands on the ivory keys
  Strayed in a fitful fantasy,
Like the silver gleam when the poplar trees
  Rustle their pale-leaves listlessly,
Or the drifting foam of a restless sea
When the waves show their teeth in the flying breeze.

Her gold hair fell on the wall of gold
  Like the delicate gossamer tangles spun
On the burnished disk of the marigold,
  Or the sunflower turning to meet the sun

When the gloom of the dark blue night is done,

And the spear of the lily is aureoled.

And her sweet red lips on these lips of mine

    Burned like the ruby fire set

In the swinging lamp of a crimson shrine,

    Or the bleeding wounds of the pomegranate,

    Or the heart of the lotus drenched and wet

With the spilt-out blood of the rose-red wine.

BALLADE DE MARGUERITE

(NORMANDE)

I am weary of lying within the chase

When the knights are meeting in market-place.

Nay, go not thou to the red-roofed town

Lest the hoofs of the war-horse tread thee down.

But I would not go where the Squires ride,

I would only walk by my Lady's side.

Alack! and alack! thou art overbold,

A Forester's son may not eat off gold.

Will she love me the less that my Father is seen

Each Martinmas day in a doublet green?

Perchance she is sewing at tapestrie,

Spindle and loom are not meet for thee.

Ah, if she is working the arras bright

I might ravel the threads by the fire-light.

Perchance she is hunting of the deer,

How could you follow o'er hill and mere?

Ah, if she is riding with the court,

I might run beside her and wind the morte.

Perchance she is kneeling in St. Denys,

(On her soul may our Lady have gramercy!)

Ah, if she is praying in lone chapelle,

I might swing the censer and ring the bell.

Come in, my son, for you look sae pale,

The father shall fill thee a stoup of ale.

But who are these knights in bright array?

Is it a pageant the rich folks play?

'T is the King of England from over sea,

Who has come unto visit our fair countrie.

But why does the curfew toll sae low?

And why do the mourners walk a-row?

O 't is Hugh of Amiens my sister's son

Who is lying stark, for his day is done.

Nay, nay, for I see white lilies clear,

It is no strong man who lies on the bier.

O 't is old Dame Jeannette that kept the hall,

I knew she would die at the autumn fall.

Dame Jeannette had not that gold-brown hair,

Old Jeannette was not a maiden fair.

O 't is none of our kith and none of our kin,

(Her soul may our Lady assoil from sin!)

But I hear the boy's voice chaunting sweet,

'Elle est morte, la Marguerite.'

Come in, my son, and lie on the bed,

And let the dead folk bury their dead.

O mother, you know I loved her true:

O mother, hath one grave room for two?

THE DOLE OF THE KING'S DAUGHTER

(BRETON)

Seven stars in the still water,

  And seven in the sky;

Seven sins on the King's daughter,

  Deep in her soul to lie.

Red roses are at her feet,

  (Roses are red in her red-gold hair)

And O where her bosom and girdle meet

  Red roses are hidden there.

Fair is the knight who lieth slain

Amid the rush and reed,

See the lean fishes that are fain

Upon dead men to feed.

Sweet is the page that lieth there,

(Cloth of gold is goodly prey,)

See the black ravens in the air,

Black, O black as the night are they.

What do they there so stark and dead?

(There is blood upon her hand)

Why are the lilies flecked with red?

(There is blood on the river sand.)

There are two that ride from the south and east,

And two from the north and west,

For the black raven a goodly feast,

For the King's daughter rest.

There is one man who loves her true,

(Red, O red, is the stain of gore!)

He hath duggen a grave by the darksome yew,

(One grave will do for four.)

No moon in the still heaven,

In the black water none,

The sins on her soul are seven,

The sin upon his is one.

AMOR INTELLECTUALIS

Oft have we trod the vales of Castaly

And heard sweet notes of sylvan music blown

From antique reeds to common folk unknown:

And often launched our bark upon that sea

Which the nine Muses hold in empery,

And ploughed free furrows through the wave and foam,

Nor spread reluctant sail for more safe home

Till we had freighted well our argosy.

Of which despoilèd treasures these remain,

Sordello's passion, and the honeyed line

Of young Endymion, lordly Tamburlaine

Driving his pampered jades, and more than these,

The seven-fold vision of the Florentine,

And grave-browed Milton's solemn harmonies.

SANTA DECCA

The Gods are dead: no longer do we bring

To grey-eyed Pallas crowns of olive-leaves!

Demeter's child no more hath tithe of sheaves,

And in the noon the careless shepherds sing,

For Pan is dead, and all the wantoning

By secret glade and devious haunt is o'er:

Young Hylas seeks the water-springs no more;

Great Pan is dead, and Mary's son is King.

And yet—perchance in this sea-trancèd isle,

Chewing the bitter fruit of memory,

Some God lies hidden in the asphodel.

Ah Love! if such there be, then it were well

For us to fly his anger: nay, but see,

The leaves are stirring: let us watch awhile.

CORFU.

A VISION

Two crownèd Kings, and One that stood alone

With no green weight of laurels round his head,

But with sad eyes as one uncomforted,

And wearied with man's never-ceasing moan

For sins no bleating victim can atone,

And sweet long lips with tears and kisses fed.

Girt was he in a garment black and red,

And at his feet I marked a broken stone

Which sent up lilies, dove-like, to his knees.

Now at their sight, my heart being lit with flame,

I cried to Beatricé, 'Who are these?'

And she made answer, knowing well each name,

'Æschylos first, the second Sophokles,

And last (wide stream of tears!) Euripides.'

IMPRESSION DE VOYAGE

The sea was sapphire coloured, and the sky

Burned like a heated opal through the air;

We hoisted sail; the wind was blowing fair

For the blue lands that to the eastward lie.

From the steep prow I marked with quickening eye

Zakynthos, every olive grove and creek,

Ithaca's cliff, Lycaon's snowy peak,

And all the flower-strewn hills of Arcady.

The flapping of the sail against the mast,

The ripple of the water on the side,

The ripple of girls' laughter at the stern,

The only sounds:—when 'gan the West to burn,

And a red sun upon the seas to ride,

I stood upon the soil of Greece at last!

285

KATAKOLO.

THE GRAVE OF SHELLEY

Like burnt-out torches by a sick man's bed

    Gaunt cypress-trees stand round the sun-bleached stone;

    Here doth the little night-owl make her throne,

And the slight lizard show his jewelled head.

And, where the chaliced poppies flame to red,

    In the still chamber of yon pyramid

    Surely some Old-World Sphinx lurks darkly hid,

Grim warder of this pleasaunce of the dead.

Ah! sweet indeed to rest within the womb

    Of Earth, great mother of eternal sleep,

But sweeter far for thee a restless tomb

    In the blue cavern of an echoing deep,

Or where the tall ships founder in the gloom

    Against the rocks of some wave-shattered steep.

ROME.

BY THE ARNO

The oleander on the wall

Grows crimson in the dawning light,

Though the grey shadows of the night

Lie yet on Florence like a pall.

The dew is bright upon the hill,

And bright the blossoms overhead,

But ah! the grasshoppers have fled,

The little Attic song is still.

Only the leaves are gently stirred

By the soft breathing of the gale,

And in the almond-scented vale

The lonely nightingale is heard.

The day will make thee silent soon,

O nightingale sing on for love!

While yet upon the shadowy grove

Splinter the arrows of the moon.

Before across the silent lawn

In sea-green vest the morning steals,

And to love's frightened eyes reveals

The long white fingers of the dawn

Fast climbing up the eastern sky

To grasp and slay the shuddering night,

All careless of my heart's delight,

Or if the nightingale should die.

IMPRESSIONS DE THÉÂTRE

FABIEN DEI FRANCHI

To my Friend Henry Irving

The silent room, the heavy creeping shade,
  The dead that travel fast, the opening door,
  The murdered brother rising through the floor,
The ghost's white fingers on thy shoulders laid,
And then the lonely duel in the glade,
  The broken swords, the stifled scream, the gore,
  Thy grand revengeful eyes when all is o'er,—
These things are well enough,—but thou wert made
  For more august creation! frenzied Lear
  Should at thy bidding wander on the heath
  With the shrill fool to mock him, Romeo
For thee should lure his love, and desperate fear
Pluck Richard's recreant dagger from its sheath—
Thou trumpet set for Shakespeare's lips to blow!

PHÈDRE

To Sarah Bernhardt

How vain and dull this common world must seem

   To such a One as thou, who should'st have talked

At Florence with Mirandola, or walked

Through the cool olives of the Academe:

Thou should'st have gathered reeds from a green stream

   For Goat-foot Pan's shrill piping, and have played

   With the white girls in that Phæacian glade

Where grave Odysseus wakened from his dream.

Ah! surely once some urn of Attic clay

   Held thy wan dust, and thou hast come again

   Back to this common world so dull and vain,

For thou wert weary of the sunless day,

   The heavy fields of scentless asphodel,

   The loveless lips with which men kiss in Hell.

SONNETS WRITTEN AT THE LYCEUM THEATRE

I. PORTIA

To Ellen Terry

I marvel not Bassanio was so bold

   To peril all he had upon the lead,

Or that proud Aragon bent low his head

Or that Morocco's fiery heart grew cold:

For in that gorgeous dress of beaten gold

  Which is more golden than the golden sun

  No woman Veronesé looked upon

Was half so fair as thou whom I behold.

Yet fairer when with wisdom as your shield

  The sober-suited lawyer's gown you donned,

And would not let the laws of Venice yield

  Antonio's heart to that accursèd Jew—

  O Portia! take my heart: it is thy due:

I think I will not quarrel with the Bond.

II. QUEEN HENRIETTA MARIA

To Ellen Terry

In the lone tent, waiting for victory,

  She stands with eyes marred by the mists of pain,

  Like some wan lily overdrenched with rain:

The clamorous clang of arms, the ensanguined sky,

War's ruin, and the wreck of chivalry

  To her proud soul no common fear can bring:

  Bravely she tarrieth for her Lord the King,

Her soul a-flame with passionate ecstasy.

O Hair of Gold! O Crimson Lips! O Face

Made for the luring and the love of man!

With thee I do forget the toil and stress,

The loveless road that knows no resting place,

Time's straitened pulse, the soul's dread weariness,

My freedom, and my life republican!

III. CAMMA

To Ellen Terry

As one who poring on a Grecian urn

Scans the fair shapes some Attic hand hath made,

God with slim goddess, goodly man with maid,

And for their beauty's sake is loth to turn

And face the obvious day, must I not yearn

For many a secret moon of indolent bliss,

When in midmost shrine of Artemis

I see thee standing, antique-limbed, and stern?

And yet—methinks I'd rather see thee play

That serpent of old Nile, whose witchery

Made Emperors drunken,—come, great Egypt, shake

Our stage with all thy mimic pageants! Nay,

I am grown sick of unreal passions, make

The world thine Actium, me thine Anthony!

PANTHEA

Nay, let us walk from fire unto fire,

   From passionate pain to deadlier delight,—

I am too young to live without desire,

   Too young art thou to waste this summer night

Asking those idle questions which of old

Man sought of seer and oracle, and no reply was told.

For, sweet, to feel is better than to know,

   And wisdom is a childless heritage,

One pulse of passion—youth's first fiery glow,—

   Are worth the hoarded proverbs of the sage:

Vex not thy soul with dead philosophy,

Have we not lips to kiss with, hearts to love and eyes to see!

Dost thou not hear the murmuring nightingale,

   Like water bubbling from a silver jar,

So soft she sings the envious moon is pale,

   That high in heaven she is hung so far

She cannot hear that love-enraptured tune,—

   Mark how she wreathes each horn with mist, yon late and labouring moon.

White lilies, in whose cups the gold bees dream,

    The fallen snow of petals where the breeze

Scatters the chestnut blossom, or the gleam

    Of boyish limbs in water,—are not these

Enough for thee, dost thou desire more?

Alas! the Gods will give nought else from their eternal store.

For our high Gods have sick and wearied grown

    Of all our endless sins, our vain endeavour

For wasted days of youth to make atone

    By pain or prayer or priest, and never, never,

Hearken they now to either good or ill,

But send their rain upon the just and the unjust at will.

They sit at ease, our Gods they sit at ease,

    Strewing with leaves of rose their scented wine,

They sleep, they sleep, beneath the rocking trees

    Where asphodel and yellow lotus twine,

Mourning the old glad days before they knew

What evil things the heart of man could dream, and dreaming do.

And far beneath the brazen floor they see

Like swarming flies the crowd of little men,

The bustle of small lives, then wearily

Back to their lotus-haunts they turn again

Kissing each others' mouths, and mix more deep

The poppy-seeded draught which brings soft purple-lidded sleep.

There all day long the golden-vestured sun,

Their torch-bearer, stands with his torch ablaze,

And, when the gaudy web of noon is spun

By its twelve maidens, through the crimson haze

Fresh from Endymion's arms comes forth the moon,

And the immortal Gods in toils of mortal passions swoon.

There walks Queen Juno through some dewy mead,

Her grand white feet flecked with the saffron dust

Of wind-stirred lilies, while young Ganymede

Leaps in the hot and amber-foaming must,

His curls all tossed, as when the eagle bare

The frightened boy from Ida through the blue Ionian air.

There in the green heart of some garden close

Queen Venus with the shepherd at her side,

Her warm soft body like the briar rose

Which would be white yet blushes at its pride,

Laughs low for love, till jealous Salmacis

Peers through the myrtle-leaves and sighs for pain of lonely bliss.

There never does that dreary north-wind blow

    Which leaves our English forests bleak and bare,

Nor ever falls the swift white-feathered snow,

    Nor ever doth the red-toothed lightning dare

To wake them in the silver-fretted night

When we lie weeping for some sweet sad sin, some dead delight.

Alas! they know the far Lethæan spring,

    The violet-hidden waters well they know,

Where one whose feet with tired wandering

    Are faint and broken may take heart and go,

And from those dark depths cool and crystalline

Drink, and draw balm, and sleep for sleepless souls, and anodyne.

But we oppress our natures, God or Fate

    Is our enemy, we starve and feed

On vain repentance—O we are born too late!

    What balm for us in bruisèd poppy seed

Who crowd into one finite pulse of time

The joy of infinite love and the fierce pain of infinite crime.

O we are wearied of this sense of guilt,

   Wearied of pleasure's paramour despair,

Wearied of every temple we have built,

   Wearied of every right, unanswered prayer,

For man is weak; God sleeps: and heaven is high:

One fiery-coloured moment: one great love; and lo! we die.

Ah! but no ferry-man with labouring pole

   Nears his black shallop to the flowerless strand,

No little coin of bronze can bring the soul

   Over Death's river to the sunless land,

Victim and wine and vow are all in vain,

The tomb is sealed; the soldiers watch; the dead rise not again.

We are resolved into the supreme air,

   We are made one with what we touch and see,

With our heart's blood each crimson sun is fair,

   With our young lives each spring-impassioned tree

Flames into green, the wildest beasts that range

The moor our kinsmen are, all life is one, and all is change.

With beat of systole and of diastole

One grand great life throbs through earth's giant heart,

And mighty waves of single Being roll

 From nerveless germ to man, for we are part

Of every rock and bird and beast and hill,

One with the things that prey on us, and one with what we kill.

From lower cells of waking life we pass

 To full perfection; thus the world grows old:

We who are godlike now were once a mass

 Of quivering purple flecked with bars of gold,

Unsentient or of joy or misery,

And tossed in terrible tangles of some wild and wind-swept sea.

This hot hard flame with which our bodies burn

 Will make some meadow blaze with daffodil,

Ay! and those argent breasts of thine will turn

 To water-lilies; the brown fields men till

Will be more fruitful for our love to-night,

Nothing is lost in nature, all things live in Death's despite.

The boy's first kiss, the hyacinth's first bell,

 The man's last passion, and the last red spear

That from the lily leaps, the asphodel

Which will not let its blossoms blow for fear

Of too much beauty, and the timid shame

Of the young bridegroom at his lover's eyes,—these with the same

One sacrament are consecrate, the earth

   Not we alone hath passions hymeneal,

The yellow buttercups that shake for mirth

   At daybreak know a pleasure not less real

Than we do, when in some fresh-blossoming wood,

We draw the spring into our hearts, and feel that life is good.

So when men bury us beneath the yew

   Thy crimson-stainèd mouth a rose will be,

And thy soft eyes lush bluebells dimmed with dew,

   And when the white narcissus wantonly

Kisses the wind its playmate some faint joy

Will thrill our dust, and we will be again fond maid and boy.

And thus without life's conscious torturing pain

   In some sweet flower we will feel the sun,

And from the linnet's throat will sing again,

   And as two gorgeous-mailèd snakes will run

Over our graves, or as two tigers creep

Through the hot jungle where the yellow-eyed huge lions sleep

And give them battle! How my heart leaps up
  To think of that grand living after death
In beast and bird and flower, when this cup,
  Being filled too full of spirit, bursts for breath,
And with the pale leaves of some autumn day
The soul earth's earliest conqueror becomes earth's last great prey.

O think of it! We shall inform ourselves
  Into all sensuous life, the goat-foot Faun,
The Centaur, or the merry bright-eyed Elves
  That leave their dancing rings to spite the dawn
Upon the meadows, shall not be more near
Than you and I to nature's mysteries, for we shall hear

The thrush's heart beat, and the daisies grow,
  And the wan snowdrop sighing for the sun
On sunless days in winter, we shall know
  By whom the silver gossamer is spun,
Who paints the diapered fritillaries,
On what wide wings from shivering pine to pine the eagle flies.

Ay! had we never loved at all, who knows

301

If yonder daffodil had lured the bee

Into its gilded womb, or any rose

Had hung with crimson lamps its little tree!

Methinks no leaf would ever bud in spring,

But for the lovers' lips that kiss, the poets' lips that sing.

Is the light vanished from our golden sun,

Or is this dædal-fashioned earth less fair,

That we are nature's heritors, and one

With every pulse of life that beats the air?

Rather new suns across the sky shall pass,

New splendour come unto the flower, new glory to the grass.

And we two lovers shall not sit afar,

Critics of nature, but the joyous sea

Shall be our raiment, and the bearded star

Shoot arrows at our pleasure! We shall be

Part of the mighty universal whole,

And through all æons mix and mingle with the Kosmic Soul!

We shall be notes in that great Symphony

Whose cadence circles through the rhythmic spheres,

And all the live World's throbbing heart shall be

One with our heart; the stealthy creeping years

Have lost their terrors now, we shall not die,

The Universe itself shall be our Immortality.

THE FOURTH MOVEMENT

IMPRESSION: LE RÉVEILLON

The sky is laced with fitful red,

The circling mists and shadows flee,

The dawn is rising from the sea,

Like a white lady from her bed.

And jagged brazen arrows fall

Athwart the feathers of the night,

And a long wave of yellow light

Breaks silently on tower and hall,

And spreading wide across the wold

Wakes into flight some fluttering bird,

And all the chestnut tops are stirred,

And all the branches streaked with gold.

AT VERONA

How steep the stairs within Kings' houses are

For exile-wearied feet as mine to tread,

And O how salt and bitter is the bread

Which falls from this Hound's table,—better far

That I had died in the red ways of war,

Or that the gate of Florence bare my head,

Than to live thus, by all things comraded

Which seek the essence of my soul to mar.

'Curse God and die: what better hope than this?

He hath forgotten thee in all the bliss

Of his gold city, and eternal day'—

Nay peace: behind my prison's blinded bars

I do possess what none can take away

My love, and all the glory of the stars.

APOLOGIA

Is it thy will that I should wax and wane,

Barter my cloth of gold for hodden grey,

And at thy pleasure weave that web of pain

Whose brightest threads are each a wasted day?

Is it thy will—Love that I love so well—

That my Soul's House should be a tortured spot

Wherein, like evil paramours, must dwell

The quenchless flame, the worm that dieth not?

Nay, if it be thy will I shall endure,

    And sell ambition at the common mart,

And let dull failure be my vestiture,

    And sorrow dig its grave within my heart.

Perchance it may be better so—at least

    I have not made my heart a heart of stone,

Nor starved my boyhood of its goodly feast,

    Nor walked where Beauty is a thing unknown.

Many a man hath done so; sought to fence

    In straitened bonds the soul that should be free,

Trodden the dusty road of common sense,

    While all the forest sang of liberty,

Not marking how the spotted hawk in flight

    Passed on wide pinion through the lofty air,

To where some steep untrodden mountain height

    Caught the last tresses of the Sun God's hair.

Or how the little flower he trod upon,

    The daisy, that white-feathered shield of gold,

Followed with wistful eyes the wandering sun

Content if once its leaves were aureoled.

But surely it is something to have been

The best belovèd for a little while,

To have walked hand in hand with Love, and seen

His purple wings flit once across thy smile.

Ay! though the gorgèd asp of passion feed

On my boy's heart, yet have I burst the bars,

Stood face to face with Beauty, known indeed

The Love which moves the Sun and all the stars!

QUIA MULTUM AMAVI

Dear Heart, I think the young impassioned priest

When first he takes from out the hidden shrine

His God imprisoned in the Eucharist,

And eats the bread, and drinks the dreadful wine,

Feels not such awful wonder as I felt

When first my smitten eyes beat full on thee,

And all night long before thy feet I knelt

Till thou wert wearied of Idolatry.

Ah! hadst thou liked me less and loved me more,

Through all those summer days of joy and rain,

I had not now been sorrow's heritor,

Or stood a lackey in the House of Pain.

Yet, though remorse, youth's white-faced seneschal,

Tread on my heels with all his retinue,

I am most glad I loved thee—think of all

The suns that go to make one speedwell blue!

SILENTIUM AMORIS

As often-times the too resplendent sun

Hurries the pallid and reluctant moon

Back to her sombre cave, ere she hath won

A single ballad from the nightingale,

So doth thy Beauty make my lips to fail,

And all my sweetest singing out of tune.

And as at dawn across the level mead

On wings impetuous some wind will come,

And with its too harsh kisses break the reed

Which was its only instrument of song,

So my too stormy passions work me wrong,

And for excess of Love my Love is dumb.

But surely unto Thee mine eyes did show

  Why I am silent, and my lute unstrung;

Else it were better we should part, and go,

  Thou to some lips of sweeter melody,

  And I to nurse the barren memory

Of unkissed kisses, and songs never sung.

HER VOICE

The wild bee reels from bough to bough

  With his furry coat and his gauzy wing,

Now in a lily-cup, and now

  Setting a jacinth bell a-swing,

    In his wandering;

Sit closer love: it was here I trow

    I made that vow,

Swore that two lives should be like one

  As long as the sea-gull loved the sea,

As long as the sunflower sought the sun,—

  It shall be, I said, for eternity

    'Twixt you and me!

Dear friend, those times are over and done;

Love's web is spun.

Look upward where the poplar trees
Sway and sway in the summer air,
Here in the valley never a breeze
Scatters the thistledown, but there
Great winds blow fair
From the mighty murmuring mystical seas,
And the wave-lashed leas.

Look upward where the white gull screams,
What does it see that we do not see?
Is that a star? or the lamp that gleams
On some outward voyaging argosy,—
Ah! can it be
We have lived our lives in a land of dreams!
How sad it seems.

Sweet, there is nothing left to say
But this, that love is never lost,
Keen winter stabs the breasts of May
Whose crimson roses burst his frost,
Ships tempest-tossed

Will find a harbour in some bay,

    And so we may.

And there is nothing left to do

    But to kiss once again, and part,

Nay, there is nothing we should rue,

    I have my beauty,—you your Art,

        Nay, do not start,

One world was not enough for two

    Like me and you.

MY VOICE

Within this restless, hurried, modern world

    We took our hearts' full pleasure—You and I,

And now the white sails of our ship are furled,

    And spent the lading of our argosy.

Wherefore my cheeks before their time are wan,

    For very weeping is my gladness fled,

Sorrow has paled my young mouth's vermilion,

    And Ruin draws the curtains of my bed.

But all this crowded life has been to thee

    No more than lyre, or lute, or subtle spell

Of viols, or the music of the sea

That sleeps, a mimic echo, in the shell.

TÆDIUM VITÆ

To stab my youth with desperate knives, to wear

This paltry age's gaudy livery,

To let each base hand filch my treasury,

To mesh my soul within a woman's hair,

And be mere Fortune's lackeyed groom,—I swear

I love it not! these things are less to me

Than the thin foam that frets upon the sea,

Less than the thistledown of summer air

Which hath no seed: better to stand aloof

Far from these slanderous fools who mock my life

Knowing me not, better the lowliest roof

Fit for the meanest hind to sojourn in,

Than to go back to that hoarse cave of strife

Where my white soul first kissed the mouth of sin.

HUMANITAD

It is full winter now: the trees are bare,

   Save where the cattle huddle from the cold

Beneath the pine, for it doth never wear

   The autumn's gaudy livery whose gold

Her jealous brother pilfers, but is true

To the green doublet; bitter is the wind, as though it blew

From Saturn's cave; a few thin wisps of hay

   Lie on the sharp black hedges, where the wain

Dragged the sweet pillage of a summer's day

   From the low meadows up the narrow lane;

Upon the half-thawed snow the bleating sheep

Press close against the hurdles, and the shivering house-dogs creep

From the shut stable to the frozen stream

   And back again disconsolate, and miss

The bawling shepherds and the noisy team;

   And overhead in circling listlessness

The cawing rooks whirl round the frosted stack,

Or crowd the dripping boughs; and in the fen the ice-pools crack

Where the gaunt bittern stalks among the reeds

And flaps his wings, and stretches back his neck,

And hoots to see the moon; across the meads

Limps the poor frightened hare, a little speck;

And a stray seamew with its fretful cry

Flits like a sudden drift of snow against the dull grey sky.

Full winter: and the lusty goodman brings

His load of faggots from the chilly byre,

And stamps his feet upon the hearth, and flings

The sappy billets on the waning fire,

And laughs to see the sudden lightening scare

His children at their play, and yet,—the spring is in the air;

Already the slim crocus stirs the snow,

And soon yon blanchèd fields will bloom again

With nodding cowslips for some lad to mow,

For with the first warm kisses of the rain

The winter's icy sorrow breaks to tears,

And the brown thrushes mate, and with bright eyes the rabbit peers

From the dark warren where the fir-cones lie,

And treads one snowdrop under foot, and runs

Over the mossy knoll, and blackbirds fly

Across our path at evening, and the suns

Stay longer with us; ah! how good to see

Grass-girdled spring in all her joy of laughing greenery

Dance through the hedges till the early rose,

  (That sweet repentance of the thorny briar!)

Burst from its sheathèd emerald and disclose

  The little quivering disk of golden fire

Which the bees know so well, for with it come

Pale boy's-love, sops-in-wine, and daffadillies all in bloom.

Then up and down the field the sower goes,

  While close behind the laughing younker scares

With shrilly whoop the black and thievish crows,

  And then the chestnut-tree its glory wears,

And on the grass the creamy blossom falls

In odorous excess, and faint half-whispered madrigals

Steal from the bluebells' nodding carillons

  Each breezy morn, and then white jessamine,

That star of its own heaven, snap-dragons

  With lolling crimson tongues, and eglantine

In dusty velvets clad usurp the bed

And woodland empery, and when the lingering rose hath shed

Red leaf by leaf its folded panoply,
  And pansies closed their purple-lidded eyes,
Chrysanthemums from gilded argosy
  Unload their gaudy scentless merchandise,
And violets getting overbold withdraw
From their shy nooks, and scarlet berries dot the leafless haw.

O happy field! and O thrice happy tree!
  Soon will your queen in daisy-flowered smock
And crown of flower-de-luce trip down the lea,
  Soon will the lazy shepherds drive their flock
Back to the pasture by the pool, and soon
Through the green leaves will float the hum of murmuring bees at noon.

Soon will the glade be bright with bellamour,
  The flower which wantons love, and those sweet nuns
Vale-lilies in their snowy vestiture
  Will tell their beaded pearls, and carnations
With mitred dusky leaves will scent the wind,
And straggling traveller's-joy each hedge with yellow stars will bind.

Dear bride of Nature and most bounteous spring,

That canst give increase to the sweet-breath'd kine,

And to the kid its little horns, and bring

The soft and silky blossoms to the vine,

Where is that old nepenthe which of yore

Man got from poppy root and glossy-berried mandragore!

There was a time when any common bird

Could make me sing in unison, a time

When all the strings of boyish life were stirred

To quick response or more melodious rhyme

By every forest idyll;—do I change?

Or rather doth some evil thing through thy fair pleasaunce range?

Nay, nay, thou art the same: 'tis I who seek

To vex with sighs thy simple solitude,

And because fruitless tears bedew my cheek

Would have thee weep with me in brotherhood;

Fool! shall each wronged and restless spirit dare

To taint such wine with the salt poison of own despair!

Thou art the same: 'tis I whose wretched soul

Takes discontent to be its paramour,

And gives its kingdom to the rude control

Of what should be its servitor,—for sure

Wisdom is somewhere, though the stormy sea

Contain it not, and the huge deep answer ''Tis not in me.'

To burn with one clear flame, to stand erect

   In natural honour, not to bend the knee

In profitless prostrations whose effect

   Is by itself condemned, what alchemy

Can teach me this? what herb Medea brewed

Will bring the unexultant peace of essence not subdued?

The minor chord which ends the harmony,

   And for its answering brother waits in vain

Sobbing for incompleted melody,

   Dies a swan's death; but I the heir of pain,

A silent Memnon with blank lidless eyes,

Wait for the light and music of those suns which never rise.

The quenched-out torch, the lonely cypress-gloom,

   The little dust stored in the narrow urn,

The gentle XAIPE of the Attic tomb,—

   Were not these better far than to return

To my old fitful restless malady,

Or spend my days within the voiceless cave of misery?

Nay! for perchance that poppy-crownèd god

   Is like the watcher by a sick man's bed

Who talks of sleep but gives it not; his rod

   Hath lost its virtue, and, when all is said,

Death is too rude, too obvious a key

To solve one single secret in a life's philosophy.

And Love! that noble madness, whose august

   And inextinguishable might can slay

The soul with honeyed drugs,—alas! I must

   From such sweet ruin play the runaway,

Although too constant memory never can

Forget the archèd splendour of those brows Olympian

Which for a little season made my youth

   So soft a swoon of exquisite indolence

That all the chiding of more prudent Truth

   Seemed the thin voice of jealousy,—O hence

Thou huntress deadlier than Artemis!

Go seek some other quarry! for of thy too perilous bliss.

My lips have drunk enough,—no more, no more,—

Though Love himself should turn his gilded prow

Back to the troubled waters of this shore

   Where I am wrecked and stranded, even now

The chariot wheels of passion sweep too near,

Hence! Hence! I pass unto a life more barren, more austere.

More barren—ay, those arms will never lean

   Down through the trellised vines and draw my soul

In sweet reluctance through the tangled green;

   Some other head must wear that aureole,

For I am hers who loves not any man

Whose white and stainless bosom bears the sign Gorgonian.

Let Venus go and chuck her dainty page,

   And kiss his mouth, and toss his curly hair,

With net and spear and hunting equipage

   Let young Adonis to his tryst repair,

But me her fond and subtle-fashioned spell

Delights no more, though I could win her dearest citadel.

Ay, though I were that laughing shepherd boy

   Who from Mount Ida saw the little cloud

Pass over Tenedos and lofty Troy

And knew the coming of the Queen, and bowed

In wonder at her feet, not for the sake

Of a new Helen would I bid her hand the apple take.

Then rise supreme Athena argent-limbed!

　And, if my lips be musicless, inspire

At least my life: was not thy glory hymned

　By One who gave to thee his sword and lyre

Like Æschylos at well-fought Marathon,

And died to show that Milton's England still could bear a son!

And yet I cannot tread the Portico

　And live without desire, fear and pain,

Or nurture that wise calm which long ago

　The grave Athenian master taught to men,

Self-poised, self-centred, and self-comforted,

To watch the world's vain phantasies go by with unbowed head.

Alas! that serene brow, those eloquent lips,

　Those eyes that mirrored all eternity,

Rest in their own Colonos, an eclipse

　Hath come on Wisdom, and Mnemosyne

Is childless; in the night which she had made

For lofty secure flight Athena's owl itself hath strayed.

Nor much with Science do I care to climb,

    Although by strange and subtle witchery

She drew the moon from heaven: the Muse Time

    Unrolls her gorgeous-coloured tapestry

To no less eager eyes; often indeed

In the great epic of Polymnia's scroll I love to read

How Asia sent her myriad hosts to war

    Against a little town, and panoplied

In gilded mail with jewelled scimitar,

    White-shielded, purple-crested, rode the Mede

Between the waving poplars and the sea

Which men call Artemisium, till he saw Thermopylæ

Its steep ravine spanned by a narrow wall,

    And on the nearer side a little brood

Of careless lions holding festival!

    And stood amazèd at such hardihood,

And pitched his tent upon the reedy shore,

And stayed two days to wonder, and then crept at midnight o'er

Some unfrequented height, and coming down

The autumn forests treacherously slew

What Sparta held most dear and was the crown

   Of far Eurotas, and passed on, nor knew

How God had staked an evil net for him

In the small bay at Salamis,—and yet, the page grows dim,

Its cadenced Greek delights me not, I feel

   With such a goodly time too out of tune

To love it much: for like the Dial's wheel

   That from its blinded darkness strikes the noon

Yet never sees the sun, so do my eyes

Restlessly follow that which from my cheated vision flies.

O for one grand unselfish simple life

   To teach us what is Wisdom! speak ye hills

Of lone Helvellyn, for this note of strife

   Shunned your untroubled crags and crystal rills,

Where is that Spirit which living blamelessly

Yet dared to kiss the smitten mouth of his own century!

Speak ye Rydalian laurels! where is he

   Whose gentle head ye sheltered, that pure soul

Whose gracious days of uncrowned majesty

Through lowliest conduct touched the lofty goal

Where love and duty mingle! Him at least

The most high Laws were glad of, he had sat at Wisdom's feast;

But we are Learning's changelings, know by rote

   The clarion watchword of each Grecian school

And follow none, the flawless sword which smote

   The pagan Hydra is an effete tool

Which we ourselves have blunted, what man now

Shall scale the august ancient heights and to old Reverence bow?

One such indeed I saw, but, Ichabod!

   Gone is that last dear son of Italy,

Who being man died for the sake of God,

   And whose unrisen bones sleep peacefully,

O guard him, guard him well, my Giotto's tower,

Thou marble lily of the lily town! let not the lour

Of the rude tempest vex his slumber, or

   The Arno with its tawny troubled gold

O'er-leap its marge, no mightier conqueror

   Clomb the high Capitol in the days of old

When Rome was indeed Rome, for Liberty

Walked like a bride beside him, at which sight pale Mystery

Fled shrieking to her farthest sombrest cell

   With an old man who grabbled rusty keys,

Fled shuddering, for that immemorial knell

   With which oblivion buries dynasties

Swept like a wounded eagle on the blast,

As to the holy heart of Rome the great triumvir passed.

He knew the holiest heart and heights of Rome,

   He drave the base wolf from the lion's lair,

And now lies dead by that empyreal dome

   Which overtops Valdarno hung in air

By Brunelleschi—O Melpomene

Breathe through thy melancholy pipe thy sweetest threnody!

Breathe through the tragic stops such melodies

   That Joy's self may grow jealous, and the Nine

Forget awhile their discreet emperies,

   Mourning for him who on Rome's lordliest shrine

Lit for men's lives the light of Marathon,

And bare to sun-forgotten fields the fire of the sun!

O guard him, guard him well, my Giotto's tower!

Let some young Florentine each eventide

Bring coronals of that enchanted flower

Which the dim woods of Vallombrosa hide,

And deck the marble tomb wherein he lies

Whose soul is as some mighty orb unseen of mortal eyes;

Some mighty orb whose cycled wanderings,

Being tempest-driven to the farthest rim

Where Chaos meets Creation and the wings

Of the eternal chanting Cherubim

Are pavilioned on Nothing, passed away

Into a moonless void,—and yet, though he is dust and clay,

He is not dead, the immemorial Fates

Forbid it, and the closing shears refrain.

Lift up your heads ye everlasting gates!

Ye argent clarions, sound a loftier strain

For the vile thing he hated lurks within

Its sombre house, alone with God and memories of sin.

Still what avails it that she sought her cave

That murderous mother of red harlotries?

At Munich on the marble architrave

    The Grecian boys die smiling, but the seas

Which wash Ægina fret in loneliness

Not mirroring their beauty; so our lives grow colourless

For lack of our ideals, if one star

    Flame torch-like in the heavens the unjust

Swift daylight kills it, and no trump of war

    Can wake to passionate voice the silent dust

Which was Mazzini once! rich Niobe

For all her stony sorrows hath her sons; but Italy,

What Easter Day shall make her children rise,

    Who were not Gods yet suffered? what sure feet

Shall find their grave-clothes folded? what clear eyes

    Shall see them bodily? O it were meet

To roll the stone from off the sepulchre

And kiss the bleeding roses of their wounds, in love of her,

Our Italy! our mother visible!

    Most blessed among nations and most sad,

For whose dear sake the young Calabrian fell

    That day at Aspromonte and was glad

That in an age when God was bought and sold

One man could die for Liberty! but we, burnt out and cold,

See Honour smitten on the cheek and gyves

   Bind the sweet feet of Mercy: Poverty

Creeps through our sunless lanes and with sharp knives

   Cuts the warm throats of children stealthily,

And no word said:—O we are wretched men

Unworthy of our great inheritance! where is the pen

Of austere Milton? where the mighty sword

   Which slew its master righteously? the years

Have lost their ancient leader, and no word

   Breaks from the voiceless tripod on our ears:

While as a ruined mother in some spasm

Bears a base child and loathes it, so our best enthusiasm

Genders unlawful children, Anarchy

   Freedom's own Judas, the vile prodigal

Licence who steals the gold of Liberty

   And yet has nothing, Ignorance the real

One Fraticide since Cain, Envy the asp

That stings itself to anguish, Avarice whose palsied grasp

Is in its extent stiffened, moneyed Greed

For whose dull appetite men waste away

Amid the whirr of wheels and are the seed

Of things which slay their sower, these each day

Sees rife in England, and the gentle feet

Of Beauty tread no more the stones of each unlovely street.

What even Cromwell spared is desecrated

By weed and worm, left to the stormy play

Of wind and beating snow, or renovated

By more destructful hands: Time's worst decay

Will wreathe its ruins with some loveliness,

But these new Vandals can but make a rain-proof barrenness.

Where is that Art which bade the Angels sing

Through Lincoln's lofty choir, till the air

Seems from such marble harmonies to ring

With sweeter song than common lips can dare

To draw from actual reed? ah! where is now

The cunning hand which made the flowering hawthorn branches bow

For Southwell's arch, and carved the House of One

Who loved the lilies of the field with all

Our dearest English flowers? the same sun

Rises for us: the seasons natural

Weave the same tapestry of green and grey:

The unchanged hills are with us: but that Spirit hath passed away.

And yet perchance it may be better so,

For Tyranny is an incestuous Queen,

Murder her brother is her bedfellow,

And the Plague chambers with her: in obscene

And bloody paths her treacherous feet are set;

Better the empty desert and a soul inviolate!

For gentle brotherhood, the harmony

Of living in the healthful air, the swift

Clean beauty of strong limbs when men are free

And women chaste, these are the things which lift

Our souls up more than even Agnolo's

Gaunt blinded Sibyl poring o'er the scroll of human woes,

Or Titian's little maiden on the stair

White as her own sweet lily and as tall,

Or Mona Lisa smiling through her hair,—

Ah! somehow life is bigger after all

Than any painted angel, could we see

The God that is within us! The old Greek serenity

Which curbs the passion of that level line

   Of marble youths, who with untroubled eyes

And chastened limbs ride round Athena's shrine

   And mirror her divine economies,

And balanced symmetry of what in man

Would else wage ceaseless warfare,—this at least within the span

Between our mother's kisses and the grave

   Might so inform our lives, that we could win

Such mighty empires that from her cave

   Temptation would grow hoarse, and pallid Sin

Would walk ashamed of his adulteries,

And Passion creep from out the House of Lust with startled eyes.

To make the body and the spirit one

   With all right things, till no thing live in vain

From morn to noon, but in sweet unison

   With every pulse of flesh and throb of brain

The soul in flawless essence high enthroned,

Against all outer vain attack invincibly bastioned,

Mark with serene impartiality
   The strife of things, and yet be comforted,
Knowing that by the chain causality
   All separate existences are wed
Into one supreme whole, whose utterance
Is joy, or holier praise! ah! surely this were governance

Of Life in most august omnipresence,
   Through which the rational intellect would find
In passion its expression, and mere sense,
   Ignoble else, lend fire to the mind,
And being joined with it in harmony
More mystical than that which binds the stars planetary,

Strike from their several tones one octave chord
   Whose cadence being measureless would fly
Through all the circling spheres, then to its Lord
   Return refreshed with its new empery
And more exultant power,—this indeed
Could we but reach it were to find the last, the perfect creed.

Ah! it was easy when the world was young

To keep one's life free and inviolate,

From our sad lips another song is rung,

    By our own hands our heads are desecrate,

Wanderers in drear exile, and dispossessed

Of what should be our own, we can but feed on wild unrest.

Somehow the grace, the bloom of things has flown,

    And of all men we are most wretched who

Must live each other's lives and not our own

    For very pity's sake and then undo

All that we lived for—it was otherwise

When soul and body seemed to blend in mystic symphonies.

But we have left those gentle haunts to pass

    With weary feet to the new Calvary,

Where we behold, as one who in a glass

    Sees his own face, self-slain Humanity,

And in the dumb reproach of that sad gaze

Learn what an awful phantom the red hand of man can raise.

O smitten mouth! O forehead crowned with thorn!

    O chalice of all common miseries!

Thou for our sakes that loved thee not hast borne

An agony of endless centuries,

And we were vain and ignorant nor knew

That when we stabbed thy heart it was our own real hearts we slew.

Being ourselves the sowers and the seeds,

   The night that covers and the lights that fade,

The spear that pierces and the side that bleeds,

   The lips betraying and the life betrayed;

The deep hath calm: the moon hath rest: but we

Lords of the natural world are yet our own dread enemy.

Is this the end of all that primal force

   Which, in its changes being still the same,

From eyeless Chaos cleft its upward course,

   Through ravenous seas and whirling rocks and flame,

Till the suns met in heaven and began

Their cycles, and the morning stars sang, and the Word was Man!

Nay, nay, we are but crucified, and though

   The bloody sweat falls from our brows like rain

Loosen the nails—we shall come down I know,

   Staunch the red wounds—we shall be whole again,

No need have we of hyssop-laden rod,

That which is purely human, that is godlike, that is God.

FLOWER OF LOVE

ΓΛΥΚΥΠΙΚΡΟΣ ΕΡΩΣ

Sweet, I blame you not, for mine the fault

was, had I not been made of common clay

I had climbed the higher heights unclimbed

yet, seen the fuller air, the larger day.

From the wildness of my wasted passion I had

struck a better, clearer song,

Lit some lighter light of freer freedom, battled

with some Hydra-headed wrong.

Had my lips been smitten into music by the

kisses that but made them bleed,

You had walked with Bice and the angels on

that verdant and enamelled mead.

I had trod the road which Dante treading saw

the suns of seven circles shine,

Ay! perchance had seen the heavens opening,

as they opened to the Florentine.

And the mighty nations would have crowned

    me, who am crownless now and without name,

And some orient dawn had found me kneeling

    on the threshold of the House of Fame.

I had sat within that marble circle where the

    oldest bard is as the young,

And the pipe is ever dropping honey, and the

    lyre's strings are ever strung.

Keats had lifted up his hymeneal curls from out

    the poppy-seeded wine,

With ambrosial mouth had kissed my forehead,

    clasped the hand of noble love in mine.

And at springtide, when the apple-blossoms brush

    the burnished bosom of the dove,

Two young lovers lying in an orchard would

    have read the story of our love.

Would have read the legend of my passion,

known the bitter secret of my heart,

Kissed as we have kissed, but never parted as

we two are fated now to part.

For the crimson flower of our life is eaten by

the cankerworm of truth,

And no hand can gather up the fallen withered

petals of the rose of youth.

Yet I am not sorry that I loved you—ah! what

else had I a boy to do,—

For the hungry teeth of time devour, and the

silent-footed years pursue.

Rudderless, we drift athwart a tempest, and

when once the storm of youth is past,

Without lyre, without lute or chorus, Death

the silent pilot comes at last.

And within the grave there is no pleasure, for

the blindworm battens on the root,

And Desire shudders into ashes, and the tree of

Passion bears no fruit.

Ah! what else had I to do but love you, God's

  own mother was less dear to me,

And less dear the Cytheræan rising like an

  argent lily from the sea.

I have made my choice, have lived my poems,

  and, though youth is gone in wasted days,

I have found the lover's crown of myrtle better

  than the poet's crown of bays.

UNCOLLECTED POEMS

FROM SPRING DAYS TO WINTER
(FOR MUSIC)

In the glad springtime when leaves were green,
  O merrily the throstle sings!
I sought, amid the tangled sheen,
Love whom mine eyes had never seen,
  O the glad dove has golden wings!

Between the blossoms red and white,
  O merrily the throstle sings!
My love first came into my sight,
O perfect vision of delight,
  O the glad dove has golden wings!

The yellow apples glowed like fire,
  O merrily the throstle sings!
O Love too great for lip or lyre,
Blown rose of love and of desire,
  O the glad dove has golden wings!

But now with snow the tree is grey,

Ah, sadly now the throstle sings!

My love is dead: ah! well-a-day,

See at her silent feet I lay

A dove with broken wings!

Ah, Love! ah, Love! that thou wert slain—

Fond Dove, fond Dove return again!

TRISTITÆ

Αἴλινον, αἴλινον εἰπέ, τὸ δ' εὖ νικάτω

O well for him who lives at ease

With garnered gold in wide domain,

Nor heeds the splashing of the rain,

The crashing down of forest trees.

O well for him who ne'er hath known

The travail of the hungry years,

A father grey with grief and tears,

A mother weeping all alone.

But well for him whose foot hath trod

The weary road of toil and strife,

Yet from the sorrows of his life.

Builds ladders to be nearer God.

THE TRUE KNOWLEDGE

... ἀναγκαίως δ' ἔχει

Βίον θερίζειν ὥστε κάρπιμον στάχυν,

καὶ τὸν γὲν εἶναι τὸν δὲ γῇ.

Thou knowest all; I seek in vain

    What lands to till or sow with seed—

    The land is black with briar and weed,

Nor cares for falling tears or rain.

Thou knowest all; I sit and wait

    With blinded eyes and hands that fail,

    Till the last lifting of the veil

And the first opening of the gate.

Thou knowest all; I cannot see.

    I trust I shall not live in vain,

    I know that we shall meet again

In some divine eternity.

IMPRESSIONS

I. LE JARDIN

The lily's withered chalice falls

    Around its rod of dusty gold,

    And from the beech-trees on the wold

The last wood-pigeon coos and calls.

The gaudy leonine sunflower

    Hangs black and barren on its stalk,

    And down the windy garden walk

The dead leaves scatter,—hour by hour.

Pale privet-petals white as milk

    Are blown into a snowy mass:

    The roses lie upon the grass

Like little shreds of crimson silk.

II. LA MER

A white mist drifts across the shrouds,

    A wild moon in this wintry sky

    Gleams like an angry lion's eye

Out of a mane of tawny clouds.

The muffled steersman at the wheel

Is but a shadow in the gloom;—

And in the throbbing engine-room

Leap the long rods of polished steel.

The shattered storm has left its trace

Upon this huge and heaving dome,

For the thin threads of yellow foam

Float on the waves like ravelled lace.

UNDER THE BALCONY

O beautiful star with the crimson mouth!

O moon with the brows of gold!

Rise up, rise up, from the odorous south!

And light for my love her way,

Lest her little feet should stray

On the windy hill and the wold!

O beautiful star with the crimson mouth!

O moon with the brows of gold!

O ship that shakes on the desolate sea!

O ship with the wet, white sail!

Put in, put in, to the port to me!

For my love and I would go

To the land where the daffodils blow

In the heart of a violet dale!

O ship that shakes on the desolate sea!

O ship with the wet, white sail!

O rapturous bird with the low, sweet note!

O bird that sits on the spray!

Sing on, sing on, from your soft brown throat!

And my love in her little bed

Will listen, and lift her head

From the pillow, and come my way!

O rapturous bird with the low, sweet note!

O bird that sits on the spray!

O blossom that hangs in the tremulous air!

O blossom with lips of snow!

Come down, come down, for my love to wear!

You will die on her head in a crown,

You will die in a fold of her gown,

To her little light heart you will go!

O blossom that hangs in the tremulous air!

O blossom with lips of snow!

THE HARLOT'S HOUSE

We caught the tread of dancing feet,

We loitered down the moonlit street,

And stopped beneath the harlot's house.

Inside, above the din and fray,

We heard the loud musicians play

The 'Treues Liebes Herz' of Strauss.

Like strange mechanical grotesques,

Making fantastic arabesques,

The shadows raced across the blind.

We watched the ghostly dancers spin

To sound of horn and violin,

Like black leaves wheeling in the wind.

Like wire-pulled automatons,

Slim silhouetted skeletons

Went sidling through the slow quadrille,

Then took each other by the hand,

And danced a stately saraband;

Their laughter echoed thin and shrill.

Sometimes a clockwork puppet pressed

A phantom lover to her breast,

Sometimes they seemed to try to sing.

Sometimes a horrible marionette

Came out, and smoked its cigarette

Upon the steps like a live thing.

Then, turning to my love, I said,

'The dead are dancing with the dead,

The dust is whirling with the dust.'

But she—she heard the violin,

And left my side, and entered in:

Love passed into the house of lust.

Then suddenly the tune went false,

The dancers wearied of the waltz,

The shadows ceased to wheel and whirl.

And down the long and silent street,

The dawn, with silver-sandalled feet,

Crept like a frightened girl.

346

LE JARDIN DES TUILERIES

This winter air is keen and cold,

    And keen and cold this winter sun,

    But round my chair the children run

Like little things of dancing gold.

Sometimes about the painted kiosk

    The mimic soldiers strut and stride,

    Sometimes the blue-eyed brigands hide

In the bleak tangles of the bosk.

And sometimes, while the old nurse cons

    Her book, they steal across the square,

    And launch their paper navies where

Huge Triton writhes in greenish bronze.

And now in mimic flight they flee,

    And now they rush, a boisterous band—

    And, tiny hand on tiny hand,

Climb up the black and leafless tree.

Ah! cruel tree! if I were you,

    And children climbed me, for their sake

Though it be winter I would break

Into spring blossoms white and blue!

ON THE SALE BY AUCTION OF KEATS' LOVE LETTERS

These are the letters which Endymion wrote

To one he loved in secret, and apart.

And now the brawlers of the auction mart

Bargain and bid for each poor blotted note,

Ay! for each separate pulse of passion quote

The merchant's price. I think they love not art

Who break the crystal of a poet's heart

That small and sickly eyes may glare and gloat.

Is it not said that many years ago,

In a far Eastern town, some soldiers ran

With torches through the midnight, and began

To wrangle for mean raiment, and to throw

Dice for the garments of a wretched man,

Not knowing the God's wonder, or His woe?

THE NEW REMORSE

The sin was mine; I did not understand.

So now is music prisoned in her cave,

Save where some ebbing desultory wave

Frets with its restless whirls this meagre strand.

And in the withered hollow of this land

   Hath Summer dug herself so deep a grave,

   That hardly can the leaden willow crave

One silver blossom from keen Winter's hand.

But who is this who cometh by the shore?

(Nay, love, look up and wonder!) Who is this

   Who cometh in dyed garments from the South?

It is thy new-found Lord, and he shall kiss

   The yet unravished roses of thy mouth,

And I shall weep and worship, as before.

FANTAISIES DÉCORATIVES

I. LE PANNEAU

Under the rose-tree's dancing shade

   There stands a little ivory girl,

   Pulling the leaves of pink and pearl

With pale green nails of polished jade.

The red leaves fall upon the mould,

   The white leaves flutter, one by one,

   Down to a blue bowl where the sun,

Like a great dragon, writhes in gold.

The white leaves float upon the air,

The red leaves flutter idly down,

Some fall upon her yellow gown,

And some upon her raven hair.

She takes an amber lute and sings,

And as she sings a silver crane

Begins his scarlet neck to strain,

And flap his burnished metal wings.

She takes a lute of amber bright,

And from the thicket where he lies

Her lover, with his almond eyes,

Watches her movements in delight.

And now she gives a cry of fear,

And tiny tears begin to start:

A thorn has wounded with its dart

The pink-veined sea-shell of her ear.

And now she laughs a merry note:

There has fallen a petal of the rose

Just where the yellow satin shows

The blue-veined flower of her throat.

With pale green nails of polished jade,

Pulling the leaves of pink and pearl,

There stands a little ivory girl

Under the rose-tree's dancing shade.

II. LES BALLONS

Against these turbid turquoise skies

The light and luminous balloons

Dip and drift like satin moons,

Drift like silken butterflies;

Reel with every windy gust,

Rise and reel like dancing girls,

Float like strange transparent pearls,

Fall and float like silver dust.

Now to the low leaves they cling,

Each with coy fantastic pose,

Each a petal of a rose

Straining at a gossamer string.

Then to the tall trees they climb,

Like thin globes of amethyst,

Wandering opals keeping tryst

With the rubies of the lime.

CANZONET

I have no store

Of gryphon-guarded gold;

Now, as before,

Bare is the shepherd's fold.

Rubies nor pearls

Have I to gem thy throat;

Yet woodland girls

Have loved the shepherd's note.

Then pluck a reed

And bid me sing to thee,

For I would feed

Thine ears with melody,

Who art more fair

Than fairest fleur-de-lys,

More sweet and rare

Than sweetest ambergris.

What dost thou fear?

Young Hyacinth is slain,

Pan is not here,

And will not come again.

No hornèd Faun

Treads down the yellow leas,

No God at dawn

Steals through the olive trees.

Hylas is dead,

Nor will he e'er divine

Those little red

Rose-petalled lips of thine.

On the high hill

No ivory dryads play,

Silver and still

Sinks the sad autumn day.

SYMPHONY IN YELLOW

An omnibus across the bridge

Crawls like a yellow butterfly,

And, here and there, a passer-by

Shows like a little restless midge.

Big barges full of yellow hay
Are moored against the shadowy wharf,
And, like a yellow silken scarf,
The thick fog hangs along the quay.

The yellow leaves begin to fade
And flutter from the Temple elms,
And at my feet the pale green Thames
Lies like a rod of rippled jade.

IN THE FOREST

Out of the mid-wood's twilight
Into the meadow's dawn,
Ivory limbed and brown-eyed,
Flashes my Faun!

He skips through the copses singing,
And his shadow dances along,
And I know not which I should follow,
Shadow or song!

O Hunter, snare me his shadow!
O Nightingale, catch me his strain!

Else moonstruck with music and madness

I track him in vain!

TO MY WIFE: WITH A COPY OF MY POEMS

I can write no stately proem

As a prelude to my lay;

From a poet to a poem

I would dare to say.

For if of these fallen petals

One to you seem fair,

Love will waft it till it settles

On your hair.

And when wind and winter harden

All the loveless land,

It will whisper of the garden,

You will understand.

WITH A COPY OF 'A HOUSE OF POMEGRANATES'

Go, little book,

To him who, on a lute with horns of pearl,

Sang of the white feet of the Golden Girl:

And bid him look

Into thy pages: it may hap that he

May find that golden maidens dance through thee.

ROSES AND RUE

(To L. L.)

Could we dig up this long-buried treasure,

    Were it worth the pleasure,

We never could learn love's song,

    We are parted too long.

Could the passionate past that is fled

    Call back its dead,

Could we live it all over again,

    Were it worth the pain!

I remember we used to meet

    By an ivied seat,

And you warbled each pretty word

    With the air of a bird;

And your voice had a quaver in it,

    Just like a linnet,

And shook, as the blackbird's throat

With its last big note;

And your eyes, they were green and grey

Like an April day,

But lit into amethyst

When I stooped and kissed;

And your mouth, it would never smile

For a long, long while,

Then it rippled all over with laughter

Five minutes after.

You were always afraid of a shower,

Just like a flower:

I remember you started and ran

When the rain began.

I remember I never could catch you,

For no one could match you,

You had wonderful, luminous, fleet,

Little wings to your feet.

I remember your hair—did I tie it?

357

For it always ran riot—

Like a tangled sunbeam of gold:

These things are old.

I remember so well the room,

And the lilac bloom

That beat at the dripping pane

In the warm June rain;

And the colour of your gown,

It was amber-brown,

And two yellow satin bows

From your shoulders rose.

And the handkerchief of French lace

Which you held to your face—

Had a small tear left a stain?

Or was it the rain?

On your hand as it waved adieu

There were veins of blue;

In your voice as it said good-bye

Was a petulant cry,

'You have only wasted your life.'

   (Ah, that was the knife!)

When I rushed through the garden gate

   It was all too late.

Could we live it over again,

   Were it worth the pain,

Could the passionate past that is fled

   Call back its dead!

Well, if my heart must break,

   Dear love, for your sake,

It will break in music, I know,

   Poets' hearts break so.

But strange that I was not told

   That the brain can hold

In a tiny ivory cell

   God's heaven and hell.

DÉSESPOIR

The seasons send their ruin as they go,

For in the spring the narciss shows its head

Nor withers till the rose has flamed to red,

And in the autumn purple violets blow,

And the slim crocus stirs the winter snow;

Wherefore yon leafless trees will bloom again

And this grey land grow green with summer rain

And send up cowslips for some boy to mow.

But what of life whose bitter hungry sea

Flows at our heels, and gloom of sunless night

Covers the days which never more return?

Ambition, love and all the thoughts that burn

We lose too soon, and only find delight

In withered husks of some dead memory.

PAN: DOUBLE VILLANELLE

I

O goat-foot God of Arcady!

This modern world is grey and old,

And what remains to us of thee?

No more the shepherd lads in glee

Throw apples at thy wattled fold,

O goat-foot God of Arcady!

Nor through the laurels can one see

Thy soft brown limbs, thy beard of gold,

And what remains to us of thee?

And dull and dead our Thames would be,

For here the winds are chill and cold,

O goat-foot God of Arcady!

Then keep the tomb of Helice,

Thine olive-woods, thy vine-clad wold,

And what remains to us of thee?

Though many an unsung elegy

Sleeps in the reeds our rivers hold,

O goat-foot God of Arcady!

Ah, what remains to us of thee?

II

Ah, leave the hills of Arcady,

Thy satyrs and their wanton play,

This modern world hath need of thee.

No nymph or Faun indeed have we,

For Faun and nymph are old and grey,

Ah, leave the hills of Arcady!

This is the land where liberty

Lit grave-browed Milton on his way,

This modern world hath need of thee!

A land of ancient chivalry

Where gentle Sidney saw the day,

Ah, leave the hills of Arcady!

This fierce sea-lion of the sea,

This England lacks some stronger lay,

This modern world hath need of thee!

Then blow some trumpet loud and free,

And give thine oaten pipe away,

Ah, leave the hills of Arcady!

This modern world hath need of thee!

THE SPHINX

TO

MARCEL SCHWOB

IN FRIENDSHIP

AND

IN ADMIRATION

THE SPHINX

In a dim corner of my room for longer than my fancy thinks

A beautiful and silent Sphinx has watched me through the shifting gloom.

Inviolate and immobile she does not rise she does not stir

For silver moons are naught to her and naught to her the suns that reel.

Red follows grey across the air, the waves of moonlight ebb and flow

But with the Dawn she does not go and in the night-time she is there.

Dawn follows Dawn and Nights grow old and all the while this curious cat

Lies couching on the Chinese mat with eyes of satin rimmed with gold.

Upon the mat she lies and leers and on the tawny throat of her

Flutters the soft and silky fur or ripples to her pointed ears.

Come forth, my lovely seneschal! so somnolent, so statuesque!
Come forth you exquisite grotesque! half woman and half animal!

Come forth my lovely languorous Sphinx! and put your head upon my knee!
And let me stroke your throat and see your body spotted like the Lynx!

And let me touch those curving claws of yellow ivory and grasp
The tail that like a monstrous Asp coils round your heavy velvet paws!

A thousand weary centuries are thine while I have hardly seen
Some twenty summers cast their green for Autumn's gaudy liveries.

But you can read the Hieroglyphs on the great sandstone obelisks,
And you have talked with Basilisks, and you have looked on Hippogriffs.

O tell me, were you standing by when Isis to Osiris knelt?
And did you watch the Egyptian melt her union for Antony

And drink the jewel-drunken wine and bend her head in mimic awe
To see the huge proconsul draw the salted tunny from the brine?

And did you mark the Cyprian kiss white Adon on his catafalque?

And did you follow Amenalk, the God of Heliopolis?

And did you talk with Thoth, and did you hear the moon-horned Io weep?

And know the painted kings who sleep beneath the wedge-shaped Pyramid?

Lift up your large black satin eyes which are like cushions where one sinks!

Fawn at my feet, fantastic Sphinx! and sing me all your memories!

Sing to me of the Jewish maid who wandered with the Holy Child,

And how you led them through the wild, and how they slept beneath your shade.

Sing to me of that odorous green eve when crouching by the marge

You heard from Adrian's gilded barge the laughter of Antinous

And lapped the stream and fed your drouth and watched with hot and hungry stare

The ivory body of that rare young slave with his pomegranate mouth!

Sing to me of the Labyrinth in which the twi-formed bull was stalled!

Sing to me of the night you crawled across the temple's granite plinth

When through the purple corridors the screaming scarlet Ibis flew

In terror, and a horrid dew dripped from the moaning Mandragores,

And the great torpid crocodile within the tank shed slimy tears,

And tare the jewels from his ears and staggered back into the Nile,

And the priests cursed you with shrill psalms as in your claws you seized their snake

And crept away with it to slake your passion by the shuddering palms.

Who were your lovers? who were they who wrestled for you in the dust?

Which was the vessel of your Lust? What Leman had you, every day?

Did giant Lizards come and crouch before you on the reedy banks?

Did Gryphons with great metal flanks leap on you in your trampled couch?

Did monstrous hippopotami come sidling toward you in the mist?

Did gilt-scaled dragons writhe and twist with passion as you passed them by?

And from the brick-built Lycian tomb what horrible Chimera came

With fearful heads and fearful flame to breed new wonders from your womb?

Or had you shameful secret quests and did you harry to your home

Some Nereid coiled in amber foam with curious rock crystal breasts?

Or did you treading through the froth call to the brown Sidonian

For tidings of Leviathan, Leviathan or Behemoth?

Or did you when the sun was set climb up the cactus-covered slope

To meet your swarthy Ethiop whose body was of polished jet?

Or did you while the earthen skiffs dropped down the grey Nilotic flats

At twilight and the flickering bats flew round the temple's triple glyphs

Steal to the border of the bar and swim across the silent lake

And slink into the vault and make the Pyramid your lúpanar

Till from each black sarcophagus rose up the painted swathèd dead?

Or did you lure unto your bed the ivory-horned Tragelaphos?

Or did you love the god of flies who plagued the Hebrews and was splashed

With wine unto the waist? or Pasht, who had green beryls for her eyes?

Or that young god, the Tyrian, who was more amorous than the dove

Of Ashtaroth? or did you love the god of the Assyrian

Whose wings, like strange transparent talc, rose high above his hawk-faced head,

    Painted with silver and with red and ribbed with rods of Oreichalch?

    Or did huge Apis from his car leap down and lay before your feet

Big blossoms of the honey-sweet and honey-coloured nenuphar?

    How subtle-secret is your smile! Did you love none then? Nay, I know

Great Ammon was your bedfellow! He lay with you beside the Nile!

    The river-horses in the slime trumpeted when they saw him come

Odorous with Syrian galbanum and smeared with spikenard and with thyme.

    He came along the river bank like some tall galley argent-sailed,

He strode across the waters, mailed in beauty, and the waters sank.

    He strode across the desert sand: he reached the valley where you lay:

He waited till the dawn of day: then touched your black breasts with his hand.

    You kissed his mouth with mouths of flame: you made the hornèd god your own:

You stood behind him on his throne: you called him by his secret name.

You whispered monstrous oracles into the caverns of his ears:

With blood of goats and blood of steers you taught him monstrous miracles.

White Ammon was your bedfellow! Your chamber was the steaming Nile!

And with your curved archaic smile you watched his passion come and go.

With Syrian oils his brows were bright: and wide-spread as a tent at noon

His marble limbs made pale the moon and lent the day a larger light.

His long hair was nine cubits' span and coloured like that yellow gem

Which hidden in their garment's hem the merchants bring from Kurdistan.

His face was as the must that lies upon a vat of new-made wine:

The seas could not insapphirine the perfect azure of his eyes.

His thick soft throat was white as milk and threaded with thin veins of blue:

And curious pearls like frozen dew were broidered on his flowing silk.

On pearl and porphyry pedestalled he was too bright to look upon:

For on his ivory breast there shone the wondrous ocean-emerald,

That mystic moonlit jewel which some diver of the Colchian caves

Had found beneath the blackening waves and carried to the Colchian witch.

Before his gilded galiot ran naked vine-wreathed corybants,

And lines of swaying elephants knelt down to draw his chariot,

And lines of swarthy Nubians bare up his litter as he rode

Down the great granite-paven road between the nodding peacock-fans.

The merchants brought him steatite from Sidon in their painted ships:

The meanest cup that touched his lips was fashioned from a chrysolite.

The merchants brought him cedar chests of rich apparel bound with cords:

His train was borne by Memphian lords: young kings were glad to be his guests.

Ten hundred shaven priests did bow to Ammon's altar day and night,

Ten hundred lamps did wave their light through Ammon's carven house—and now

Foul snake and speckled adder with their young ones crawl from stone to stone

For ruined is the house and prone the great rose-marble monolith!

Wild ass or trotting jackal comes and couches in the mouldering gates:

Wild satyrs call unto their mates across the fallen fluted drums.

And on the summit of the pile the blue-faced ape of Horus sits

And gibbers while the fig-tree splits the pillars of the peristyle

The god is scattered here and there: deep hidden in the windy sand

I saw his giant granite hand still clenched in impotent despair.

And many a wandering caravan of stately negroes silken-shawled,

Crossing the desert, halts appalled before the neck that none can span.

And many a bearded Bedouin draws back his yellow-striped burnous

To gaze upon the Titan thews of him who was thy paladin.

Go, seek his fragments on the moor and wash them in the evening dew,

And from their pieces make anew thy mutilated paramour!

Go, seek them where they lie alone and from their broken pieces make

Thy bruisèd bedfellow! And wake mad passions in the senseless stone!

Charm his dull ear with Syrian hymns! he loved your body! oh, be kind,

Pour spikenard on his hair, and wind soft rolls of linen round his limbs!

Wind round his head the figured coins! stain with red fruits those pallid lips!

Weave purple for his shrunken hips! and purple for his barren loins!

Away to Egypt! Have no fear. Only one God has ever died.

Only one God has let His side be wounded by a soldier's spear.

But these, thy lovers, are not dead. Still by the hundred-cubit gate

Dog-faced Anubis sits in state with lotus-lilies for thy head.

Still from his chair of porphyry gaunt Memnon strains his lidless eyes

Across the empty land, and cries each yellow morning unto thee.

And Nilus with his broken horn lies in his black and oozy bed

And till thy coming will not spread his waters on the withering corn.

Your lovers are not dead, I know. They will rise up and hear your voice

And clash their cymbals and rejoice and run to kiss your mouth! And so,

Set wings upon your argosies! Set horses to your ebon car!

Back to your Nile! Or if you are grown sick of dead divinities

Follow some roving lion's spoor across the copper-coloured plain,

Reach out and hale him by the mane and bid him be your paramour!

Couch by his side upon the grass and set your white teeth in his throat

And when you hear his dying note lash your long flanks of polished brass

And take a tiger for your mate, whose amber sides are flecked with black,

And ride upon his gilded back in triumph through the Theban gate,

And toy with him in amorous jests, and when he turns, and snarls, and gnaws,

O smite him with your jasper claws! and bruise him with your agate breasts!

Why are you tarrying? Get hence! I weary of your sullen ways,

I weary of your steadfast gaze, your somnolent magnificence.

Your horrible and heavy breath makes the light flicker in the lamp,

And on my brow I feel the damp and dreadful dews of night and death.

Your eyes are like fantastic moons that shiver in some stagnant lake,

Your tongue is like a scarlet snake that dances to fantastic tunes,

Your pulse makes poisonous melodies, and your black throat is like the hole

Left by some torch or burning coal on Saracenic tapestries.

Away! The sulphur-coloured stars are hurrying through the Western gate!

Away! Or it may be too late to climb their silent silver cars!

See, the dawn shivers round the grey gilt-dialled towers, and the rain

Streams down each diamonded pane and blurs with tears the wannish day.

What snake-tressed fury fresh from Hell, with uncouth gestures and unclean,

Stole from the poppy-drowsy queen and led you to a student's cell?

What songless tongueless ghost of sin crept through the curtains of the night,

And saw my taper burning bright, and knocked, and bade you enter in?

Are there not others more accursed, whiter with leprosies than I?

Are Abana and Pharphar dry that you come here to slake your thirst?

Get hence, you loathsome mystery! Hideous animal, get hence!

You wake in me each bestial sense, you make me what I would not be.

You make my creed a barren sham, you wake foul dreams of sensual life,

And Atys with his blood-stained knife were better than the thing I am.

False Sphinx! False Sphinx! By reedy Styx old Charon, leaning on his oar,

Waits for my coin. Go thou before, and leave me to my crucifix,

Whose pallid burden, sick with pain, watches the world with wearied eyes,

And weeps for every soul that dies, and weeps for every soul in vain.

THE BALLAD OF READING GAOL

IN MEMORIAM

C. T. W.

SOMETIME TROOPER OF THE ROYAL HORSE GUARDS

OBIIT H.M. PRISON, READING, BERKSHIRE

JULY 7, 1896

THE BALLAD OF READING GAOL

I

He did not wear his scarlet coat,
  For blood and wine are red,
And blood and wine were on his hands
  When they found him with the dead,
The poor dead woman whom he loved,
  And murdered in her bed.

He walked amongst the Trial Men
  In a suit of shabby grey;
A cricket cap was on his head,
  And his step seemed light and gay;
But I never saw a man who looked

So wistfully at the day.

I never saw a man who looked
  With such a wistful eye
Upon that little tent of blue
  Which prisoners call the sky,
And at every drifting cloud that went
  With sails of silver by.

I walked, with other souls in pain,
  Within another ring,
And was wondering if the man had done
  A great or little thing,
When a voice behind me whispered low,
  'That fellow's got to swing.'

Dear Christ! the very prison walls
  Suddenly seemed to reel,
And the sky above my head became
  Like a casque of scorching steel;
And, though I was a soul in pain,
  My pain I could not feel.

I only knew what hunted thought

Quickened his step, and why

He looked upon the garish day

With such a wistful eye;

The man had killed the thing he loved,

And so he had to die.

Yet each man kills the thing he loves,

By each let this be heard,

Some do it with a bitter look,

Some with a flattering word,

The coward does it with a kiss,

The brave man with a sword!

Some kill their love when they are young,

And some when they are old;

Some strangle with the hands of Lust,

Some with the hands of Gold:

The kindest use a knife, because

The dead so soon grow cold.

Some love too little, some too long,

Some sell, and others buy;

Some do the deed with many tears,

And some without a sigh:

For each man kills the thing he loves,

    Yet each man does not die.

He does not die a death of shame

    On a day of dark disgrace,

Nor have a noose about his neck,

    Nor a cloth upon his face,

Nor drop feet foremost through the floor

    Into an empty space.

He does not sit with silent men

    Who watch him night and day;

Who watch him when he tries to weep,

    And when he tries to pray;

Who watch him lest himself should rob

    The prison of its prey.

He does not wake at dawn to see

    Dread figures throng his room,

The shivering Chaplain robed in white,

    The Sheriff stern with gloom,

And the Governor all in shiny black,

With the yellow face of Doom.

He does not rise in piteous haste

    To put on convict-clothes,

While some coarse-mouthed Doctor gloats, and notes

    Each new and nerve-twitched pose,

Fingering a watch whose little ticks

    Are like horrible hammer-blows.

He does not know that sickening thirst

    That sands one's throat, before

The hangman with his gardener's gloves

    Slips through the padded door,

And binds one with three leathern thongs,

    That the throat may thirst no more.

He does not bend his head to hear

    The Burial Office read,

Nor, while the terror of his soul

    Tells him he is not dead,

Cross his own coffin, as he moves

    Into the hideous shed.

He does not stare upon the air

Through a little roof of glass:
He does not pray with lips of clay
    For his agony to pass;
Nor feel upon his shuddering cheek
    The kiss of Caiaphas.

II

Six weeks our guardsman walked the yard,
    In the suit of shabby grey:
His cricket cap was on his head,
    And his step seemed light and gay,
But I never saw a man who looked
    So wistfully at the day.

I never saw a man who looked
    With such a wistful eye
Upon that little tent of blue
    Which prisoners call the sky,
And at every wandering cloud that trailed
    Its ravelled fleeces by.

He did not wring his hands, as do
    Those witless men who dare

To try to rear the changeling Hope

In the cave of black Despair:

He only looked upon the sun,

And drank the morning air.

He did not wring his hands nor weep,

Nor did he peek or pine,

But he drank the air as though it held

Some healthful anodyne;

With open mouth he drank the sun

As though it had been wine!

And I and all the souls in pain,

Who tramped the other ring,

Forgot if we ourselves had done

A great or little thing,

And watched with gaze of dull amaze

The man who had to swing.

And strange it was to see him pass

With a step so light and gay,

And strange it was to see him look

So wistfully at the day,

And strange it was to think that he

    Had such a debt to pay.

For oak and elm have pleasant leaves

    That in the springtime shoot:

But grim to see is the gallows-tree,

    With its adder-bitten root,

And, green or dry, a man must die

    Before it bears its fruit!

The loftiest place is that seat of grace

    For which all worldlings try:

But who would stand in hempen band

    Upon a scaffold high,

And through a murderer's collar take

    His last look at the sky?

It is sweet to dance to violins

    When Love and Life are fair:

To dance to flutes, to dance to lutes

    Is delicate and rare:

But it is not sweet with nimble feet

    To dance upon the air!

So with curious eyes and sick surmise
　　We watched him day by day,
And wondered if each one of us
　　Would end the self-same way,
For none can tell to what red Hell
　　His sightless soul may stray.

At last the dead man walked no more
　　Amongst the Trial Men,
And I knew that he was standing up
　　In the black dock's dreadful pen,
And that never would I see his face
　　In God's sweet world again.

Like two doomed ships that pass in storm
　　We had crossed each other's way:
But we made no sign, we said no word,
　　We had no word to say;
For we did not meet in the holy night,
　　But in the shameful day.

A prison wall was round us both,

Two outcast men we were:

The world had thrust us from its heart,

   And God from out His care:

And the iron gin that waits for Sin

   Had caught us in its snare.

III

In Debtors' Yard the stones are hard,

   And the dripping wall is high,

So it was there he took the air

   Beneath the leaden sky,

And by each side a Warder walked,

   For fear the man might die.

Or else he sat with those who watched

   His anguish night and day;

Who watched him when he rose to weep,

   And when he crouched to pray;

Who watched him lest himself should rob

   Their scaffold of its prey.

The Governor was strong upon

   The Regulations Act:

The Doctor said that Death was but

    A scientific fact:

And twice a day the Chaplain called,

    And left a little tract.

And twice a day he smoked his pipe,

    And drank his quart of beer:

His soul was resolute, and held

    No hiding-place for fear;

He often said that he was glad

    The hangman's hands were near.

But why he said so strange a thing

    No Warder dared to ask:

For he to whom a watcher's doom

    Is given as his task,

Must set a lock upon his lips,

    And make his face a mask.

Or else he might be moved, and try

    To comfort or console:

And what should Human Pity do

    Pent up in Murderers' Hole?

What word of grace in such a place

Could help a brother's soul?

With slouch and swing around the ring

We trod the Fools' Parade!

We did not care: we knew we were

The Devil's Own Brigade:

And shaven head and feet of lead

Make a merry masquerade.

We tore the tarry rope to shreds

With blunt and bleeding nails;

We rubbed the doors, and scrubbed the floors,

And cleaned the shining rails:

And, rank by rank, we soaped the plank,

And clattered with the pails.

We sewed the sacks, we broke the stones,

We turned the dusty drill:

We banged the tins, and bawled the hymns,

And sweated on the mill:

But in the heart of every man

Terror was lying still.

So still it lay that every day

    Crawled like a weed-clogged wave:

And we forgot the bitter lot

    That waits for fool and knave,

Till once, as we tramped in from work,

    We passed an open grave.

With yawning mouth the yellow hole

    Gaped for a living thing;

The very mud cried out for blood

    To the thirsty asphalte ring:

And we knew that ere one dawn grew fair

    Some prisoner had to swing.

Right in we went, with soul intent

    On Death and Dread and Doom:

The hangman, with his little bag,

    Went shuffling through the gloom:

And each man trembled as he crept

    Into his numbered tomb.

That night the empty corridors

Were full of forms of Fear,

And up and down the iron town

    Stole feet we could not hear,

And through the bars that hide the stars

    White faces seemed to peer.

He lay as one who lies and dreams

    In a pleasant meadow-land,

The watchers watched him as he slept,

    And could not understand

How one could sleep so sweet a sleep

    With a hangman close at hand.

But there is no sleep when men must weep

    Who never yet have wept:

So we—the fool, the fraud, the knave—

    That endless vigil kept,

And through each brain on hands of pain

    Another's terror crept.

Alas! it is a fearful thing

    To feel another's guilt!

For, right within, the sword of Sin

Pierced to its poisoned hilt,

And as molten lead were the tears we shed

For the blood we had not spilt.

The Warders with their shoes of felt

Crept by each padlocked door,

And peeped and saw, with eyes of awe,

Grey figures on the floor,

And wondered why men knelt to pray

Who never prayed before.

All through the night we knelt and prayed,

Mad mourners of a corse!

The troubled plumes of midnight were

The plumes upon a hearse:

And bitter wine upon a sponge

Was the savour of Remorse.

The grey cock crew, the red cock crew,

But never came the day:

And crooked shapes of Terror crouched,

In the corners where we lay:

And each evil sprite that walks by night

    Before us seemed to play.

They glided past, they glided fast,

    Like travellers through a mist:

They mocked the moon in a rigadoon

    Of delicate turn and twist,

And with formal pace and loathsome grace

    The phantoms kept their tryst.

With mop and mow, we saw them go,

    Slim shadows hand in hand:

About, about, in ghostly rout

    They trod a saraband:

And the damned grotesques made arabesques,

    Like the wind upon the sand!

With the pirouettes of marionettes,

    They tripped on pointed tread:

But with flutes of Fear they filled the ear,

    As their grisly masque they led,

And loud they sang, and long they sang,

    For they sang to wake the dead.

'Oho!' they cried, 'The world is wide,

But fettered limbs go lame!

And once, or twice, to throw the dice

Is a gentlemanly game,

But he does not win who plays with Sin

In the secret House of Shame.'

No things of air these antics were,

That frolicked with such glee:

To men whose lives were held in gyves,

And whose feet might not go free,

Ah! wounds of Christ! they were living things,

Most terrible to see.

Around, around, they waltzed and wound;

Some wheeled in smirking pairs;

With the mincing step of a demirep

Some sidled up the stairs:

And with subtle sneer, and fawning leer,

Each helped us at our prayers.

The morning wind began to moan,

But still the night went on:

Through its giant loom the web of gloom

   Crept till each thread was spun:

And, as we prayed, we grew afraid

   Of the Justice of the Sun.

The moaning wind went wandering round

   The weeping prison-wall:

Till like a wheel of turning steel

   We felt the minutes crawl:

O moaning wind! what had we done

   To have such a seneschal?

At last I saw the shadowed bars,

   Like a lattice wrought in lead,

Move right across the whitewashed wall

   That faced my three-plank bed,

And I knew that somewhere in the world

   God's dreadful dawn was red.

At six o'clock we cleaned our cells,

   At seven all was still,

But the sough and swing of a mighty wing

The prison seemed to fill,

For the Lord of Death with icy breath

Had entered in to kill.

He did not pass in purple pomp,

Nor ride a moon-white steed.

Three yards of cord and a sliding board

Are all the gallows' need:

So with rope of shame the Herald came

To do the secret deed.

We were as men who through a fen

Of filthy darkness grope:

We did not dare to breathe a prayer,

Or to give our anguish scope:

Something was dead in each of us,

And what was dead was Hope.

For Man's grim Justice goes its way,

And will not swerve aside:

It slays the weak, it slays the strong,

It has a deadly stride:

With iron heel it slays the strong,

The monstrous parricide!

We waited for the stroke of eight:
  Each tongue was thick with thirst:
For the stroke of eight is the stroke of Fate
  That makes a man accursed,
And Fate will use a running noose
  For the best man and the worst.

We had no other thing to do,
  Save to wait for the sign to come:
So, like things of stone in a valley lone,
  Quiet we sat and dumb:
But each man's heart beat thick and quick,
  Like a madman on a drum!

With sudden shock the prison-clock
  Smote on the shivering air,
And from all the gaol rose up a wail
  Of impotent despair,
Like the sound that frightened marshes hear
  From some leper in his lair.

And as one sees most fearful things

In the crystal of a dream,

We saw the greasy hempen rope

   Hooked to the blackened beam,

And heard the prayer the hangman's snare

   Strangled into a scream.

And all the woe that moved him so

   That he gave that bitter cry,

And the wild regrets, and the bloody sweats,

   None knew so well as I:

For he who lives more lives than one

   More deaths than one must die.

IV

There is no chapel on the day

   On which they hang a man:

The Chaplain's heart is far too sick,

   Or his face is far too wan,

Or there is that written in his eyes

   Which none should look upon.

So they kept us close till nigh on noon,

   And then they rang the bell,

And the Warders with their jingling keys

    Opened each listening cell,

And down the iron stair we tramped,

    Each from his separate Hell.

Out into God's sweet air we went,

    But not in wonted way,

For this man's face was white with fear,

    And that man's face was grey,

And I never saw sad men who looked

    So wistfully at the day.

I never saw sad men who looked

    With such a wistful eye

Upon that little tent of blue

    We prisoners called the sky,

And at every careless cloud that passed

    In happy freedom by.

But there were those amongst us all

    Who walked with downcast head,

And knew that, had each got his due,

    They should have died instead:

He had but killed a thing that lived,

Whilst they had killed the dead.

For he who sins a second time

Wakes a dead soul to pain,

And draws it from its spotted shroud,

And makes it bleed again,

And makes it bleed great gouts of blood,

And makes it bleed in vain!

Like ape or clown, in monstrous garb

With crooked arrows starred,

Silently we went round and round

The slippery asphalte yard;

Silently we went round and round,

And no man spoke a word.

Silently we went round and round,

And through each hollow mind

The Memory of dreadful things

Rushed like a dreadful wind,

And Horror stalked before each man,

And Terror crept behind.

The Warders strutted up and down,
  And kept their herd of brutes,
Their uniforms were spick and span,
  And they wore their Sunday suits,
But we knew the work they had been at,
  By the quicklime on their boots.

For where a grave had opened wide,
  There was no grave at all:
Only a stretch of mud and sand
  By the hideous prison-wall,
And a little heap of burning lime,
  That the man should have his pall.

For he has a pall, this wretched man,
  Such as few men can claim:
Deep down below a prison-yard,
  Naked for greater shame,
He lies, with fetters on each foot,
  Wrapt in a sheet of flame!

And all the while the burning lime

Eats flesh and bone away,

It eats the brittle bone by night,

And the soft flesh by day,

It eats the flesh and bone by turns,

But it eats the heart alway.

For three long years they will not sow

Or root or seedling there:

For three long years the unblessed spot

Will sterile be and bare,

And look upon the wondering sky

With unreproachful stare.

They think a murderer's heart would taint

Each simple seed they sow.

It is not true! God's kindly earth

Is kindlier than men know,

And the red rose would but blow more red,

The white rose whiter blow.

Out of his mouth a red, red rose!

Out of his heart a white!

For who can say by what strange way,

Christ brings His will to light,
Since the barren staff the pilgrim bore
Bloomed in the great Pope's sight?

But neither milk-white rose nor red
May bloom in prison-air;
The shard, the pebble, and the flint,
Are what they give us there:
For flowers have been known to heal
A common man's despair.

So never will wine-red rose or white,
Petal by petal, fall
On that stretch of mud and sand that lies
By the hideous prison-wall,
To tell the men who tramp the yard
That God's Son died for all.

Yet though the hideous prison-wall
Still hems him round and round,
And a spirit may not walk by night
That is with fetters bound,
And a spirit may but weep that lies

In such unholy ground,

He is at peace—this wretched man—
 At peace, or will be soon:
There is no thing to make him mad,
 Nor does Terror walk at noon,
For the lampless Earth in which he lies
 Has neither Sun nor Moon.

They hanged him as a beast is hanged:
 They did not even toll
A requiem that might have brought
 Rest to his startled soul,
But hurriedly they took him out,
 And hid him in a hole.

They stripped him of his canvas clothes,
 And gave him to the flies:
They mocked the swollen purple throat,
 And the stark and staring eyes:
And with laughter loud they heaped the shroud
 In which their convict lies.

The Chaplain would not kneel to pray

By his dishonoured grave:
Nor mark it with that blessed Cross
  That Christ for sinners gave,
Because the man was one of those
  Whom Christ came down to save.

Yet all is well; he has but passed
  To Life's appointed bourne:
And alien tears will fill for him
  Pity's long-broken urn,
For his mourners will be outcast men,
  And outcasts always mourn

V

I know not whether Laws be right,
  Or whether Laws be wrong;
All that we know who lie in gaol
  Is that the wall is strong;
And that each day is like a year,
  A year whose days are long.

But this I know, that every Law
  That men have made for Man,

Since first Man took his brother's life,

And the sad world began,

But straws the wheat and saves the chaff

With a most evil fan.

This too I know—and wise it were

If each could know the same—

That every prison that men build

Is built with bricks of shame,

And bound with bars lest Christ should see

How men their brothers maim.

With bars they blur the gracious moon,

And blind the goodly sun:

And they do well to hide their Hell,

For in it things are done

That Son of God nor son of Man

Ever should look upon!

The vilest deeds like poison weeds,

Bloom well in prison-air;

It is only what is good in Man

That wastes and withers there:

Pale Anguish keeps the heavy gate,

   And the Warder is Despair.

For they starve the little frightened child

   Till it weeps both night and day:

And they scourge the weak, and flog the fool,

   And gibe the old and grey,

And some grow mad, and all grow bad,

   And none a word may say.

Each narrow cell in which we dwell

   Is a foul and dark latrine,

And the fetid breath of living Death

   Chokes up each grated screen,

And all, but Lust, is turned to dust

   In Humanity's machine.

The brackish water that we drink

   Creeps with a loathsome slime,

And the bitter bread they weigh in scales

   Is full of chalk and lime,

And Sleep will not lie down, but walks

   Wild-eyed, and cries to Time.

But though lean Hunger and green Thirst

  Like asp with adder fight,

We have little care of prison fare,

  For what chills and kills outright

Is that every stone one lifts by day

  Becomes one's heart by night.

With midnight always in one's heart,

  And twilight in one's cell,

We turn the crank, or tear the rope,

  Each in his separate Hell,

And the silence is more awful far

  Than the sound of a brazen bell.

And never a human voice comes near

  To speak a gentle word:

And the eye that watches through the door

  Is pitiless and hard:

And by all forgot, we rot and rot,

  With soul and body marred.

And thus we rust Life's iron chain

Degraded and alone:

And some men curse, and some men weep,

And some men make no moan:

But God's eternal Laws are kind

And break the heart of stone.

And every human heart that breaks,

In prison-cell or yard,

Is as that broken box that gave

Its treasure to the Lord,

And filled the unclean leper's house

With the scent of costliest nard.

Ah! happy they whose hearts can break

And peace of pardon win!

How else may man make straight his plan

And cleanse his soul from Sin?

How else but through a broken heart

May Lord Christ enter in?

And he of the swollen purple throat,

And the stark and staring eyes,

Waits for the holy hands that took

The Thief to Paradise;

And a broken and a contrite heart

The Lord will not despise.

The man in red who reads the Law

Gave him three weeks of life,

Three little weeks in which to heal

His soul of his soul's strife,

And cleanse from every blot of blood

The hand that held the knife.

And with tears of blood he cleansed the hand,

The hand that held the steel:

For only blood can wipe out blood,

And only tears can heal:

And the crimson stain that was of Cain

Became Christ's snow-white seal.

VI

In Reading gaol by Reading town

There is a pit of shame,

And in it lies a wretched man

Eaten by teeth of flame,
In a burning winding-sheet he lies,
  And his grave has got no name.

And there, till Christ call forth the dead,
  In silence let him lie:
No need to waste the foolish tear,
  Or heave the windy sigh:
The man had killed the thing he loved,
  And so he had to die.

And all men kill the thing they love,
  By all let this be heard,
Some do it with a bitter look,
  Some with a flattering word,
The coward does it with a kiss,
  The brave man with a sword!

RAVENNA

Newdigate Prize Poem

Recited in the Sheldonian Theatre

Oxford

June 26th, 1878

TO MY FRIEND

GEORGE FLEMING

AUTHOR OF

'THE NILE NOVEL' AND 'MIRAGE'

Ravenna, March 1877

Oxford, March 1878

RAVENNA

I.

A year ago I breathed the Italian air,—

And yet, methinks this northern Spring is fair,—

These fields made golden with the flower of March,

The throstle singing on the feathered larch,

The cawing rooks, the wood-doves fluttering by,

The little clouds that race across the sky;

And fair the violet's gentle drooping head,

The primrose, pale for love uncomforted,

The rose that burgeons on the climbing briar,

The crocus-bed, (that seems a moon of fire

Round-girdled with a purple marriage-ring);

And all the flowers of our English Spring,

Fond snowdrops, and the bright-starred daffodil.

Up starts the lark beside the murmuring mill,

And breaks the gossamer-threads of early dew;

And down the river, like a flame of blue,

Keen as an arrow flies the water-king,

While the brown linnets in the greenwood sing.

A year ago!—it seems a little time

Since last I saw that lordly southern clime,

Where flower and fruit to purple radiance blow,

And like bright lamps the fabled apples glow.

Full Spring it was—and by rich flowering vines,

Dark olive-groves and noble forest-pines,

I rode at will; the moist glad air was sweet,

The white road rang beneath my horse's feet,

And musing on Ravenna's ancient name,

I watched the day till, marked with wounds of flame,

The turquoise sky to burnished gold was turned.

O how my heart with boyish passion burned,

When far away across the sedge and mere

I saw that Holy City rising clear,

Crowned with her crown of towers!—On and on

I galloped, racing with the setting sun,

And ere the crimson after-glow was passed,

I stood within Ravenna's walls at last!

II.

How strangely still! no sound of life or joy

Startles the air; no laughing shepherd-boy

Pipes on his reed, nor ever through the day

Comes the glad sound of children at their play:

O sad, and sweet, and silent! surely here

A man might dwell apart from troublous fear,

Watching the tide of seasons as they flow

From amorous Spring to Winter's rain and snow,

And have no thought of sorrow;—here, indeed,

Are Lethe's waters, and that fatal weed

Which makes a man forget his fatherland.

Ay! amid lotus-meadows dost thou stand,

Like Proserpine, with poppy-laden head,

Guarding the holy ashes of the dead.

For though thy brood of warrior sons hath ceased,

Thy noble dead are with thee!—they at least

Are faithful to thine honour:—guard them well,

O childless city! for a mighty spell,

To wake men's hearts to dreams of things sublime,

Are the lone tombs where rest the Great of Time.

III.

Yon lonely pillar, rising on the plain,

Marks where the bravest knight of France was slain,—

The Prince of chivalry, the Lord of war,

Gaston de Foix: for some untimely star

Led him against thy city, and he fell,

As falls some forest-lion fighting well.

Taken from life while life and love were new,

He lies beneath God's seamless veil of blue;

Tall lance-like reeds wave sadly o'er his head,

And oleanders bloom to deeper red,

Where his bright youth flowed crimson on the ground.

Look farther north unto that broken mound,—

There, prisoned now within a lordly tomb

Raised by a daughter's hand, in lonely gloom,

Huge-limbed Theodoric, the Gothic king,

Sleeps after all his weary conquering.

Time hath not spared his ruin,—wind and rain

Have broken down his stronghold; and again

We see that Death is mighty lord of all,

And king and clown to ashen dust must fall

Mighty indeed their glory! yet to me

Barbaric king, or knight of chivalry,

Or the great queen herself, were poor and vain,

Beside the grave where Dante rests from pain.

His gilded shrine lies open to the air;

And cunning sculptor's hands have carven there

The calm white brow, as calm as earliest morn,

The eyes that flashed with passionate love and scorn,

The lips that sang of Heaven and of Hell,

The almond-face which Giotto drew so well,

The weary face of Dante;—to this day,

Here in his place of resting, far away

414

From Arno's yellow waters, rushing down

Through the wide bridges of that fairy town,

Where the tall tower of Giotto seems to rise

A marble lily under sapphire skies!

Alas! my Dante! thou hast known the pain

Of meaner lives,—the exile's galling chain,

How steep the stairs within kings' houses are,

And all the petty miseries which mar

Man's nobler nature with the sense of wrong.

Yet this dull world is grateful for thy song;

Our nations do thee homage,—even she,

That cruel queen of vine-clad Tuscany,

Who bound with crown of thorns thy living brow,

Hath decked thine empty tomb with laurels now,

And begs in vain the ashes of her son.

O mightiest exile! all thy grief is done:

Thy soul walks now beside thy Beatrice;

Ravenna guards thine ashes: sleep in peace.

<u>IV.</u>

How lone this palace is; how grey the walls!

No minstrel now wakes echoes in these halls.

The broken chain lies rusting on the door,

And noisome weeds have split the marble floor:

Here lurks the snake, and here the lizards run

By the stone lions blinking in the sun.

Byron dwelt here in love and revelry

For two long years—a second Anthony,

Who of the world another Actium made!

Yet suffered not his royal soul to fade,

Or lyre to break, or lance to grow less keen,

'Neath any wiles of an Egyptian queen.

For from the East there came a mighty cry,

And Greece stood up to fight for Liberty,

And called him from Ravenna: never knight

Rode forth more nobly to wild scenes of fight!

None fell more bravely on ensanguined field,

Borne like a Spartan back upon his shield!

O Hellas! Hellas! in thine hour of pride,

Thy day of might, remember him who died

To wrest from off thy limbs the trammelling chain:

O Salamis! O lone Platæan plain!

O tossing waves of wild Euboean sea!

O wind-swept heights of lone Thermopylæ!

He loved you well—ay, not alone in word,

Who freely gave to thee his lyre and sword,

Like Æschylos at well-fought Marathon:

  And England, too, shall glory in her son,

Her warrior-poet, first in song and fight.

No longer now shall Slander's venomed spite

Crawl like a snake across his perfect name,

Or mar the lordly scutcheon of his fame.

  For as the olive-garland of the race,

Which lights with joy each eager runner's face,

As the red cross which saveth men in war,

As a flame-bearded beacon seen from far

By mariners upon a storm-tossed sea,—

Such was his love for Greece and Liberty!

  Byron, thy crowns are ever fresh and green:

Red leaves of rose from Sapphic Mitylene

Shall bind thy brows; the myrtle blooms for thee,

In hidden glades by lonely Castaly;

The laurels wait thy coming: all are thine,

And round thy head one perfect wreath will twine.

V.

The pine-tops rocked before the evening breeze

With the hoarse murmur of the wintry seas,

And the tall stems were streaked with amber bright;—

I wandered through the wood in wild delight,

Some startled bird, with fluttering wings and fleet,

Made snow of all the blossoms; at my feet,

Like silver crowns, the pale narcissi lay,

And small birds sang on every twining spray.

O waving trees, O forest liberty!

Within your haunts at least a man is free,

And half forgets the weary world of strife:

The blood flows hotter, and a sense of life

Wakes i' the quickening veins, while once again

The woods are filled with gods we fancied slain.

Long time I watched, and surely hoped to see

Some goat-foot Pan make merry minstrelsy

Amid the reeds! some startled Dryad-maid

In girlish flight! or lurking in the glade,

The soft brown limbs, the wanton treacherous face

Of woodland god! Queen Dian in the chase,

White-limbed and terrible, with look of pride,

And leash of boar-hounds leaping at her side!

Or Hylas mirrored in the perfect stream.

O idle heart! O fond Hellenic dream!

Ere long, with melancholy rise and swell,

The evening chimes, the convent's vesper bell,

Struck on mine ears amid the amorous flowers.

Alas! alas! these sweet and honied hours

Had whelmed my heart like some encroaching sea,

And drowned all thoughts of black Gethsemane.

VI.

O lone Ravenna! many a tale is told

Of thy great glories in the days of old:

Two thousand years have passed since thou didst see

Cæsar ride forth to royal victory.

Mighty thy name when Rome's lean eagles flew

From Britain's isles to far Euphrates blue;

And of the peoples thou wast noble queen,

Till in thy streets the Goth and Hun were seen.

Discrowned by man, deserted by the sea,

Thou sleepest, rocked in lonely misery!

No longer now upon thy swelling tide,

Pine-forest-like, thy myriad galleys ride!

For where the brass-beaked ships were wont to float,

The weary shepherd pipes his mournful note;

And the white sheep are free to come and go

Where Adria's purple waters used to flow.

O fair! O sad! O Queen uncomforted!

In ruined loveliness thou liest dead,

Alone of all thy sisters; for at last

Italia's royal warrior hath passed

Rome's lordliest entrance, and hath worn his crown

In the high temples of the Eternal Town!

The Palatine hath welcomed back her king,

And with his name the seven mountains ring!

And Naples hath outlived her dream of pain,

And mocks her tyrant! Venice lives again,

New risen from the waters! and the cry

Of Light and Truth, of Love and Liberty,

Is heard in lordly Genoa, and where

The marble spires of Milan wound the air,

Rings from the Alps to the Sicilian shore,

And Dante's dream is now a dream no more.

But thou, Ravenna, better loved than all,

Thy ruined palaces are but a pall

That hides thy fallen greatness! and thy name

Burns like a grey and flickering candle-flame

Beneath the noonday splendour of the sun

Of new Italia! for the night is done,

The night of dark oppression, and the day

Hath dawned in passionate splendour: far away

The Austrian hounds are hunted from the land,

Beyond those ice-crowned citadels which stand

Girdling the plain of royal Lombardy,

From the far West unto the Eastern sea.

I know, indeed, that sons of thine have died

In Lissa's waters, by the mountain-side

Of Aspromonte, on Novara's plain,—

Nor have thy children died for thee in vain:

And yet, methinks, thou hast not drunk this wine

From grapes new-crushed of Liberty divine,

Thou hast not followed that immortal Star

Which leads the people forth to deeds of war.

Weary of life, thou liest in silent sleep,

As one who marks the lengthening shadows creep,

Careless of all the hurrying hours that run,

Mourning some day of glory, for the sun

Of Freedom hath not shewn to thee his face,

And thou hast caught no flambeau in the race.

Yet wake not from thy slumbers,—rest thee well,

Amidst thy fields of amber asphodel,

Thy lily-sprinkled meadows,—rest thee there,

To mock all human greatness: who would dare

To vent the paltry sorrows of his life

Before thy ruins, or to praise the strife

Of kings' ambition, and the barren pride

Of warring nations! wert not thou the Bride

Of the wild Lord of Adria's stormy sea!

The Queen of double Empires! and to thee

Were not the nations given as thy prey!

And now—thy gates lie open night and day,

The grass grows green on every tower and hall,

The ghastly fig hath cleft thy bastioned wall;

And where thy mailèd warriors stood at rest

The midnight owl hath made her secret nest.

O fallen! fallen! from thy high estate,

O city trammelled in the toils of Fate,

Doth nought remain of all thy glorious days,

But a dull shield, a crown of withered bays!

Yet who beneath this night of wars and fears,

From tranquil tower can watch the coming years;

Who can foretell what joys the day shall bring,

Or why before the dawn the linnets sing?

Thou, even thou, mayst wake, as wakes the rose

To crimson splendour from its grave of snows;

As the rich corn-fields rise to red and gold

From these brown lands, now stiff with Winter's cold;

As from the storm-rack comes a perfect star!

O much-loved city! I have wandered far

From the wave-circled islands of my home;

Have seen the gloomy mystery of the Dome

Rise slowly from the drear Campagna's way,

Clothed in the royal purple of the day:

I from the city of the violet crown

Have watched the sun by Corinth's hill go down,

And marked the 'myriad laughter' of the sea

From starlit hills of flower-starred Arcady;

Yet back to thee returns my perfect love,

As to its forest-nest the evening dove.

O poet's city! one who scarce has seen

Some twenty summers cast their doublets green

For Autumn's livery, would seek in vain

To wake his lyre to sing a louder strain,

Or tell thy days of glory;—poor indeed

Is the low murmur of the shepherd's reed,

Where the loud clarion's blast should shake the sky,

And flame across the heavens! and to try

Such lofty themes were folly: yet I know

That never felt my heart a nobler glow

Than when I woke the silence of thy street

With clamorous trampling of my horse's feet,

And saw the city which now I try to sing,

After long days of weary travelling.

VII.

Adieu, Ravenna! but a year ago,

I stood and watched the crimson sunset glow

From the lone chapel on thy marshy plain:

The sky was as a shield that caught the stain

Of blood and battle from the dying sun,

And in the west the circling clouds had spun

A royal robe, which some great God might wear,

While into ocean-seas of purple air

Sank the gold galley of the Lord of Light.

Yet here the gentle stillness of the night

Brings back the swelling tide of memory,

And wakes again my passionate love for thee:

Now is the Spring of Love, yet soon will come

On meadow and tree the Summer's lordly bloom;

And soon the grass with brighter flowers will blow,

And send up lilies for some boy to mow.

Then before long the Summer's conqueror,

Rich Autumn-time, the season's usurer,

Will lend his hoarded gold to all the trees,

And see it scattered by the spendthrift breeze;

And after that the Winter cold and drear.

So runs the perfect cycle of the year.

And so from youth to manhood do we go,

And fall to weary days and locks of snow.

Love only knows no winter; never dies:

Nor cares for frowning storms or leaden skies

And mine for thee shall never pass away,

Though my weak lips may falter in my lay.

Adieu! Adieu! yon silent evening star,

The night's ambassador, doth gleam afar,

And bid the shepherd bring his flocks to fold.

Perchance before our inland seas of gold

Are garnered by the reapers into sheaves,

Perchance before I see the Autumn leaves,

I may behold thy city; and lay down

Low at thy feet the poet's laurel crown.

Adieu! Adieu! yon silver lamp, the moon,

Which turns our midnight into perfect noon,

Doth surely light thy towers, guarding well

Where Dante sleeps, where Byron loved to dwell.

About Author

Oscar Fingal O'Flahertie Wills Wilde (16 October 1854 – 30 November 1900) was an Irish poet and playwright. After writing in different forms throughout the 1880s, the early 1890s saw him become one of the most popular playwrights in London. He is best remembered for his epigrams and plays, his novel The Picture of Dorian Gray, and the circumstances of his criminal conviction for "gross indecency", imprisonment, and early death at age 46.

Wilde's parents were successful Anglo-Irish intellectuals in Dublin. A young Wilde learned to speak fluent French and German. At university, Wilde read Greats; he demonstrated himself to be an exceptional classicist, first at Trinity College Dublin, then at Oxford. He became associated with the emerging philosophy of aestheticism, led by two of his tutors, Walter Pater and John Ruskin. After university, Wilde moved to London into fashionable cultural and social circles.

As a spokesman for aestheticism, he tried his hand at various literary activities: he published a book of poems, lectured in the United States and Canada on the new "English Renaissance in Art" and interior decoration, and then returned to London where he worked prolifically as a journalist. Known for his biting wit, flamboyant dress and glittering conversational skill, Wilde became one of the best-known personalities of his day. At the turn of the 1890s, he refined his ideas about the supremacy of art in a series of dialogues and essays, and incorporated themes of decadence, duplicity, and beauty into what would be his only novel, The Picture of Dorian Gray (1890). The opportunity to construct aesthetic details precisely, and combine them with larger social themes, drew Wilde to write drama. He wrote Salome (1891) in French while in Paris but it was refused a licence for England due to an absolute prohibition on the portrayal of Biblical subjects on the English stage. Unperturbed, Wilde produced four society comedies in the early 1890s, which made him one of the most successful playwrights of late-Victorian London.

At the height of his fame and success, while The Importance of Being Earnest (1895) was still being performed in London, Wilde had the Marquess of Queensberry prosecuted for criminal libel. The Marquess was the father of Wilde's lover, Lord Alfred Douglas. The libel trial unearthed evidence that caused Wilde to drop his charges and led to his own arrest and trial for gross indecency with men. After two more trials he was convicted and sentenced to two years' hard labour, the maximum penalty, and was jailed from 1895 to 1897. During his last year in prison, he wrote De Profundis (published posthumously in 1905), a long letter which discusses his spiritual journey through his trials, forming a dark counterpoint to his earlier philosophy of pleasure. On his release, he left immediately for France, never to return to Ireland or Britain. There he wrote his last work, The Ballad of Reading Gaol (1898), a long poem commemorating the harsh rhythms of prison life.

Early life

Oscar Wilde was born at 21 Westland Row, Dublin (now home of the Oscar Wilde Centre, Trinity College), the second of three children born to Anglo-Irish Sir William Wilde and Jane Wilde, two years behind his brother William ("Willie"). Wilde's mother had distant Italian ancestry, and under the pseudonym "Speranza" (the Italian word for 'hope'), wrote poetry for the revolutionary Young Irelanders in 1848; she was a lifelong Irish nationalist. She read the Young Irelanders' poetry to Oscar and Willie, inculcating a love of these poets in her sons. Lady Wilde's interest in the neo-classical revival showed in the paintings and busts of ancient Greece and Rome in her home.

William Wilde was Ireland's leading oto-ophthalmologic (ear and eye) surgeon and was knighted in 1864 for his services as medical adviser and assistant commissioner to the censuses of Ireland. He also wrote books about Irish archaeology and peasant folklore. A renowned philanthropist, his dispensary for the care of the city's poor at the rear of Trinity College, Dublin, was the forerunner of the Dublin Eye and Ear Hospital, now located at Adelaide Road. On his father's side Wilde was descended from a Dutchman, Colonel de Wilde, who went to Ireland with King William of Orange's invading army in 1690, and numerous Anglo-Irish ancestors. On his mother's side, Wilde's ancestors included a bricklayer from County Durham, who emigrated to Ireland sometime in the 1770s.

Wilde was baptised as an infant in St. Mark's Church, Dublin, the local Church of Ireland (Anglican) church. When the church was closed, the records were moved to the nearby St. Ann's Church, Dawson Street. Davis Coakley mentions a second baptism by a Catholic priest, Father Prideaux Fox, who befriended Oscar's mother circa 1859. According to Fox's testimony in Donahoe's Magazine in 1905, Jane Wilde would visit his chapel in Glencree, County Wicklow, for Mass and would take her sons with her. She asked Father Fox in this period to baptise her sons.

Fox described it in this way:

> "I am not sure if she ever became a Catholic herself but it was not long before she asked me to instruct two of her children, one of them being the future erratic genius, Oscar Wilde. After a few weeks I baptized these two children, Lady Wilde herself being present on the occasion.

In addition to his children with his wife, Sir William Wilde was the father of three children born out of wedlock before his marriage: Henry Wilson, born in 1838 to one woman, and Emily and Mary Wilde, born in 1847 and 1849, respectively, to a second woman. Sir William acknowledged paternity of his illegitimate or "natural" children and provided for their education, arranging for them to be reared by his relatives rather than with his legitimate children in his family household with his wife.

In 1855, the family moved to No. 1 Merrion Square, where Wilde's sister, Isola, was born in 1857. The Wildes' new home was larger. With both his parents' success and delight in social life, the house soon became the site of a "unique medical and cultural milieu". Guests at their salon included Sheridan Le Fanu, Charles Lever, George Petrie, Isaac Butt, William Rowan Hamilton and Samuel Ferguson.

Until he was nine, Oscar Wilde was educated at home, where a French nursemaid and a German governess taught him their languages. He attended Portora Royal School in Enniskillen, County Fermanagh, from 1864 to 1871. Until his early twenties, Wilde summered at the villa, Moytura House, which his father had built in Cong, County Mayo. There the young Wilde and his brother Willie played with George Moore.

Isola died at age nine of meningitis. Wilde's poem "Requiescat" is written to her memory.

"Tread lightly, she is near

Under the snow

Speak gently, she can hear

the daisies grow"

University education: 1870s

Trinity College, Dublin

Wilde left Portora with a royal scholarship to read classics at Trinity College, Dublin, from 1871 to 1874, sharing rooms with his older brother Willie Wilde. Trinity, one of the leading classical schools, placed him with scholars such as R. Y. Tyrell, Arthur Palmer, Edward Dowden and his tutor, Professor J. P. Mahaffy, who inspired his interest in Greek literature. As a student Wilde worked with Mahaffy on the latter's book Social Life in Greece. Wilde, despite later reservations, called Mahaffy "my first and best teacher" and "the scholar who showed me how to love Greek things".For his part, Mahaffy boasted of having created Wilde; later, he said Wilde was "the only blot on my tutorship".

The University Philosophical Society also provided an education, as members discussed intellectual and artistic subjects such as Dante Gabriel Rossetti and Algernon Charles Swinburne weekly. Wilde quickly became an established member – the members' suggestion book for 1874 contains two pages of banter (sportingly) mocking Wilde's emergent aestheticism. He presented a paper titled "Aesthetic Morality". At Trinity, Wilde established himself as an outstanding student: he came first in his class in his first year, won a scholarship by competitive examination in his second and, in his finals, won the Berkeley Gold Medal in Greek, the University's highest academic award. He was encouraged to compete for a demyship to Magdalen College, Oxford – which he won easily, having already studied Greek for over nine years.

Magdalen College, Oxford

At Magdalen, he read Greats from 1874 to 1878, and from there he applied to join the Oxford Union, but failed to be elected.

Attracted by its dress, secrecy, and ritual, Wilde petitioned the Apollo Masonic Lodge at Oxford, and was soon raised to the "Sublime Degree of Master Mason".During a resurgent interest in Freemasonry in his third year, he commented he "would be awfully sorry to give it up if I secede from the Protestant Heresy". Wilde's active involvement in Freemasonry lasted only for the time he spent at Oxford; he allowed his membership of the Apollo University Lodge to lapse after failing to pay subscriptions.

Catholicism deeply appealed to him, especially its rich liturgy, and he discussed converting to it with clergy several times. In 1877, Wilde was left speechless after an audience with Pope Pius IX in Rome.He eagerly read the books of Cardinal Newman, a noted Anglican priest who had converted to Catholicism and risen in the church hierarchy. He became more serious in 1878, when he met the Reverend Sebastian Bowden, a priest in the Brompton Oratory who had received some high-profile converts. Neither his father, who threatened to cut off his funds, nor Mahaffy thought much of the plan; but mostly Wilde, the supreme individualist, balked at the last minute from pledging himself to any formal creed. On the appointed day of his baptism, Wilde sent Father Bowden a bunch of altar lilies instead. Wilde did retain a lifelong interest in Catholic theology and liturgy.

While at Magdalen College, Wilde became particularly well known for his role in the aesthetic and decadent movements. He wore his hair long, openly scorned "manly" sports though he occasionally boxed, and he decorated his rooms with peacock feathers, lilies, sunflowers, blue china and other objets d'art. He once remarked to friends, whom he entertained lavishly, "I find it harder and harder every day to live up to my blue china." The line quickly became famous, accepted as a slogan by aesthetes but used against them by critics who sensed in it a terrible vacuousness. Some elements disdained the aesthetes, but their languishing attitudes and showy costumes became a recognised pose. Wilde was once physically attacked by a group of four fellow students, and dealt with them single-handedly, surprising critics. By his third year Wilde had truly begun to develop himself and his myth, and considered his learning to be more expansive than what was within the prescribed texts. This attitude resulted in his being rusticated for one term, after he had returned late to a college term from a trip to Greece with Mahaffy.

Wilde did not meet Walter Pater until his third year, but had been enthralled by his Studies in the History of the Renaissance, published during Wilde's final year in Trinity. Pater argued that man's sensibility to beauty should be refined above all else, and that each moment should be felt to its fullest extent. Years later, in De Profundis, Wilde described Pater's Studies... as "that book that has had such a strange influence over my life".He learned tracts of the book by heart, and carried it with him on travels in later years. Pater gave Wilde his sense of almost flippant devotion to art, though he gained a purpose for it through the lectures and writings of critic John Ruskin. Ruskin despaired at the self-validating aestheticism of Pater, arguing that the importance of art lies in its potential for the betterment of society. Ruskin admired beauty, but believed it must be allied with, and applied to, moral good. When Wilde eagerly attended Ruskin's lecture series The Aesthetic and Mathematic Schools of Art in Florence, he learned about aesthetics as the non-mathematical elements of painting. Despite being given to neither early rising nor manual labour, Wilde volunteered for Ruskin's project to convert a swampy country lane into a smart road neatly edged with flowers.

Wilde won the 1878 Newdigate Prize for his poem "Ravenna", which reflected on his visit there the year before, and he duly read it at Encaenia. In November 1878, he graduated with a double first in his B.A. of Classical Moderations and Literae Humaniores (Greats). Wilde wrote to a friend, "The dons are 'astonied' beyond words – the Bad Boy doing so well in the end!"

Apprenticeship of an aesthete: 1880s

Debut in society

After graduation from Oxford, Wilde returned to Dublin, where he met again Florence Balcombe, a childhood sweetheart. She became engaged to Bram Stoker and they married in 1878. Wilde was disappointed but stoic:

he wrote to her, remembering "the two sweet years – the sweetest years of all my youth" during which they had been close. He also stated his intention to "return to England, probably for good." This he did in 1878, only briefly visiting Ireland twice after that.

Unsure of his next step, Wilde wrote to various acquaintances enquiring about Classics positions at Oxford or Cambridge. The Rise of Historical Criticism was his submission for the Chancellor's Essay prize of 1879, which, though no longer a student, he was still eligible to enter. Its subject, "Historical Criticism among the Ancients" seemed ready-made for Wilde – with both his skill in composition and ancient learning – but he struggled to find his voice with the long, flat, scholarly style. Unusually, no prize was awarded that year.

With the last of his inheritance from the sale of his father's houses, he set himself up as a bachelor in London. The 1881 British Census listed Wilde as a boarder at 1 (now 44) Tite Street, Chelsea, where Frank Miles, a society painter, was the head of the household. Wilde spent the next six years in London and Paris, and in the United States, where he travelled to deliver lectures.

He had been publishing lyrics and poems in magazines since entering Trinity College, especially in Kottabos and the Dublin University Magazine. In mid-1881, at 27 years old, he published Poems, which collected, revised and expanded his poems.

The book was generally well received, and sold out its first print run of 750 copies. Punch was less enthusiastic, saying "The poet is Wilde, but his poetry's tame". By a tight vote, the Oxford Union condemned the book for alleged plagiarism. The librarian, who had requested the book for the library, returned the presentation copy to Wilde with a note of apology. Biographer Richard Ellmann argues that Wilde's poem "Hélas!" was a sincere, though flamboyant, attempt to explain the dichotomies the poet saw in himself; one line reads: "To drift with every passion till my soul

Is a stringed lute on which all winds can play".

The book had further printings in 1882. It was bound in a rich, enamel parchment cover (embossed with gilt blossom) and printed on hand-made Dutch paper; over the next few years, Wilde presented many copies to the dignitaries and writers who received him during his lecture tours.

America: 1882

Aestheticism was sufficiently in vogue to be caricatured by Gilbert and Sullivan in Patience (1881). Richard D'Oyly Carte, an English impresario, invited Wilde to make a lecture tour of North America, simultaneously priming the pump for the US tour of Patience and selling this most charming aesthete to the American public. Wilde journeyed on the SS Arizona, arriving 2 January 1882, and disembarking the following day. Originally planned to last four months, it continued for almost a year due to the commercial success. Wilde sought to transpose the beauty he saw in art into daily life. This was a practical as well as philosophical project: in Oxford he had surrounded himself with blue china and lilies, and now one of his lectures was on interior design.

When asked to explain reports that he had paraded down Piccadilly in London carrying a lily, long hair flowing, Wilde replied, "It's not whether I did it or not that's important, but whether people believed I did it". Wilde believed that the artist should hold forth higher ideals, and that pleasure and beauty would replace utilitarian ethics.

Wilde and aestheticism were both mercilessly caricatured and criticised in the press; the Springfield Republican, for instance, commented on Wilde's behaviour during his visit to Boston to lecture on aestheticism, suggesting that Wilde's conduct was more a bid for notoriety rather than devotion to beauty and the aesthetic. T. W. Higginson, a cleric and abolitionist, wrote in "Unmanly Manhood" of his general concern that Wilde, "whose only distinction is that he has written a thin volume of very mediocre verse", would improperly influence the behaviour of men and women.

According to biographer Michèle Mendelssohn, Wilde was the subject of anti-Irish caricature and was portrayed as a monkey, a blackface performer and a Christy's Minstrel throughout his career. "Harper's Weekly put a sunflower-worshipping monkey dressed as Wilde on the front of the January 1882 issue. The magazine didn't let its reputation for quality impede its expression of what are now considered odious ethnic and racial ideologies. The drawing stimulated other American maligners and, in England, had a full-page reprint in the Lady's Pictorial. ... When the National Republican discussed Wilde, it was to explain 'a few items as to the animal's pedigree.' And on 22 January 1882 the Washington Post illustrated the Wild Man of Borneo alongside Oscar Wilde of England and asked 'How far is it from this to this?' "Though his press reception was hostile, Wilde was well received in diverse settings across America; he drank whiskey with miners in Leadville, Colorado, and was fêted at the most fashionable salons in many cities he visited.

London life and marriage

His earnings, plus expected income from The Duchess of Padua, allowed him to move to Paris between February and mid-May 1883. While there he met Robert Sherard, whom he entertained constantly. "We are dining on the Duchess tonight", Wilde would declare before taking him to an expensive restaurant. In August he briefly returned to New York for the production of Vera, his first play, after it was turned down in London. He reportedly entertained the other passengers with "Ave Imperatrix!, A Poem on England", about the rise and fall of empires. E. C. Stedman, in Victorian Poets, describes this "lyric to England" as "manly verse – a poetic and eloquent invocation". The play was initially well received by the audience, but when the critics wrote lukewarm reviews, attendance fell sharply and the play closed a week after it had opened.

Wilde had to return to England, where he continued to lecture on topics including Personal Impressions of America, The Value of Art in Modern Life, and Dress.

In London, he had been introduced in 1881 to Constance Lloyd, daughter of Horace Lloyd, a wealthy Queen's Counsel, and his wife. She happened to be visiting Dublin in 1884, when Wilde was lecturing at the Gaiety Theatre. He proposed to her, and they married on 29 May 1884 at the Anglican St James's Church, Paddington, in London. Although Constance had an annual allowance of £250, which was generous for a young woman (equivalent to about £25,600 in current value), the Wildes had relatively luxurious tastes. They had preached to others for so long on the subject of design that people expected their home to set new standards. No. 16, Tite Street was duly renovated in seven months at considerable expense. The couple had two sons together, Cyril (1885) and Vyvyan (1886). Wilde became the sole literary signatory of George Bernard Shaw's petition for a pardon of the anarchists arrested (and later executed) after the Haymarket massacre in Chicago in 1886.

Robert Ross had read Wilde's poems before they met at Oxford in 1886. He seemed unrestrained by the Victorian prohibition against homosexuality, and became estranged from his family. By Richard Ellmann's account, he was a precocious seventeen-year-old who "so young and yet so knowing, was determined to seduce Wilde". According to Daniel Mendelsohn, Wilde, who had long alluded to Greek love, was "initiated into homosexual sex" by Ross, while his "marriage had begun to unravel after his wife's second pregnancy, which left him physically repelled".

Prose writing: 1886–91

Journalism and editorship: 1886–89

Criticism over artistic matters in The Pall Mall Gazette provoked a letter in self-defence, and soon Wilde was a contributor to that and other journals during 1885–87. He enjoyed reviewing and journalism; the form suited his style. He could organise and share his views on art, literature and life, yet in a format less tedious than lecturing. Buoyed up, his reviews were largely chatty and positive. Wilde, like his parents before him, also supported the cause of Irish nationalism. When Charles Stewart Parnell was falsely accused of inciting murder, Wilde wrote a series of astute columns defending him in the Daily Chronicle.

His flair, having previously been put mainly into socialising, suited journalism and rapidly attracted notice. With his youth nearly over, and a family to support, in mid-1887 Wilde became the editor of The Lady's World magazine, his name prominently appearing on the cover. He promptly renamed it as The Woman's World and raised its tone, adding serious articles on parenting, culture, and politics, while keeping discussions of fashion and arts. Two pieces of fiction were usually included, one to be read to children, the other for the ladies themselves. Wilde worked hard to solicit good contributions from his wide artistic acquaintance, including those of Lady Wilde and his wife Constance, while his own "Literary and Other Notes" were themselves popular and amusing.

The initial vigour and excitement which he brought to the job began to fade as administration, commuting and office life became tedious. At the same time as Wilde's interest flagged, the publishers became concerned anew about circulation: sales, at the relatively high price of one shilling, remained low. Increasingly sending instructions to the magazine by letter, Wilde began a new period of creative work and his own column appeared less regularly.In October 1889, Wilde had finally found his voice in prose and, at the end of the second volume, Wilde left The Woman's World. The magazine outlasted him by one issue.

If Wilde's period at the helm of the magazine was a mixed success from an organizational point of view, it played a pivotal role in his development as a writer and facilitated his ascent to fame. Whilst Wilde the journalist supplied articles under the guidance of his editors, Wilde the editor was forced to learn to manipulate the literary marketplace on his own terms.

During the late 1880s, Wilde was a close friend of the artist James NcNeill Whistler and they dined together on many occasions. At one of these dinners, Whistler said a bon mot that Wilde found particularly witty, Wilde exclaimed that he wished that he had said it, and Whistler retorted "You will, Oscar, you will".Herbert Vivian—a mutual friend of Wilde and Whistler—attended the dinner and recorded it in his article The Reminiscences of a Short Life which appeared in The Sun in 1889. The article alleged that Wilde had a habit of passing off other people's witticisms as his own—especially Whistler's. Wilde considered Vivian's article to be a scurrilous betrayal, and it directly caused the broken friendship between Wilde and Whistler. The Reminiscences also caused great acrimony between Wilde and Vivian, Wilde accusing Vivian of "the inaccuracy of an eavesdropper with the method of a blackmailer" and banishing Vivian from his circle.

Shorter fiction

Wilde published The Happy Prince and Other Tales in 1888, and had been regularly writing fairy stories for magazines. In 1891 he published two more collections, Lord Arthur Savile's Crime and Other Stories, and in September A House of Pomegranates was dedicated "To Constance Mary Wilde". "The Portrait of Mr. W. H.", which Wilde had begun in 1887, was first published in Blackwood's Edinburgh Magazine in July 1889. It is a short story, which reports a conversation, in which the theory that Shakespeare's sonnets were written out of the poet's love of the boy actor "Willie Hughes", is advanced, retracted, and then propounded again. The only evidence for this is two supposed puns within the sonnets themselves.

The anonymous narrator is at first sceptical, then believing, finally flirtatious with the reader: he concludes that "there is really a great deal to be said of the Willie Hughes theory of Shakespeare's sonnets." By the end fact and fiction have melded together. Arthur Ransome wrote that Wilde "read something of himself into Shakespeare's sonnets" and became fascinated with the "Willie Hughes theory" despite the lack of biographical evidence for the historical William Hughes' existence. Instead of writing a short but serious essay on the question, Wilde tossed the theory amongst the three characters of the story, allowing it to unfold as background to the plot. The story thus is an early masterpiece of Wilde's combining many elements that interested him: conversation, literature and the idea that to shed oneself of an idea one must first convince another of its truth. Ransome concludes that Wilde succeeds precisely because the literary criticism is unveiled with such a deft touch.

Though containing nothing but "special pleading", it would not, he says "be possible to build an airier castle in Spain than this of the imaginary William Hughes" we continue listening nonetheless to be charmed by the telling. "You must believe in Willie Hughes," Wilde told an acquaintance, "I almost do, myself."

Essays and dialogues

Wilde, having tired of journalism, had been busy setting out his aesthetic ideas more fully in a series of longer prose pieces which were published in the

440

major literary-intellectual journals of the day. In January 1889, The Decay of Lying: A Dialogue appeared in The Nineteenth Century, and Pen, Pencil and Poison, a satirical biography of Thomas Griffiths Wainewright, in The Fortnightly Review, edited by Wilde's friend Frank Harris. Two of Wilde's four writings on aesthetics are dialogues: though Wilde had evolved professionally from lecturer to writer, he retained an oral tradition of sorts. Having always excelled as a wit and raconteur, he often composed by assembling phrases, bons mots and witticisms into a longer, cohesive work.

Wilde was concerned about the effect of moralising on art; he believed in art's redemptive, developmental powers: "Art is individualism, and individualism is a disturbing and disintegrating force. There lies its immense value. For what it seeks is to disturb monotony of type, slavery of custom, tyranny of habit, and the reduction of man to the level of a machine." In his only political text, The Soul of Man Under Socialism, he argued political conditions should establish this primacy – private property should be abolished, and cooperation should be substituted for competition. At the same time, he stressed that the government most amenable to artists was no government at all. Wilde envisioned a society where mechanisation has freed human effort from the burden of necessity, effort which can instead be expended on artistic creation. George Orwell summarised, "In effect, the world will be populated by artists, each striving after perfection in the way that seems best to him."

This point of view did not align him with the Fabians, intellectual socialists who advocated using state apparatus to change social conditions, nor did it endear him to the monied classes whom he had previously entertained. Hesketh Pearson, introducing a collection of Wilde's essays in 1950, remarked how The Soul of Man Under Socialism had been an inspirational text for revolutionaries in Tsarist Russia but laments that in the Stalinist era "it is doubtful whether there are any uninspected places in which it could now be hidden".

Wilde considered including this pamphlet and The Portrait of Mr. W.H., his essay-story on Shakespeare's sonnets, in a new anthology in 1891, but eventually decided to limit it to purely aesthetic subjects. Intentions packaged revisions of four essays: The Decay of Lying, Pen, Pencil and Poison, The Truth of Masks (first published 1885), and The Critic as Artist in two parts. For Pearson the biographer, the essays and dialogues exhibit every aspect of Wilde's genius and character: wit, romancer, talker, lecturer, humanist and scholar and concludes that "no other productions of his have as varied an appeal". 1891 turned out to be Wilde's annus mirabilis; apart from his three collections he also produced his only novel.

The Picture of Dorian Gray

The first version of The Picture of Dorian Gray was published as the lead story in the July 1890 edition of Lippincott's Monthly Magazine, along with five others. The story begins with a man painting a picture of Gray. When Gray, who has a "face like ivory and rose leaves", sees his finished portrait, he breaks down. Distraught that his beauty will fade while the portrait stays beautiful, he inadvertently makes a Faustian bargain in which only the painted image grows old while he stays beautiful and young. For Wilde, the purpose of art would be to guide life as if beauty alone were its object. As Gray's portrait allows him to escape the corporeal ravages of his hedonism, Wilde sought to juxtapose the beauty he saw in art with daily life.

Reviewers immediately criticised the novel's decadence and homosexual allusions; The Daily Chronicle for example, called it "unclean", "poisonous", and "heavy with the mephitic odours of moral and spiritual putrefaction". Which he clarified his stance on ethics and aesthetics in art – "If a work of art is rich and vital and complete, those who have artistic instincts will see its beauty and those to whom ethics appeal more strongly will see its moral lesson." He nevertheless revised it extensively for book publication in 1891: six new chapters were added, some overtly decadent passages and homo-eroticism excised, and a preface was included consisting of twenty two epigrams, such as "Books are well written, or badly written. That is all."

Contemporary reviewers and modern critics have postulated numerous possible sources of the story, a search Jershua McCormack argues is futile because Wilde "has tapped a root of Western folklore so deep and ubiquitous that the story has escaped its origins and returned to the oral tradition." Wilde claimed the plot was "an idea that is as old as the history of literature but to which I have given a new form".Modern critic Robin McKie considered the novel to be technically mediocre, saying that the conceit of the plot had guaranteed its fame, but the device is never pushed to its full.On the other hand, Robert McCrum of The Guardian deemed it the 27th best novel ever written in English, calling it "an arresting, and slightly camp, exercise in late-Victorian gothic."

Theatrical career: 1892–95

Salomé

The 1891 census records the Wildes' residence at 16 Tite Street, where he lived with his wife Constance and two sons. Wilde though, not content with being better known than ever in London, returned to Paris in October 1891, this time as a respected writer. He was received at the salons littéraires, including the famous mardis of Stéphane Mallarmé, a renowned symbolist poet of the time. Wilde's two plays during the 1880s, Vera; or, The Nihilists and The Duchess of Padua, had not met with much success. He had continued his interest in the theatre and now, after finding his voice in prose, his thoughts turned again to the dramatic form as the biblical iconography of Salome filled his mind. One evening, after discussing depictions of Salome throughout history, he returned to his hotel and noticed a blank copybook lying on the desk, and it occurred to him to write in it what he had been saying. The result was a new play, Salomé, written rapidly and in French.

A tragedy, it tells the story of Salome, the stepdaughter of the tetrarch Herod Antipas, who, to her stepfather's dismay but mother's delight, requests the head of Jokanaan (John the Baptist) on a silver platter as a reward for dancing the Dance of the Seven Veils. When Wilde returned to London just before Christmas the Paris Echo referred to him as "le great event" of the season. Rehearsals of the play, starring Sarah Bernhardt, began but the play was refused a licence by the Lord Chamberlain, since it depicted biblical characters. Salome was published jointly in Paris and London in 1893, but was not performed until 1896 in Paris, during Wilde's later incarceration.

Comedies of society

Wilde, who had first set out to irritate Victorian society with his dress and talking points, then outrage it with Dorian Gray, his novel of vice hidden beneath art, finally found a way to critique society on its own terms. Lady Windermere's Fan was first performed on 20 February 1892 at St James's Theatre, packed with the cream of society. On the surface a witty comedy, there is subtle subversion underneath: "it concludes with collusive concealment rather than collective disclosure". The audience, like Lady Windermere, are forced to soften harsh social codes in favour of a more nuanced view. The play was enormously popular, touring the country for months, but largely trashed by conservative critics. It was followed by A Woman of No Importance in 1893, another Victorian comedy, revolving around the spectre of illegitimate births, mistaken identities and late revelations. Wilde was commissioned to write two more plays and An Ideal Husband, written in 1894, followed in January 1895.

Peter Raby said these essentially English plays were well-pitched, "Wilde, with one eye on the dramatic genius of Ibsen, and the other on the commercial competition in London's West End, targeted his audience with adroit precision".

Queensberry family

In mid-1891 Lionel Johnson introduced Wilde to Lord Alfred Douglas, Johnson's cousin and an undergraduate at Oxford at the time. Known to his family and friends as "Bosie", he was a handsome and spoilt young man. An intimate friendship sprang up between Wilde and Douglas and by 1893 Wilde was infatuated with Douglas and they consorted together regularly in a tempestuous affair. If Wilde was relatively indiscreet, even flamboyant, in the way he acted, Douglas was reckless in public. Wilde, who was earning up to £100 a week from his plays (his salary at The Woman's World had been £6), indulged Douglas's every whim: material, artistic or sexual.

Douglas soon initiated Wilde into the Victorian underground of gay prostitution and Wilde was introduced to a series of young working-class male prostitutes from 1892 onwards by Alfred Taylor. These infrequent rendezvous usually took the same form: Wilde would meet the boy, offer him gifts, dine him privately and then take him to a hotel room. Unlike Wilde's idealised relations with Ross, John Gray, and Douglas, all of whom remained part of his aesthetic circle, these consorts were uneducated and knew nothing of literature. Soon his public and private lives had become sharply divided; in De Profundis he wrote to Douglas that "It was like feasting with panthers; the danger was half the excitement... I did not know that when they were to strike at me it was to be at another's piping and at another's pay."

Douglas and some Oxford friends founded a journal, The Chameleon, to which Wilde "sent a page of paradoxes originally destined for the Saturday Review". "Phrases and Philosophies for the Use of the Young" was to come under attack six months later at Wilde's trial, where he was forced to defend the magazine to which he had sent his work.In any case, it became unique: The Chameleon was not published again.

Lord Alfred's father, the Marquess of Queensberry, was known for his outspoken atheism, brutish manner and creation of the modern rules of boxing. Queensberry, who feuded regularly with his son, confronted Wilde and Lord Alfred about the nature of their relationship several times, but Wilde was able to mollify him. In June 1894, he called on Wilde at 16 Tite Street, without an appointment, and clarified his stance: "I do not say that you are it, but you look it, and pose at it, which is just as bad. And if I catch you and my son again in any public restaurant I will thrash you" to which Wilde responded: "I don't know what the Queensberry rules are, but the Oscar Wilde rule is to shoot on sight".His account in De Profundis was less triumphant: "It was when, in my library at Tite Street, waving his small hands in the air in epileptic fury, your father... stood uttering every foul word his foul mind could think of, and screaming the loathsome threats he afterwards with such cunning carried out". Queensberry only described the scene once, saying Wilde had "shown him the white feather", meaning he had acted in a cowardly way. Though trying to remain calm, Wilde saw that he was becoming ensnared in a brutal family quarrel. He did not wish to bear Queensberry's insults, but he knew to confront him could lead to disaster were his liaisons disclosed publicly.

The Importance of Being Earnest

Wilde's final play again returns to the theme of switched identities: the play's two protagonists engage in "bunburying" (the maintenance of alternative personas in the town and country) which allows them to escape Victorian social mores.Earnest is even lighter in tone than Wilde's earlier comedies. While their characters often rise to serious themes in moments of crisis, Earnest lacks the by-now stock Wildean characters: there is no "woman with a past", the principals are neither villainous nor cunning, simply idle cultivés, and the idealistic young women are not that innocent. Mostly set in drawing rooms and almost completely lacking in action or violence, Earnest lacks the self-conscious decadence found in The Picture of Dorian Gray and Salome.

The play, now considered Wilde's masterpiece, was rapidly written in Wilde's artistic maturity in late 1894. It was first performed on 14 February 1895, at St James's Theatre in London, Wilde's second collaboration with George Alexander, the actor-manager. Both author and producer assiduously revised, prepared and rehearsed every line, scene and setting in the months before the premiere, creating a carefully constructed representation of late-Victorian society, yet simultaneously mocking it. During rehearsal Alexander requested that Wilde shorten the play from four acts to three, which the author did. Premieres at St James's seemed like "brilliant parties", and the opening of The Importance of Being Earnest was no exception. Allan Aynesworth (who played Algernon) recalled to Hesketh Pearson, "In my fifty-three years of acting, I never remember a greater triumph than [that] first night."Earnest's immediate reception as Wilde's best work to date finally crystallised his fame into a solid artistic reputation. The Importance of Being Earnest remains his most popular play.

Wilde's professional success was mirrored by an escalation in his feud with Queensberry. Queensberry had planned to insult Wilde publicly by throwing a bouquet of rotting vegetables onto the stage; Wilde was tipped off and had Queensberry barred from entering the theatre.Fifteen weeks later Wilde was in prison.

Trials

446

Wilde v. Queensberry

On 18 February 1895, the Marquess left his calling card at Wilde's club, the Albemarle, inscribed: "For Oscar Wilde, posing somdomite" Wilde, encouraged by Douglas and against the advice of his friends, initiated a private prosecution against Queensberry for libel, since the note amounted to a public accusation that Wilde had committed the crime of sodomy.

Queensberry was arrested for criminal libel; a charge carrying a possible sentence of up to two years in prison. Under the 1843 Libel Act, Queensberry could avoid conviction for libel only by demonstrating that his accusation was in fact true, and furthermore that there was some "public benefit" to having made the accusation openly. Queensberry's lawyers thus hired private detectives to find evidence of Wilde's homosexual liaisons.

Wilde's friends had advised him against the prosecution at a Saturday Review meeting at the Café Royal on 24 March 1895; Frank Harris warned him that "they are going to prove sodomy against you" and advised him to flee to France. Wilde and Douglas walked out in a huff, Wilde saying "it is at such moments as these that one sees who are one's true friends". The scene was witnessed by George Bernard Shaw who recalled it to Arthur Ransome a day or so before Ransome's trial for libelling Douglas in 1913. To Ransome it confirmed what he had said in his 1912 book on Wilde; that Douglas's rivalry for Wilde with Robbie Ross and his arguments with his father had resulted in Wilde's public disaster; as Wilde wrote in De Profundis. Douglas lost his case. Shaw included an account of the argument between Harris, Douglas and Wilde in the preface to his play The Dark Lady of the Sonnets.

The libel trial became a cause célèbre as salacious details of Wilde's private life with Taylor and Douglas began to appear in the press. A team of private detectives had directed Queensberry's lawyers, led by Edward Carson QC, to the world of the Victorian underground. Wilde's association with blackmailers and male prostitutes, cross-dressers and homosexual brothels was recorded, and various persons involved were interviewed, some being coerced to appear as witnesses since they too were accomplices to the crimes of which Wilde was accused.

The trial opened on 3 April 1895 before Justice Richard Henn Collins amid scenes of near hysteria both in the press and the public galleries. The extent of the evidence massed against Wilde forced him to declare meekly, "I am the prosecutor in this case"Wilde's lawyer, Sir Edward George Clarke, opened the case by pre-emptively asking Wilde about two suggestive letters Wilde had written to Douglas, which the defence had in its possession. He characterised the first as a "prose sonnet" and admitted that the "poetical language" might seem strange to the court but claimed its intent was innocent. Wilde stated that the letters had been obtained by blackmailers who had attempted to extort money from him, but he had refused, suggesting they should take the £60 (equal to £6,800 today) offered, "unusual for a prose piece of that length". He claimed to regard the letters as works of art rather than something of which to be ashamed.

Carson, a fellow Dubliner who had attended Trinity College, Dublin at the same time as Wilde, cross-examined Wilde on how he perceived the moral content of his works. Wilde replied with characteristic wit and flippancy, claiming that works of art are not capable of being moral or immoral but only well or poorly made, and that only "brutes and illiterates", whose views on art "are incalculably stupid", would make such judgements about art. Carson, a leading barrister, diverged from the normal practice of asking closed questions. Carson pressed Wilde on each topic from every angle, squeezing out nuances of meaning from Wilde's answers, removing them from their aesthetic context and portraying Wilde as evasive and decadent. While Wilde won the most laughs from the court, Carson scored the most legal points. To undermine Wilde's credibility, and to justify Queensberry's description of Wilde as a "posing somdomite", Carson drew from the witness an admission of his capacity for "posing", by demonstrating that he had lied about his age on oath. Playing on this, he returned to the topic throughout his cross-examination. Carson also tried to justify Queensberry's characterisation by quoting from Wilde's novel, The Picture of Dorian Gray, referring in particular to a scene in the second chapter, in which Lord Henry Wotton explains his decadent philosophy to Dorian, an "innocent young man", in Carson's words.

448

Carson then moved to the factual evidence and questioned Wilde about his friendships with younger, lower-class men. Wilde admitted being on a first-name basis and lavishing gifts upon them, but insisted that nothing untoward had occurred and that the men were merely good friends of his. Carson repeatedly pointed out the unusual nature of these relationships and insinuated that the men were prostitutes. Wilde replied that he did not believe in social barriers, and simply enjoyed the society of young men. Then Carson asked Wilde directly whether he had ever kissed a certain servant boy, Wilde responded, "Oh, dear no. He was a particularly plain boy – unfortunately ugly – I pitied him for it." Carson pressed him on the answer, repeatedly asking why the boy's ugliness was relevant. Wilde hesitated, then for the first time became flustered: "You sting me and insult me and try to unnerve me; and at times one says things flippantly when one ought to speak more seriously."

In his opening speech for the defence, Carson announced that he had located several male prostitutes who were to testify that they had had sex with Wilde. On the advice of his lawyers, Wilde dropped the prosecution. Queensberry was found not guilty, as the court declared that his accusation that Wilde was "posing as a Somdomite " was justified, "true in substance and in fact".Under the Libel Act 1843, Queensberry's acquittal rendered Wilde legally liable for the considerable expenses Queensberry had incurred in his defence, which left Wilde bankrupt.

Regina v. Wilde

After Wilde left the court, a warrant for his arrest was applied for on charges of sodomy and gross indecency. Robbie Ross found Wilde at the Cadogan Hotel, Pont Street, Knightsbridge, with Reginald Turner; both men advised Wilde to go at once to Dover and try to get a boat to France; his mother advised him to stay and fight. Wilde, lapsing into inaction, could only say, "The train has gone. It's too late."On 6 April 1895, Wilde was arrested for "gross indecency" under Section 11 of the Criminal Law Amendment Act 1885, a term meaning homosexual acts not amounting to buggery (an offence under a separate statute). At Wilde's instruction, Ross and Wilde's butler forced their way into the bedroom and library of 16 Tite Street, packing some personal effects, manuscripts, and letters. Wilde was then imprisoned on remand at Holloway, where he received daily visits from Douglas.

Events moved quickly and his prosecution opened on 26 April 1895, before Mr Justice Charles. Wilde pleaded not guilty. He had already begged Douglas to leave London for Paris, but Douglas complained bitterly, even wanting to give evidence; he was pressed to go and soon fled to the Hotel du Monde. Fearing persecution, Ross and many others also left the United Kingdom during this time. Under cross examination Wilde was at first hesitant, then spoke eloquently:

> **Charles Gill** (prosecuting): What is "the love that dare not speak its name"?
>
> **Wilde:** "The love that dare not speak its name" in this century is such a great affection of an elder for a younger man as there was between David and Jonathan, such as Plato made the very basis of his philosophy, and such as you find in the sonnets of Michelangelo and Shakespeare. It is that deep spiritual affection that is as pure as it is perfect. It dictates and pervades great works of art, like those of Shakespeare and Michelangelo, and those two letters of mine, such as they are. It is in this century misunderstood, so much misunderstood that it may be described as "the love that dare not speak its name", and on that account of it I am placed where I am now. It is beautiful, it is fine, it is the noblest form of affection. There is nothing unnatural about it. It is intellectual, and it repeatedly exists between an older and a younger man, when the older man has intellect, and the younger man has all the joy, hope and glamour of life before him. That it should be so, the world does not understand. The world mocks at it, and sometimes puts one in the pillory for it.

This response was counter-productive in a legal sense as it only served to reinforce the charges of homosexual behaviour.

The trial ended with the jury unable to reach a verdict. Wilde's counsel, Sir Edward Clarke, was finally able to get a magistrate to allow Wilde and his friends to post bail. The Reverend Stewart Headlam put up most of the £5,000 surety required by the court, having disagreed with Wilde's treatment by the press and the courts. Wilde was freed from Holloway and, shunning attention, went into hiding at the house of Ernest and Ada Leverson, two of his firm friends. Edward Carson approached Frank Lockwood QC, the Solicitor General and asked "Can we not let up on the fellow now?" Lockwood answered that he would like to do so, but feared that the case had become too politicised to be dropped.

The final trial was presided over by Mr Justice Wills. On 25 May 1895 Wilde and Alfred Taylor were convicted of gross indecency and sentenced to two years' hard labour. The judge described the sentence, the maximum allowed, as "totally inadequate for a case such as this", and that the case was "the worst case I have ever tried". Wilde's response "And I? May I say nothing, my Lord?" was drowned out in cries of "Shame" in the courtroom.

Imprisonment

When first I was put into prison some people advised me to try and forget who I was. It was ruinous advice. It is only by realising what I am that I have found comfort of any kind. Now I am advised by others to try on my release to forget that I have ever been in a prison at all. I know that would be equally fatal. It would mean that I would always be haunted by an intolerable sense of disgrace, and that those things that are meant for me as much as for anybody else – the beauty of the sun and moon, the pageant of the seasons, the music of daybreak and the silence of great nights, the rain falling through the leaves, or the dew creeping over the grass and making it silver – would all be tainted for me, and lose their healing power, and their power of communicating joy. To regret one's own experiences is to arrest one's own development. To deny one's own experiences is to put a lie into the lips of one's own life. It is no less than a denial of the soul.

De Profundis

Wilde was incarcerated from 25 May 1895 to 18 May 1897.

He first entered Newgate Prison in London for processing, then was moved to Pentonville Prison, where the "hard labour" to which he had been sentenced consisted of many hours of walking a treadmill and picking oakum (separating the fibres in scraps of old navy ropes), and where prisoners were allowed to read only the Bible and The Pilgrim's Progress.

A few months later he was moved to Wandsworth Prison in London. Inmates there also followed the regimen of "hard labour, hard fare and a hard bed", which wore harshly on Wilde's delicate health. In November he collapsed during chapel from illness and hunger. His right ear drum was ruptured in the fall, an injury that later contributed to his death. He spent two months in the infirmary.

Richard B. Haldane, the Liberal MP and reformer, visited Wilde and had him transferred in November to Reading Gaol, 30 miles (48 km) west of London on 23 November 1895. The transfer itself was the lowest point of his incarceration, as a crowd jeered and spat at him on the railway platform. He spent the remainder of his sentence there, addressed and identified only as "C33" – the occupant of the third cell on the third floor of C ward.

About five months after Wilde arrived at Reading Gaol, Charles Thomas Wooldridge, a trooper in the Royal Horse Guards, was brought to Reading to await his trial for murdering his wife on 29 March 1896; on 17 June Wooldridge was sentenced to death and returned to Reading for his execution, which took place on Tuesday, 7 July 1896 – the first hanging at Reading in 18 years. From Wooldridge's hanging, Wilde later wrote The Ballad of Reading Gaol.

Wilde was not, at first, even allowed paper and pen but Haldane eventually succeeded in allowing access to books and writing materials. Wilde requested, among others: the Bible in French; Italian and German grammars; some Ancient Greek texts, Dante's Divine Comedy, Joris-Karl Huysmans's new French novel about Christian redemption En route, and essays by St Augustine, Cardinal Newman and Walter Pater.

Between January and March 1897 Wilde wrote a 50,000-word letter to Douglas. He was not allowed to send it, but was permitted to take it with him when released from prison. In reflective mode, Wilde coldly examines his career to date, how he had been a colourful agent provocateur in Victorian society, his art, like his paradoxes, seeking to subvert as well as sparkle. His own estimation of himself was: one who "stood in symbolic relations to the art and culture of my age". It was from these heights that his life with Douglas began, and Wilde examines that particularly closely, repudiating him for what Wilde finally sees as his arrogance and vanity: he had not forgotten Douglas' remark, when he was ill, "When you are not on your pedestal you are not interesting." Wilde blamed himself, though, for the ethical degradation of character that he allowed Douglas to bring about in him and took responsibility for his own fall, "I am here for having tried to put your father in prison." The first half concludes with Wilde forgiving Douglas, for his own sake as much as Douglas's. The second half of the letter traces Wilde's spiritual journey of redemption and fulfilment through his prison reading. He realised that his ordeal had filled his soul with the fruit of experience, however bitter it tasted at the time.

> ... I wanted to eat of the fruit of all the trees in the garden of the world ... And so, indeed, I went out, and so I lived. My only mistake was that I confined myself so exclusively to the trees of what seemed to me the sun-lit side of the garden, and shunned the other side for its shadow and its gloom.

Wilde was released from prison on 19 May 1897 and sailed that evening for Dieppe, France. He never returned to the UK.

On his release, he gave the manuscript to Ross, who may or may not have carried out Wilde's instructions to send a copy to Douglas (who later denied having received it). The letter was partially published in 1905 as De Profundis; its complete and correct publication first occurred in 1962 in The Letters of Oscar Wilde.

Decline: 1897–1900

Exile

Though Wilde's health had suffered greatly from the harshness and diet of prison, he had a feeling of spiritual renewal. He immediately wrote to the Society of Jesus requesting a six-month Catholic retreat; when the request was denied, Wilde wept. "I intend to be received into the Catholic Church before long", Wilde told a journalist who asked about his religious intentions.

He spent his last three years impoverished and in exile. He took the name "Sebastian Melmoth", after Saint Sebastian and the titular character of Melmoth the Wanderer (a Gothic novel by Charles Maturin, Wilde's great-uncle).Wilde wrote two long letters to the editor of the Daily Chronicle, describing the brutal conditions of English prisons and advocating penal reform. His discussion of the dismissal of Warder Martin for giving biscuits to an anaemic child prisoner repeated the themes of the corruption and degeneration of punishment that he had earlier outlined in The Soul of Man under Socialism.

Wilde spent mid-1897 with Robert Ross in the seaside village of Berneval-le-Grand in northern France, where he wrote The Ballad of Reading Gaol, narrating the execution of Charles Thomas Wooldridge, who murdered his wife in a rage at her infidelity. It moves from an objective story-telling to symbolic identification with the prisoners. No attempt is made to assess the justice of the laws which convicted them but rather the poem highlights the brutalisation of the punishment that all convicts share. Wilde juxtaposes the executed man and himself with the line "Yet each man kills the thing he loves". He adopted the proletarian ballad form and the author was credited as "C33", Wilde's cell number in Reading Gaol. He suggested that it be published in Reynolds' Magazine, "because it circulates widely among the criminal classes – to which I now belong – for once I will be read by my peers – a new experience for me". It was an immediate roaring commercial success, going through seven editions in less than two years, only after which "[Oscar" was added to the title page, though many in literary circles had known Wilde to be the author. It brought him a small amount of money.

Although Douglas had been the cause of his misfortunes, he and Wilde were reunited in August 1897 at Rouen. This meeting was disapproved of by the friends and families of both men. Constance Wilde was already refusing to meet Wilde or allow him to see their sons, though she sent him money – three pounds a week. During the latter part of 1897, Wilde and Douglas lived together near Naples for a few months until they were separated by their families under the threat of cutting off all funds.

Wilde's final address was at the dingy Hôtel d'Alsace (now known as L'Hôtel), on rue des Beaux-Arts in Saint-Germain-des-Prés, Paris. "This poverty really breaks one's heart: it is so sale , so utterly depressing, so hopeless. Pray do what you can" he wrote to his publisher. He corrected and published An Ideal Husband and The Importance of Being Earnest, the proofs of which, according to Ellmann, show a man "very much in command of himself and of the play" but he refused to write anything else: "I can write, but have lost the joy of writing".

He wandered the boulevards alone and spent what little money he had on alcohol. A series of embarrassing chance encounters with hostile English visitors, or Frenchmen he had known in better days, drowned his spirit. Soon Wilde was sufficiently confined to his hotel to joke, on one of his final trips outside, "My wallpaper and I are fighting a duel to the death. One of us has got to go". On 12 October 1900 he sent a telegram to Ross: "Terribly weak. Please come". His moods fluctuated; Max Beerbohm relates how their mutual friend Reginald 'Reggie' Turner had found Wilde very depressed after a nightmare. "I dreamt that I had died, and was supping with the dead!" "I am sure", Turner replied, "that you must have been the life and soul of the party." Turner was one of the few of the old circle who remained with Wilde to the end and was at his bedside when he died.

Death

By 25 November 1900 Wilde had developed meningitis, then called "cerebral meningitis". Robbie Ross arrived on 29 November, sent for a priest, and Wilde was conditionally baptised into the Catholic Church by Fr Cuthbert Dunne, a Passionist priest from Dublin, Wilde having been baptised in the Church of Ireland and having moreover a recollection of Catholic baptism as a child, a fact later attested to by the minister of the sacrament, Fr Lawrence Fox. Fr Dunne recorded the baptism,

As the voiture rolled through the dark streets that wintry night, the sad story of Oscar Wilde was in part repeated to me... Robert Ross knelt by the bedside, assisting me as best he could while I administered conditional baptism, and afterwards answering the responses while I gave Extreme Unction to the prostrate man and recited the prayers for the dying. As the man was in a semi-comatose condition, I did not venture to administer the Holy Viaticum; still I must add that he could be roused and was roused from this state in my presence. When roused, he gave signs of being inwardly conscious... Indeed I was fully satisfied that he understood me when told that I was about to receive him into the Catholic Church and gave him the Last Sacraments... And when I repeated close to his ear the Holy Names, the Acts of Contrition, Faith, Hope and Charity, with acts of humble resignation to the Will of God, he tried all through to say the words after me.

Wilde died of meningitis on 30 November 1900. Different opinions are given as to the cause of the disease: Richard Ellmann claimed it was syphilitic; Merlin Holland, Wilde's grandson, thought this to be a misconception, noting that Wilde's meningitis followed a surgical intervention, perhaps a mastoidectomy; Wilde's physicians, Dr Paul Cleiss and A'Court Tucker, reported that the condition stemmed from an old suppuration of the right ear (from the prison injury, see above) treated for several years (une ancienne suppuration de l'oreille droite d'ailleurs en traitement depuis plusieurs années) and made no allusion to syphilis.

Burial

Wilde was initially buried in the Cimetière de Bagneux outside Paris; in 1909 his remains were disinterred and transferred to Père Lachaise Cemetery, inside the city. His tomb there was designed by Sir Jacob Epstein. It was commissioned by Robert Ross, who asked for a small compartment to be made for his own ashes, which were duly transferred in 1950. The modernist angel depicted as a relief on the tomb was originally complete with male genitalia, which were initially censored by French Authorities with a golden leaf. The genitals have since been vandalised; their current whereabouts are unknown. In 2000, Leon Johnson, a multimedia artist, installed a silver prosthesis to replace them. In 2011, the tomb was cleaned of the many lipstick marks left there by admirers and a glass barrier was installed to prevent further marks or damage.

The epitaph is a verse from The Ballad of Reading Gaol,

> And alien tears will fill for him
>
> Pity's long-broken urn,
>
> For his mourners will be outcast men,
>
> And outcasts always mourn.

Posthumous pardon

In 2017, Wilde was among an estimated 50,000 men who were pardoned for homosexual acts that were no longer considered offences under the Policing and Crime Act 2017. The Act is known informally as the Alan Turing law.

Honours

In 2014 Wilde was one of the inaugural honorees in the Rainbow Honor Walk, a walk of fame in San Francisco's Castro neighbourhood noting LGBTQ people who have "made significant contributions in their fields."

Biographies

Wilde's life has been the subject of numerous biographies since his death. The earliest were memoirs by those who knew him: often they are personal or impressionistic accounts which can be good character sketches, but are sometimes factually unreliable. Frank Harris, his friend and editor, wrote a biography, Oscar Wilde: His Life and Confessions (1916); though prone to exaggeration and sometimes factually inaccurate, it offers a good literary portrait of Wilde. Lord Alfred Douglas wrote two books about his relationship with Wilde. Oscar Wilde and Myself (1914), largely ghost-written by T. W. H. Crosland, vindictively reacted to Douglas's discovery that De Profundis was addressed to him and defensively tried to distance him from Wilde's scandalous reputation. Both authors later regretted their work. Later, in Oscar Wilde: A Summing Up (1939) and his Autobiography he was more sympathetic to Wilde. Of Wilde's other close friends, Robert Sherard; Robert Ross, his literary executor; and Charles Ricketts variously published biographies, reminiscences or correspondence. The first more or less objective biography of Wilde came about when Hesketh Pearson wrote Oscar Wilde: His Life and Wit (1946). In 1954 Wilde's son Vyvyan Holland published his memoir Son of Oscar Wilde, which recounts the difficulties Wilde's wife and children faced after his imprisonment. It was revised and updated by Merlin Holland in 1989.

Oscar Wilde, a critical study by Arthur Ransome was published in 1912. The book only briefly mentioned Wilde's life, but subsequently Ransome (and The Times Book Club) were sued for libel by Lord Alfred Douglas. In April 1913 Douglas lost the libel action after a reading of De Profundis refuted his claims.

Richard Ellmann wrote his 1987 biography Oscar Wilde, for which he posthumously won a National (USA) Book Critics Circle Award in 1988and a Pulitzer Prize in 1989. The book was the basis for the 1997 film Wilde, directed by Brian Gilbert and starring Stephen Fry as the title character.

Neil McKenna's 2003 biography, The Secret Life of Oscar Wilde, offers an exploration of Wilde's sexuality. Often speculative in nature, it was widely criticised for its pure conjecture and lack of scholarly rigour. Thomas Wright's Oscar's Books (2008) explores Wilde's reading from his childhood in Dublin to his death in Paris. After tracking down many books that once belonged to Wilde's Tite Street library (dispersed at the time of his trials), Wright was the first to examine Wilde's marginalia.

> Later on, I think everyone will recognise his achievements; his plays and essays will endure. Of course, you may think with others that his personality and conversation were far more wonderful than anything he wrote, so that his written works give only a pale reflection of his power. Perhaps that is so, and of course, it will be impossible to reproduce what is gone forever.

Robert Ross, 23 December 1900

In 2018, Matthew Sturgis' "Oscar: A Life," was published in London. The book incorporates rediscovered letters and other documents and is the most extensively researched biography of Wilde to appear since 1988.

Parisian literati, also produced several biographies and monographs on him. André Gide wrote In Memoriam, Oscar Wilde and Wilde also features in his journals. Thomas Louis, who had earlier translated books on Wilde into French, produced his own L'esprit d'Oscar Wilde in 1920. Modern books include Philippe Jullian's Oscar Wilde, and L'affaire Oscar Wilde, ou, Du danger de laisser la justice mettre le nez dans nos draps (The Oscar Wilde Affair, or, On the Danger of Allowing Justice to put its Nose in our Sheets) by Odon Vallet, a French religious historian. (Source: Wikipedia)

NOTABLE WORKS

The Picture of Dorian Gray (1890/1891). The first version of "The Picture of Dorian Gray" was published, in a form highly edited by the magazine, as the lead story in the July 1890 edition of Lippincott's Monthly Magazine. Wilde published the longer and revised version in book form in 1891, with an added preface.

Stories

"The Portrait of Mr. W. H." (1889)

The Happy Prince and Other Tales (1888, a collection of fairy tales) consisting of:

- "The Happy Prince"
- "The Nightingale and the Rose"
- "The Selfish Giant"
- "The Devoted Friend"
- "The Remarkable Rocket"

A House of Pomegranates (1891, fairy tales)

Lord Arthur Savile's Crime and Other Stories (1891) Including "The Canterville Ghost" first published in periodical form in 1887.

Complete Short Fiction. Penguin Classics, 2003. Edited with an Introduction and Notes by Ian Small. Contains all works listed above plus Poems in Prose (1894) and one very short 'Elder-tree' (fragment).

POEMS

Ravenna (1878) Winner of the Newdigate Prize.

Poems (1881) Wilde's collection of poetry and first publication.

The Sphinx (1894)

Poems in Prose (1894)

The Ballad of Reading Gaol (1898)

PLAYS

Vera; or, The Nihilists (1880)

The Duchess of Padua (1883)

Lady Windermere's Fan (1892)

A Woman of No Importance (1893)

Salomé (French version) (1893, first performed in Paris 1896)

Salomé: A Tragedy in One Act: Translated from the French of Oscar Wilde by Lord Alfred Douglas, illustrated by Aubrey Beardsley (1894)

An Ideal Husband (1895) (text)

The Importance of Being Earnest (1895) (text)

La Sainte Courtisane and A Florentine Tragedy Fragmentary. First published 1908 in Methuen's Collected Works

(Dates are dates of first performance, which approximate better to the probable date of composition than dates of publication.)

The Importance of Being Earnest and Other Plays. Penguin Classics, 2000. Edited with an Introduction, Commentaries and Notes by Richard Allen Cave. Contains all from above save the first two. Salome is in English.

As an appendix there is one excised scene from The Importance of Being Earnest.

POSTHUMOUS (PREVIOUSLY UNPUBLISHED)

De Profundis (Written 1895-97, in Reading Gaol). Expurgated edition published 1905; suppressed portions 1913, expanded version in The Letters of Oscar Wilde (1962).

The Rise of Historical Criticism (Written while at college) First published in 1905 (Sherwood Press, Hartford, CT) privately printed. Reprinted in Miscellanies, the last volume of the First Collected Edition (1908).

The First Collected Edition (Methuen & Co., 14 volumes) appeared in 1908 and contained many previously unpublished works.

The Second Collected Edition (Methuen & Co., 12 volumes) appeared in installments between 1909–11 and contained several other unpublished works.

The Letters of Oscar Wilde (Written 1868-1900) Published in 1962. Republished as The Complete Letters of Oscar Wilde (2000), with letters discovered since 1962, and new annotations by Merlin Holland.

The Women of Homer (Written 1876, while at college). First published in Oscar Wilde: The Women of Homer (2008) by The Oscar Wilde Society.

The Philosophy of Dress First published in The New-York Tribune (1885), published for the first time in book form in Oscar Wilde On Dress (2013).

MISATTRIBUTED

Teleny, or The Reverse of the Medal (Paris, 1893) has been attributed to Wilde, but its authorship is unclear. One theory is that it was a combined effort by several of Wilde's friends, which he may have edited.

Constance On September 14, 2011, Wilde's grandson Merlin Holland contested Wilde's claimed authorship of this play entitled Constance, scheduled to open that week in the King's Head Theatre. It was not, in fact, "Oscar Wilde's final play," as its producers were claiming. Holland said Wilde did sketch out the play's scenario in 1894, but "never wrote a word" of it, and that "it is dishonest to foist this on the public." The Artistic Director Adam Spreadbury-Maher of the King's Head Theatre and producer of Constance pointed out that Wilde's son, Vyvyan Holland, wrote in 1954, "a significant amount of the dialogue (of Constance) bears the authentic stamp of my father's hand". There is further proof that the developed scenario that Constance was reconstituted from was written by Wilde between 1897 and his death in 1900, rather than the 1894 George Alexander scenario which Merlin Holland quotes.